# We the People

## Daily Devotional
## For Loving God & Country

## Mist Carter

*Assent Books*

We the People: Daily Devotional for Loving God & Country
Copyright © 2023 by Mist Carter

Cover design by: Kathy Radich

Assent Books is an imprint of LeRue Press, LLC

For information about special discounts or bulk purchases, please contact

LeRue Press, LLC
280 Greg Street, Suite 10
Reno, NV 89502
www.Lrpnv.com


ISBN:978-1-938814-43-3

# DEDICATION

First and foremost, I want to thank God for blessing me with His gifts, guidance, and grace. I dedicate this book to my family and friends on earth and in heaven, as well as my fellow patriots. Thank you for all the support and encouragement you have provided. I am grateful for the patience and promotion I have received from Janice and Lenore from Assent Books, as well as the editing talents of Bob Chidester. I want to especially thank my friend and amazingly talented artist, Kathy Radich, who not only designed this book cover, but the cover for my previous book, *"God's Truth About America!"* Our citizens and nation desperately need prayer, and the courage to speak up and take a stand against the ungodliness America is experiencing. My hope is that we would unite each day as one body citing the same daily devotional to God throughout the year. Imagine the power of that! God bless all of you, and God bless America!

# INTRODUCTION

The concern for the future of America is deepening each day. In 2020, our country began a rapid decline of morality, and an escalation of evil and corruption. I couldn't stand by and do nothing. I had to do what I could to get the **truth** out to as many as possible, which resulted in writing two previous books about this crisis we're experiencing.

Our dysfunction and destruction is a result of one thing. We have turned our backs on God as a nation. Our Founding Fathers would be saddened to see our condition today—but they wouldn't be surprised because they warned us. James Madison is quoted, *"The future and success of America is not in this Constitution, but in the laws of God upon which this Constitution is founded."* And Benjamin Franklin warned, *"Man will ultimately be governed by God or by tyrants."*

The goal of the radical liberal agenda appears to be to dismantle our nation and our Constitution. And sadly, this is not being done by a majority of Americans—it's being done by a small, yet powerful segment of our population, such as: Corrupt politicians, Media, Big Tech, and Big Pharma that promote untruthful propaganda; an education system that expelled God and replaced Him with Marxist philosophies; reckless spending bills that have resulted in an economic crisis for each American; our foolish foreign policies, and our weak reaction when enemy nations take advantage of our weakness. Who can forget the disastrous withdrawal from Afghanistan, leaving thirteen military personnel dead and abandoning billions of dollars of military weaponry? And what about the surveilling "weather balloon" that was allowed to traverse our nation gathering military and other forms of intelligence? And look at the negative impact Big Pharma, the CDC, NIH, and all the other propagandists who lied to us and covered up the truth about untested vaccines and their deadly adverse effects, as well as COVID mandates that prevented children from receiving an adequate education.

This rapid downfall began with an executive order to make our energy independence all but vanish. To fill that void, the untruthful propaganda about the Green New Deal came at us from all angles. The "wokesters" are putting all their efforts into destroying the Christian values upon which this nation was founded and forcing Americans to put their godly views aside in order to make way for LGBTQ (and all the rest of the letters of the alphabet), and to flaunt their perverted agenda on people of all ages (again a small percentage of the population dominating everyone else). They must hate America so much that they have allowed an open border that has threatened our security, poisoned us with lethal drugs, added to the homeless crisis, destroyed the expensive hotels in which they are housed for free, overwhelmed our schools and medical facilities, and has added to the already out-of-control crime in America. This list could go on and on, but we can clearly see that kicking God out of America is not working.

The absurdity of all of these ruthless schemes with which the radical, socialist idealogues are polluting our nation revolves around two topics—race and gender! Here's a news flash: These are two physical characteristics, given to every human being by God, that are unchangeable! We can't change the color of our skin with which we were born, yet the left applies "race" to all aspects of life—how futile is that? With respect to gender, try as one may, you still will end up to be the biological gender with which you were born. I could get a double mastectomy and add a prosthetic penis, yet I would still be a biological female—with two "X" chromosomes!

So what is the answer? What is the solution? First, it will take ALL of us who truly love God and truly love this country to get involved. If a portion of our population has turned their back on God—WE HAVE NOT! Yet, we have allowed this corrupt, woke, and evil minority to run the show. Enough is enough!

Here is what we can do. We need to **pray**, and **pray** some more! That is the main reason I wrote a devotional book instead of simply continuing with laying out the truth and facts about our national condition, as I did in the previous two books. Now that we have the facts, we need to put on the Armor of God! We should "fear not" to **speak up** when this corruption and evil is in our face. We can do this by letting our elected officials (at all levels of government) know exactly how we feel, and how this corruption and evil is impacting us. It doesn't matter what party affiliation they represent, or if you voted for them or not. Their main focus is getting re-elected, so if we inundate them with our concerns, they might become concerned enough to listen to us. Remember, WE are the majority.

We need to **stand up** and let our voices be heard. The radical, socialist, "wokesters" are expecting us to roll over and take all this abuse and corruption. They are used to us <u>not</u> challenging them. When they make their outlandish claims that don't have a hint of truth in them, (like claiming something or someone is racist) we don't question them. We don't ask them to provide us with an "example" of their erroneous accusation. Next time we're faced with fallacious situations, CHALLENGE THEM! What's the worst that can happen? Oh, they might "cancel" us?... what a pity! And, we don't have to be reminded, we need to **vote** and **pray**! Never sit out an election. If there is fraud in our elections, pray to God that He will intervene. But we have to vote!

Finally, dive deeply into God's Word. I invite you to read a page every day from this book, and follow it up with reading the chapter from where the verse of the day was taken. It will feed your mind, feed your heart, and give you hope that we CAN bring God back into our nation. God Bless you all.

———§———

*"Learn the truth and never reject it. Get wisdom, self-control, and understanding."*
Proverbs 23:23 (NCV)

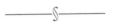

The principal document for truth is the Bible. It doesn't just contain truth—it is truth. Ultimately, truth is a Person—Jesus said, *"I am the Way and the Truth and the Life..."* John 14:6 (NLV) So, where we acquire truth does matter. Every time we read the Bible, we are engaging in a conversation with our living God. He reveals Who He is, and we apply the truths He lays out as we go about our lives.

For many, truth is relative or situational, which is based on one's experiences and opinions. This leads to the use of phrases like "your truth" or "my truth." For others, truth is based on consensus, or what the group thinks. This approach can have disastrous outcomes—a tactic in Hitler's playbook.

We are in a battle to maintain our constitutional republic. It doesn't matter if you are liberal or conservative, truth is crucial for victory. As an example, if a party's platform is pro-life, or same-sex marriage, it is imperative to seek God's truth on these types of issues, which should be our first wellspring of truth—not your favorite news source.

Learn God's truth. Teach your children His truth. Invest in it and watch it increase in value. And, never let go of it.

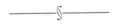

*Heavenly Father, help us to pour into your truth in all matters. You are the go-to Source for wisdom and understanding. Our prayer is that all Americans will rely on Your truth first, before allowing untruths, propaganda, and lies to influence our thinking and decisions.*

*"I am the Alpha and the Omega—the beginning and the end," says the Lord God. "I am the one who is, who always was, and who is still to come—the Almighty One."*

Revelation 1:8 (NLT)

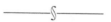

These past several years have been unsettling to say the least. It has driven us to ask questions like: "Where are we going as a nation?" "Will our economy survive the endless and reckless government spending?" "Will we get a handle on the crime and violence in our cities?" "Will our borders finally become secure?" "Will we become more self-sufficient when it comes to energy, manufacturing, and agriculture?" "Will ideology stop dividing us as a nation?" The questions are unceasing. Yet, the main question we should ask is "Who's in charge?"

The answer to that is found in this passage. The Lord Almighty is always in charge, as He has been, and will continue to be. Sadly, we often forget that truth because individually, and as a nation, we have taken our eyes off of our Creator; Protector; Provider; and Sustainer. The Old Testament is full of accounts of when God's people—Israel—did just that and paid a heavy price for doing so. Let's wake up America! Return to Him for strength and guidance to help us through these turbulent times until He returns again.

*Jesus, we praise and worship You for being with us now and always. Help us to rely on Your power to get us through the tough times as a nation. Our prayer is that we will return to our roots that are founded in You, and be a light to the world.*

# January 3                 God-Breathed Words

*"Every Scripture passage is inspired by God. All of them are useful for teaching, pointing out errors, correcting people, and training them for a life that has God's approval."*

2 Timothy 3:16 (GW)

When we finally open our Bibles and actually read the Scriptures, do we ever consider from Whom those inspired words came? The Bible is not just a potpourri of 66 books penned in antiquity. The Bible is God's revelation of Himself and His plan for humanity, which He inspired 40 different men of diverse backgrounds over the course of 1500 years. From all this diversity and lengthy span of years, we can't help but be in awe of the incredible unity and consistent messages woven throughout its divinely inspired pages.

Beyond this amazing evidence that the Bible is truly the inspiration from God, is the remarkable evidence of fulfilled prophecy. Hundreds of Bible prophecies have been fulfilled—specifically and meticulously—often long after the prophetic writer had passed away. So, is the Bible trustworthy? Yes! Yes! Yes! So, what is stopping us from feeding daily on the richness contained therein? God has given us a treasure chest of useful and invaluable information. No other book in the history of the world has the power to change lives like God's inspired Word.

*Heavenly Father, thank You for Your expression of love to us in Your precious Book. We pray that Your Holy Spirit would make us aware that we need to feed on Your living Word daily to nourish our soul. Help us to fully grasp the fact that the Bible is the only resource we need to teach us the truth, to convict us of our sins, to correct our paths, and to train us to live our life in ways that honor You and serve Your Kingdom.*

*"Peace I leave with you, My peace I give to you; not as the world gives do I give to you. Let not your heart be troubled, neither let it be afraid."*      John 14:27 (NKJV)

When our nation is struggling to find its roots in God, peace can seem unattainable. Daily we are exposed to so much noise and lies about ideas, methods, and actions that are far away from the principles upon which our country was founded. It's no wonder why we don't experience peace—especially the peace that Jesus promises. The presence of His Holy Spirit is the unbreakable link of our living relationship with God. This inner peace, which is independent of our circumstances, gives us the power to calm our greatest fear, and comfort our deepest sorrow. His peace gives the strength and courage to hold fast to our moral convictions and deepen our faith in the One Who saved us.

As Americans who love America, we aren't immune from the negative impact that inflation; open borders; human/drug trafficking; an ineffective and damaging education system; and ridiculous "woke" ideology has on us. We can experience peace even while the world is in turmoil. Jesus knows a thing or two about turmoil, suffering, and persecution. So when He says "My peace I give to You," we know that through all His suffering He experienced God's peace. The good news is that Jesus is still in the business of giving peace—to us.

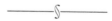

*God, fill us with your peace. Let our focus be on You and You alone. Please give us the courage and strength to grow from our troubles and circumstances, and bathe in the peace that only You can give.*

*"Your land is ruined; your cities have been burned with fire. While you watch, your enemies are stealing everything from your land; it is ruined like a country destroyed by enemies."*

Isaiah 1:7 (NCV)

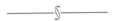

Although Isaiah wrote these words around 700 B.C. regarding the pending doom of Judah, it's like he is writing about the condition of our nation today. Just a few years ago, peaceful—*not really*—protesters burned our cities, and destroyed lives and businesses all from a mob-mentality propaganda ploy that was started by a few radical nation-haters. The incidents that spurred these protests could and should be handled civilly and justly—but when hate and evil are not held in check, the results are devastating. Look at what has happened to our nation because it has been invaded by foreigners illegally trampling on our cities; receiving countless benefits on the backs of tax-paying citizens; poisoning Americans with lethal illegal drugs; increasing the population of violent gangs; and opening the door to the heinous cartels from Mexico who have infiltrated our nation.

In Isaiah's time, God was not only placing blame on the people who had turned their backs on Him, he was placing blame on those who ruled them. When rulers are bad, bad things happen to those whom they rule. The good news is that there was a remnant of faithful in Isaiah's time—the question is, can we say the same today? Are we that remnant?

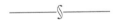

*Heavenly Father, are we living in a "history repeating itself" moment? I certainly feel that way. Our desire is that You would be restored to the Cornerstone of our nation and rid the evil that has permeated the core of who we are. We need You desperately.*

# January 6         Liar! Liar! Pants on Fire!

*"If a ruler pays attention to liars, all his advisers will be wicked."*
Proverbs 29:12 (NLT)

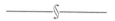

The events of January 6, 2021 were tragic in many respects. The biggest tragedy were the lies and deception put forth by media, radical leftists, and members of our own government. In spite of the numerous arrests made for supporters of the former President, none of those had been arrested for insurrection, sedition, or conspiracy to overthrow the government. A handful of bad actors had staged a plan to infiltrate the peaceful protest to turn it into a disorderly event. The media and many elected officials spewed out lie after lie, such as: police officers were killed (the only death was a female protester shot by capitol police officer); the original crowd was heavily armed (not a single gun was recovered in the riot) etc. Meanwhile, the media is virtually silent about other atrocities that had occurred in our nation in the past several years, such as: the BLM and Antifa riots that destroyed cities, business, and lives; the shooting of Republican Congressman Steve Scalise; banning the truths from *qualified* medical professionals about COVID-19; and the denial/coverup of alleged corruption of a presidential candidate prior to the 2020 elections etc.

The point is that when our leaders are not seeking guidance and wisdom from God, they are susceptible to sin and evil actions, which seeps into an entire administration or government. Seek truth; verify then trust.

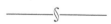

*God, we pray that our leaders would have hearts that seek Your truth and guidance. Please bless our nation with godly leaders who pursue truth and have discerning hearts.*

# January 7            What Would Jesus Do?

*"May integrity and uprightness protect me, because my hope, Lord, is in You."*
Psalm 25:21 (NIV)

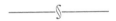

God has told us that where integrity of heart is characteristic of us, He will preserve, protect, and re-direct us. By integrity, we're talking about *wholeness* of heart toward God—not holiness. Holiness flows from wholeness, of which integrity is essential. Yet, we must decide to live an uncompromising life. What is an uncompromising life? It is a commitment to draw the lines in our life where the Word of God draws them. When we compromise, we refuse to adopt the biblical principles, which God has set before us. Integrity concerns our thoughts and our actions. God's perspective is that our thoughts and actions should be in harmony with moral values, rules, and norms.

When we substitute ourselves as the ones to be pleased, rather than God, we learn the art of compromise. We only fool ourselves when we fail to establish boundaries, and when we fail to listen to the "umpire" of our conscience, Who lets us know if our actions are "fair" or "foul." Even before we decide to cross our boundary, we can predict how our story will end. Integrity is what keeps our heart sensitive and responsive to God. When we are in any situation where we have to think if we are operating with integrity, or not, all we have to do is ask "What would Jesus Do?"—WWJD?

*Father God, we are grateful for Your protection and direction of our lives. God, we are faced with temptation each day. We ask for the same wisdom, courage, and resolve that Jesus displayed throughout His life on earth, so we may make choices in our lives that honor and please You. Help us to never compromise Your principles and truths. May our boundaries and commitment to You be faithful.*

*Then He said, "Beware! Guard against every kind of greed. Life is not measured by how much you own...Yes, a person is a fool to store up earthly wealth but not have a rich relationship with God."*

Luke 12:15; 21 (NIV)

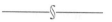

In some way, everything that is material from this planet comes out of the creation of God. So the issue is not possessions; it is our attitude toward them. The Scriptures provide numerous warnings about greed, whether it shows up as consumption or hoarding. And when we put our ceaseless allegiance to our possessions instead of God, we lose out on having a rich relationship with Him—which is spiritual bankruptcy. Whether we consume our money and/or possessions as fast as we acquire them, or anxiously hoard them for later consumption, we are living greedy and selfish lives. More importantly, we are letting God know that we do not trust Him to be our Provider, Sustainer, and Master of our life. We all need a guardrail to protect us against greed.

Greed does not only infect us as individuals, but also in corporations and all levels of government. How is it that a middle-income politician can leave office as a multi-millionaire. Many in our U.S. Congress are tied together with lobbyists from big corporations, big pharma, big tech etc. in a reciprocal, symbiotic relationship that feeds the greed—but dismisses their constituents. Vet political candidates before you vote.

*Heavenly Father, You have provided in the way that You intended. May we always put Your Kingdom first, and our kingdom second. Help us to understand that all we consume or hoard in this life, means nothing in eternity. May our greed be only confined to attaining a rich relationship with You.*

# January 9                 Godliness vs. Sin

*"Godliness makes a nation great, but sin is a disgrace to any people."*
Proverbs 14:34 (NLT)

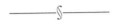

Our nation was founded on Christian principles. God has been in control of the rise and fall of every kingdom or nation from the beginning of time until now. Not one of these (including America) can stay in power longer than God allows. God judges all nations and brings judgment upon sinful nations, which is the cause of each nation's downfall. Let's examine the life of our nation. Have we drifted from our founding doctrine of godliness?

The Establishment Clause of the First Amendment was designed to prevent the establishment of a government-run church. Yet as time went on, our nation started manipulating this clause to declare a separation of church and state, which is actually not in the Constitution. The result is that we began to take God out of our founding—and our lives. The real downfall began in 1962 when we the Supreme Court ruled to remove prayer in public schools. Look where public schools are today—a far cry from godliness.

Our moral decline is on a fast-track to becoming a total disgrace to God and those who love Him. It is the responsibility of each one of us to uphold the biblical truths upon which this nation was formed, and once again have godliness front and center in our lives.

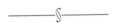

*Almighty God, forgive us for standing by as You have been removed from many aspects of our lives. Stir those in leadership to return to our founding principles. God, awaken our hearts to do what is right according to Your will and save our nation.*

# January 10           Idol Worship

*"Those who cling to worthless idols turn away from God's love for them."*
Jonah 2:8 (NIV)

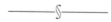

Being lured by idols, losing sight of God's good providence, and clinging instead to false security, are all part of the human condition. Idol worship happens whenever we substitute anything in the place of God, as what's most important in life. When we hear the word *idol*, we often think of statues and objects reminiscent of those worshiped by pagans in ancient cultures. However, the idols of our day often bear no resemblance to the artifacts used thousands of years ago. Today, many have replaced the *golden calf* with an insatiable drive for money or prestige or success in the eyes of the world.

We all are guilty to some degree of manufacturing little gods for ourselves. We may not have a statue or image to which we bow down, but we do have habits; traditions; activities; people; and possessions that we place ahead of God. Pleasure, riches, and honors often become man's *trinity*. These things, in and of themselves, are not bad. The problem is that we become seduced by these to point of putting our Lord on the back burner. In order to identify and tear down the idols of our soul, we must ask ourselves, "What is the object of my affections, my efforts, and my attention? On what do I spend the greatest amount of my time and resources? What is seducing my soul?" We need only worship God!

Lord, You are the giver of life and all the blessings to enjoy this life. Forgive us for elevating these good these good things to god-things. Forgive us the worshipping these created things, rather than You, our Creator. Help us to detox our soul, and be filled with the joy of loving, worshipping, and serving You—our One true God.

# Joy to the Fullest

*"I have told these things so that you can have the same joy I have and so that your joy will be the fullest possible joy."*                    John 15:11 (NCV)

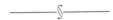

The joy that Jesus wants us to have differs from how the world views joy. Jesus said, *"I came that they may have life, and have it abundantly."* (John 10:10) So, what is the abundant life of which Jesus speaks? Is it good health; all the money we could want; all the activities that we enjoy; and no problems in life? Man's idea of joy is to be as happy as he can by leaving God out of his life.

The joy of Christ is not found in tangible things. His joy is true joy—a joy that is lasting. It is a joy that is unspeakable, unshakeable, and full of glory. It's a joy that transforms our soul and gives us new life. Jesus taught that we are blessed with real joy when we have Him in our lives as much as possible. Jesus desires nothing more than for us to just be with Him as much as we possibly can. When we do, His joy overflows and is poured out into our hearts—the kind of joy most of us have never truly experienced. So, when we really examine our *Jesus time*, we'll most likely conclude that it is pretty minimal—perhaps a daily prayer and reading His Word when we can fit it into our busy schedules. Yet, in order to have His joy to the fullest, we need to put much more effort into our communion time with Jesus. Aren't you just a bit curious to know what that kind of joy is like?

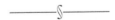

*Jesus, joy in its fullness is found in You; it is defined by You; and delivered by You. How blessed we are that You love us that much to share this magnificent gift with us. May each of us commit to being with You as much as possible each and every day through prayer; meditation; reading Your Word; worship; service; and in our thoughts and actions. May your priorities become our priorities, and may Your joy become our joy to the fullest.*

*"Do not judge others, and you will not be judged. Do not condemn others, or it will all come back against you. Forgive others, and you will be forgiven."* Luke 6:37 (NLT)

———§———

We often enthusiastically embrace the teachings of Jesus. Yet, some of His teachings challenge us to the point of finding them almost impossible to put into practice—especially in today's political climate. This verse happens to be one of them. It's a tough one to apply.

Jesus is forbidding careless, hasty, unwarranted, unjust, and unmerciful condemnation that is usually brought about by self-righteous pride. In other words, stop criticizing! Now there are several Scripture verses that instruct us to evaluate; discern; and distinguish the difference between good and evil, or between true and false doctrine. But we're not to judge or criticize the motives of others. We are not to condemn them because they don't look, speak, or act like we think they should. And too often, we are quick to judge or criticize—well before we have all the facts. There is no way we can fully know the heart of another. This leads to making an assessment of someone that is not based on reality, because we don't know the circumstances of that person—which results in judgment or criticism that is intended to tear down or destroy. How we think or speak about our neighbor reveals much about our own experience of God's grace and mercy. What Jesus is teaching us in this verse is that as we continually forgive others, we are practicing what God continually does for us.

———§———

*Heavenly Father, we thank You that You have been so gracious as to forgive us of our countless sins. You have been far more merciful with us than we are with each other. Help us to follow Your instruction, and lead us to be tender-hearted, kind, and forgiving. Help us to not set ourselves up as judges, while maintaining discernment for those times when rebuke and restoration is needed.*

# January 13           Integrity

*"I know, my God, that you examine our hearts and rejoice when you find integrity there."*
1 Chronicles 29:17 (NLT)

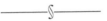

The hallmark of the Christian life is integrity. This is the virtue that holds everything in place, and without it our character crumbles. Integrity, and the lack of it, touches every area of our life—the health of our marriage; the character of our children; our testimony at work; among friends; in our church; and the vitality of our relationship with God. Our integrity is the sum of our disposition, our thoughts, our intentions, our desires, our speech and our actions. And, it is influenced and developed by our choices. Integrity is wholeness of purpose; total honesty; and a whole-hearted and blameless approach to life. For Christians, integrity means that we live our life by godly standards, godly principles, and godly values no matter where we are; whom we are with; or what our circumstances may be. Integrity is making our daily actions line up with our heart's values.

Our integrity is put to the test every day, in virtually every situation. We live in an imperfect world that seems to suggest that it is *foolishness* to be honest and righteous. All around us we encounter people who actually appear to be rewarded for their dishonesty and lack of integrity. This is a real challenge for the man or woman who decides to walk in integrity. We are being watched closely to see how we will respond to every situation in life. Is our walk matching our talk; our behavior matching our beliefs; and our character matching our confession?

*God we pray that we would all be willing to closely examine all the areas of our life and admit if we are lacking integrity in any way, shape or form. If so, God we pray that You would forgive us, and Your Holy Spirit would give us the strength to have our behavior match our belief in every pondered thought, spoken word, or action taken.*

*The wine supply ran out during the festivities, so Jesus' mother told Him, "They have no more wine." "Dear woman, that's not our problem," Jesus replied. "My time has not yet come."*

John 2:3-4 (NLT)

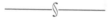

A huge social faux pas was about to take place while Jesus, His mother, and a few disciples were attending a wedding. The hosts were about to run out of wine. Mary knew before anyone that her son was the Messiah. For decades she patiently waited to share her wonderful secret with the world. Their mother/son relationship, which had existed for thirty years, was about to change. To call her "mother" would have kept that relationship kind of intact. "Woman" shows that she is now to relate, not with her son, but with the Son of God.

Jesus' response to His mother clarified three misconceptions. First, the Messiah's glory would come at the expense of His death—not as the result of a dazzling show of power. Secondly, the Messiah's glory would come from God—not from people. And thirdly, the Messiah's glory would take place on the Father's timetable—not anyone else's. Yet, Mary understood and directed the servers to follow any order Jesus might give. Somewhere between the jars and wedding coordinator, the miraculous transformation took place. Water became wine. This simple act of kindness was for the sake of love for His friends. Jesus didn't make it sideshow spectacle. In the Gospel of John, the entire life of Jesus was directed toward obeying the Father and fulfilling the hour. This was the first of many miracles by Jesus.

*Thank You God for the privilege of getting to know You through Your written Word. May we apply these teachings to our lives. May we also follow Your will and Your timetable.*

# January 15                              Holy Allegiance

*"But thanks be to God that, though you used to be slaves to sin, you have come to obey from your heart the pattern of teaching that has now claimed your allegiance. You have been set free from sin and have become slaves to righteousness."*     Romans 6:17 (NIV)

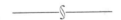

We all serve something; it's just a matter of what. Some are slaves of their work. These servants of busyness and achievement can't shut down their laptops for more than a couple of hours at a time and their electronic devices are all but surgically implanted in their hands. They take working vacations to appease neglected loved ones and miserly hoard days off they never intend to take. A balanced life always lies just beyond the current project deadline.

Some are slaves to things, possessions, temporal stuff. Driven by the fantasy that contentment can be found in having things, they cannot stop acquiring long enough to enjoy what they already own. Perhaps the increasingly common slaves are those who are enslaved to the god of self. Psychologists call them narcissists. The name comes from a figure in Roman mythology named Narcissus, who fell in love with his own reflection in a stream.

The Gospel has present, ongoing, and eternal implications. But something happens immediately when we receive the grace of God through faith. We instantly are given a new heart; a new nature that hates sin; and a new desire to obey its new master—righteousness. We become slaves to righteousness and now have holy allegiance.

*Father God, thank You for freeing us from the slavery to sin. We are not perfect, yet through Your grace and mercy, we have a new allegiance that is so fulfilling and eternal. We strive each day for Your righteousness. You are a priority over all else in our lives.*

*"But how can people call for help if they don't know who to trust? And how can they know who to trust if they haven't heard of the One who can be trusted? And how can they hear if nobody tells them?"*

Romans 10:14 (MSG)

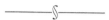

Mission is sharing Who Jesus is and the eternal salvation He offers, as well as the impact He has made on our lives. Mission takes place in the everyday and the ordinary. It is a local and global outreach to love our neighbor. We live in a world full of lost people. We can find them in a remote village half a world away; or in our neighborhoods; our workplaces; our schools; our own families; and even our government. Jesus has commanded us to go and share the Gospel with all people in the world (Matt. 28:19) — marching orders for the church to carry on His work. Why is it that we are satisfied to be saved, but not motivated to see others come to know Jesus Christ as their Lord and Savior?

Somehow, we have come to believe that our responsibility ends when we come to church each week; pray when we can; read the Bible every now and then; and live a life that is slightly cleaner than the world around us. Jesus told us exactly what He expects of us. While He may never call us to go to a foreign land to tell the story of salvation, He does expect us to tell it to those He has placed in our lives. Destinations and details will vary, but the commission is the same for all of us: *"Go and make disciples."* Mundane or magnificent, the assignment from God is given with the assurance that His Holy Spirit will be with us every step of the way. The Gospel message was meant to be spread, through going or sending.

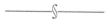

*God, set our hearts on fire and embrace our assignment to reach out to the lost, whether our mission field is near or far away. Help us to be Your hands and feet.*

# January 17  Fake News

*"Good people hate what is false, but the wicked do shameful and disgraceful things."*
Proverbs 13:5 (NCV)

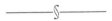

These days it seems we are inundated with lies; misinformation; disinformation; radical propaganda; and omission of truth. Our digital age emits these disgraceful things to us non-stop and at warp speed. Sadly, no matter what side of the aisle you claim to be part of, each side has its share of wicked and shameful people who engage in these antics. For example, some political leaders and news outlets—with a bias toward the left—claim our southern border is secure; while those on the right are screaming from the roof tops that we have an unmanageable crisis. As far as lies from those on the right—I have to be honest, I can't think of any at this time, but I'm sure they exist. Oh, one just popped into my mind—the Congressman from New York who was elected in 2022. He made countless claims about his background that was littered with made-up accomplishments—Now, that was some resumé!

So, what do people who hate what is false do about it? First and foremost, turn to God. Chapter six of the Book of Proverbs, lists the seven things that God hates—one of them is a *lying tongue*. Seek His guidance and wisdom. Look at all sides of an issue; situation; statement; report; or candidate; then you can determine if it falls on the side of truth or the side of lies. We will never rid our schools, businesses, and governments from evil and wickedness, but we can be discerning and seek truth—God's truth.

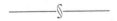

*God, set our hearts and minds on what is true. May we practice discernment and truth-seeking to detect and dismiss what is false from lying tongues, and dispel the wickedness that is so prevalent in our world.*

# January 18                                          Narrow Gate

*"You can enter God's Kingdom only through the narrow gate. The highway to hell is broad, and its gate is wide for the many who choose that way. But the gateway to life is very narrow and the road is difficult, and only a few ever find it."*    Matthew 7:13-14 (NLT)

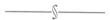

Too often, we desire to follow the crowd because we're afraid of being labeled as "weird" or have a fear of being *canceled*. However, living in a way that the world deems to be "normal" and trying to fit in, is a dangerous path. It is a reckless way of life that leaves a wake of death and destruction in so many ways: physically; emotionally; financially; relationally; and spiritually. The good news is that we were not designed to have a "normal" life. God doesn't call us to live like the rest of the world. He empowers us to live like His Son, Jesus Christ. According to Scripture passages, God's people should always feel somewhat out of place in this world. The Psalmist said, *"I am a stranger on earth..."* (Ps. 119:19) To live as a stranger means that our life is going to be morally different from the so-called normal people who are shaped by the culture and values of this world.

We don't have to accept the "woke culture" that has contaminated our nation with hate, violence, divisiveness, lies, and corruption. We can—and must—take a stand! We're all going to stand out for something—shouldn't we stand out for being a Christ follower? Let's start by embracing our "weirdness."

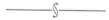

*God, You have given every human the freedom to make choices. Choosing the narrow gate is not a popular choice, and one that might be considered weird. Yet, You have given us a very clear warning if we choose the wide gate. Lord, by Your grace and power, move our hearts to come to Your truth, and embrace Your path.*

# January 19                        Only Two Genders!

*So God created human beings in His image. In the image of God He created them. He created them male and female.*                        Genesis 1:27 (NCV)

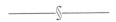

Gender is clearly defined in the Bible. "Transgender" is a made-up word by those who clearly are far from God. Everywhere in the world, babies are born each day—either male or female. It is sickening that children are being inundated—from a very young age—with brainwashing and indoctrinating messages about sexuality and gender.

This dangerous propaganda has dismissed God's creation of two genders and instead tells children they can have a "Baskin-Robbins" approach to their life by choosing from over 50 gender identities. It gets crazier—they can even identify as a plant or an animal.

Our schools have become battlegrounds that promote cultural change; a change that leads to the fall of our nation. What's worse is that schools are doing their best to hide these hideous antics from parents. We have become the laughingstock of the world with our focus being on issues like gender-identity. We need to get into the battle and eradicate this nonsense. It starts in our communities. Get involved. Attend school board meetings to see for yourself how children's minds are being manipulated with evil. Pray, pray, pray!

*Heavenly Father, how much longer will You put up with us? We know this absolutely breaks Your heart, as it does ours. Give us the guidance, strength, and courage to fight against this evil and regain control of our education system that should be based on moral truths.*

# January 20                    Ditch Diggers

*Then Elisha said, "The LORD says, to dig holes in the valley. The LORD says you will not see wind or rain, but that valley will be filled with water. Then you, your cattle and your other animals will drink."*

2 Kings 3:16-17 (NCV)

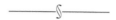

God has often called upon His people to do things that, at first, didn't seem to make any sense at all. He told Noah to build an Ark, when there had never been a need for such a big boat prior to that. God told Joshua to have the people march once a day for six days around the outer walls of Jericho. Then He told them to march around seven times on the seventh day, and the walls would simply fall down with a shout. What a crazy way to take a city, but it worked! There are many other examples, but the point is that God often asks people to do different things that no one else would do—and then wait on Him for the results. We must never forget that God never gives a command for which there is not a good reason behind it. He just wants our faith.

When the king of Israel, the king of Judah, and the king of Edom set out to go to war against the king of Moab, they soon ran out of water on route to the battle. They needed a miracle from God! Elisha the prophet was summoned to call upon God for help. Now, God could have sent rain, but He chose to use the assistance of the army to dig numerous ditches throughout the valley. Did God really need their help? No! God did so because He needed to see that they had faith. God filled the ditches with the much-needed water. Let us all dig a ditch, so that God can fill it!

*God, help us to grasp the fact that You want to see our faith become truly active, and respond to Your instruction with obedience as we experience the privilege participating in Your amazing and wondrous work.*

# January 21          Seek Truth and Wisdom

*"It is the greatness of God to keep things hidden, but it is the greatness of kings to find things out."*          Proverbs 25:2 (NLV)

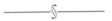

We will certainly never fully know and understand the ways of God—at least on this side of heaven. In Isaiah 55:9, God says that His ways are *"higher than"* ours. Yet God does want us to seek Him and His wisdom through our desire and effort to study; examine; research; and learn those hidden truths.

This is more imperative for those in leadership and power to pursue. When kings (and presidents) fail to properly seek truth about matters that impact those whom they lead, great harm comes to their kingdoms/nations. When a president is so filled with pride and has an agenda that is corrupt and lacks God's truth and wisdom, decay of a nation takes place. This level of arrogance causes kings or presidents to solely focus on holding on to power, instead of exercising prudence.

Before making decisions about a nation's energy production; illegal immigration; our failing education system; or our national debt; a leader should seek the truth about issues, and anticipate the consequences of decisions and actions of such. We honor God's greatness when we seek His wisdom and truth. We wish members of our government would do the same.

*Heavenly Father, we are guilty for the times we go-it-alone, and fail to seek the truth of Your Word first. God, we know that You have been removed from so much in our nation, but we pray for our leaders—that their hearts would be softened to pursue You instead of power and pride.*

*"You are the salt of the earth; but if the salt loses its flavor, how shall it be seasoned? Let your light so shine before men, that they may see your good works and glorify your Father in heaven."*
                                              Matthew 5:13,16 (NKJV)

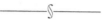

Leadership is a gift, a set of abilities given to some people by God, and developed through circumstances God has set in place uniquely preparing them to become leaders. Not everyone is a leader. On the other hand, influence is simply faithfulness at work. It can be overt or subtle, spoken or acted. *Each* one of us is an *influencer*, even in the tiniest of ways. Jesus has called each one of us to take on the role of influencer and to impact our world, as Christ's ambassadors. From a spiritual sense, salt is used as a preservative, protecting society from the effects of evil. It is a flavoring or seasoning, which gives others a taste of how life is to be lived in God's Kingdom. It is an antiseptic, where we can offer healing and help to the wounds that are the result of sin. It creates thirst when we share with others the love and eternal blessings of Jesus.

We are also called to be the light of the world. Light dispels darkness—spiritual darkness, which is so prevalent in the world. Light reveals, awakens, and warns of the dangers that exist when life is lived without God as the central focus. It is what sets us apart from the rest of the world. In order to prevent the world from affecting us and weakening our ability to be effective in our sphere of influence, we must stay in close contact with the ultimate Influencer—Christ Himself.

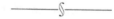

*Almighty God, help us to see that our spheres of influence are far greater than we know. Help us to be Your salt and light in this world.*

# January 23                                    Fear God

*"Sin lurks deep in the hearts of the wicked, forever urging them on to evil deeds. They have no fear of God to hold them back. Instead, in their conceit, they think they can hide their evil deeds and not get caught."*                    Psalm 36:1-2 (TLB)

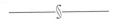

When we have no fear of God, it is revealed in three areas of our lives: our character; our conversation; and our conduct. If we were aware that all of our thoughts, words, and actions would be displayed publicly for everyone to witness, it's highly likely that would make a difference in how we live. Yet, that is simply just having the fear of man. If we have this kind of fear of other people's opinion of us, how much more should we have of the fear of God?

Sadly, some people of power in our nation don't fear God or man. Unchecked, this casualness grows dangerously risky. Sin is a consequence and condition of the absence of reverence for God. Taking its place is the pursuit of opportunities to gratify one's desire to do evil, and God is no longer part of one's life. Fearing God is revering Him; respecting Him; obeying Him; submitting to His discipline; and worshipping Him with awe. When we fear God, we fear displeasing Him. It is not only something we learn, it is something we choose. We make a conscious choice each day what place God is going to have in our life. When we fear the Lord, we flee from evil because the prospect of displeasing God is unbearable.

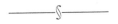

*Heavenly Father, we recognize Your might, Your power, Your holiness, and Your justice surpasses all else. God, help us to gain the perspective that fearing You, our Creator, will land us in the place where knowledge and wisdom of You is rightly employed. Help us to embrace the fact that fearing You and loving You are inseparably linked.*

*"That's why I take pleasure in my weaknesses, and in the insults, hardships, persecutions, and troubles that I suffer for Christ. For when I am weak, then I am strong."*

2 Corinthians 12:10 (NLT)

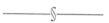

Scripture is full of promises God has made and kept. Unfortunately, many of us have misconstrued certain Biblical verses (i.e. 1 Cor. 10:13) and have heard, or even quoted such adages as: "God won't give you more than you can handle." The truth is—God never promised that! In fact, Jesus warned His disciples (and us) that, *"In this world you will have trouble and suffering."* (John 16:33) Our weakness is God's instrument. God will actually allow us to experience more than we can handle so that He—in His infinite grace—can root out our sin and replace it with a deeper love for Him and His strength. Here is the cornerstone of a Christian life: We will have trouble! Trouble is also humbling. God proved this point through Job, who was humbled to ashes, yet never lost his faith. God also uses suffering to draw us to Himself—into the intimacy of His glorious presence. God uses suffering to display His grace. In those times of tribulation, He will pour out enough of His grace so that we can endure these trials. And God will use our times of suffering to perfect His power. When we get to the place where we have lost all human ability to deal with difficulty, we've got nowhere to go. That's when we realize we are weak and unable to fix it. That is when we know we have nothing but God—and that is enough.

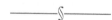

*Heavenly Father, thank You for giving us a better understanding of Your purpose for allowing the difficulties we experience in this world. Thank You for those times when You draw us to Yourself and put Your grace on display, bringing us to the end of ourselves so that our total trust is in You, and we can become powerful in our weakness. May we confirm these truths in our hearts.*

# January 25                    Love God, Not the World

*"Do not love this world nor the things it offers you, for when you love the world, you do not have the love of the Father in you."*                    1 John 2:15 (NLT)

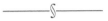

We live in crazy times, yet this has been the case since the first sin. The *world* has conceived a system of values and goals from which God is excluded. John is forbidding those things, the love of which rivals and excludes the love of God—all those immoral tendencies and pursuits, which give the world its evil character. These dangers never cease to exist, so it is imperative for believers to continue to advance along our spiritual journey by remaining in Him always.

This principle should take root and flourish in the family, first and foremost, so that godly examples are made available to follow. It's an on-going balancing act to discern the physical world, which is to be admired as the work of God, from man's sinful nature that has corrupted this world He created. Just look at the depraved condition of our nation as an example. There is so much moral decay and evil that is polluting our nation. But, we don't hear the climate change fearmongers talking about this type of pollution. Therefore, the more we put God first in our lives on a daily basis, the less likely we will succumb to worldliness.

*Lord, we thank You for Your saving grace and love for us. May Your gift of love infuse us with power for a life of godliness, and protect us from the craziness and evil of this world. Give us wisdom for guarding our hearts to protect us from the lure of putting more importance on things of this world over You. Surround us with people who are bold enough to speak truth into our lives, and give us that same courage to speak to others who may stumble.*

*"For wisdom will enter your heart, and knowledge will fill you with joy. Wise choices wi[ll] watch over you. Understanding will keep you safe."*     Proverbs 2:10-11 (NLT)

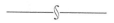

True wisdom is much more than intellectual knowledge. It's a transformation of character. When we gain wisdom, we become changed people. Obtaining wisdom requires diligence on our part in pursuing God's will—yet wisdom is a gift from God. Having such knowledge from God gives us inner joy. Therefore, wisdom must not only fill our heads, it must enter and live in our hearts in order to have a commanding power and influence on our choices and actions. Wisdom is knowing and having discernment, so that we can apply the truth of the Word of God at the right time; in the right way; with the right motive.

Godly wisdom in our hearts can protect us from making troublesome or immoral choices yielded from temptation and/or ungodly influence. Seek God's will especially when it comes to choosing relationships. God's wisdom is not subjective. It is clearly and objectively revealed in God's Word. When we make wise decisions and choices, we will experience joy, and feel safe and confident about those choices.

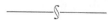

*Father God, we praise and thank You for Your gracious gift of wisdom. We pray that wisdom and discernment will reign in our hearts and that the choices and decisions that we make daily will be in alignment with Your will. We ask for your deliverance from the temptations and dangers of this world, and we would instead seek Your guidance prior to making any decisions or choices, so that those actions will be wise ones.*

# January 27                                    Faith like Joseph

*It was by faith that Joseph, when he was about to die, said confidently that the people of Israel would leave Egypt. He even commanded them to take his bones with them when they left.*                                    Hebrews 11:22 (NLT)

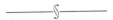

The faith of Joseph was remarkable. After the way his family treated him, as well as the ungodly influence of Egypt, you would think he would have abandoned his faith. But instead, it grew stronger—even at times when it seemed God was absent. Like his forefathers, he was not perfect, but he was devoted to God and trusted His Word. God's promises were handed down from one generation to another. Joseph believed that God would one day deliver his people from Egypt, and knew that his remains belonged in the land God had promised them. That promise of deliverance was fulfilled 359 years after Joseph's death. Despite the testing and trials of his life, his faith remained secure.

We struggle to understand the actions of our government at times. Our disdain for and frustration about those actions and decisions can boil to a crescendo that starts to erode our faith that God is actually in control. If Joseph's faith could remain secure, despite all he had endured, why can't ours?

*God, may this give us comfort in those times it seems we don't feel Your presence. You will not leave us or forsake us, and that is an amazing promise. Although we can't see or touch You, we trust that You are here with us. May our confidence and faith grow even stronger, so that we will follow You in times of uncertainty.*

*"I have treasured Your word in my heart, so I might not sin against You."*

Psalm 119:11 (TLV)

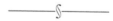

As part of our sinful nature, we experience temptation daily. If not properly dealt with, temptation will lead to sin. God does not lead us to sin—we choose to sin by giving in to our internal desire to sin. Sin takes place when the temptation strikes a pleasant chord in the human heart, to which we have no one to blame but ourselves. There is hope, however. God's Word becomes an integral part of a believer's life—it fortifies us against temptation's power. Another weapon we have to put the kibosh on temptation is prayer. In Mark 14:38, Jesus told His disciples, *"Watch and pray that you may not enter into temptation. The spirit indeed is willing, but the flesh is weak."* These are wise words from Christ to help us to seek the needed grace and strength from God, when dealing with temptation.

When we treasure something, we hold it dear to our heart and make time for it. The Word of God helps us grow spiritually; guides us when we are unsure; challenges us to live righteously in a secular world; and adds value to our life.

*Heavenly Father, we know that only good things come from You. Unfortunately, we fail to be satisfied with all Your goodness, and fail to see the big picture. We are blessed with Your promise to place limitations on the intensity of temptation; You know what we can bear. You only allow temptations that we can handle. The temptation may seem enormous, but it pales in comparison to Your love for us. God, You know our circumstances, our character, and the plan that will provide victory and new maturity. Please engrave that in our hearts so we will remember it the moment we are tempted.*

*Then Peter began to speak: "I now realize how true it is that God does not show favoritism."*

Acts 10:34 (NIV)

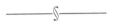

The glorious faith we have in Christ should never be associated with partiality, favoritism, or discrimination. God Himself shows no favoritism—so neither should we who put our trust in Him. We sometimes think God sees color, gender, or economic status—He only sees the heart. We are the ones who look at those things and form an unfair bias based purely on the external appearance, rather than the internal. When we do this, we miss the mind and heart of God.

Unfortunately, we live in a time where race, gender, age, political affiliation and other factors of ideology have become part of every aspect of our lives—and not in a good way. Abuse of the word "racist" or "racism" is spewed about in an ignorant manner by many individuals—which in itself is discriminatory. Jesus crossed numerous barriers and lines to spread His Good News. If Jesus had limited His message of love and eternal life solely on one's gender, race, national origin, etc., we might have missed out on His salvation. God sees only one race—the *human race*—as His favorite!

*God, we are so blessed that You love each of us equally, and have chosen us to be part of Your eternal family. You have graciously done so without bias, prejudice, and partiality because You see us from the inside out. God, we seek to have this same perspective. Forgive us when we take our eyes off of You and seek fulfillment from those things or people in the world that we think can make us better. Help us to treat people equally.*

*"Whoever has respect for the Lord lives a good life. But those who hate Him walk down an evil path."*
         Proverbs 14:2 (NIRV)

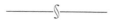

This defiance, rebellion, disobedience and even hate against God is nothing new. It has been around since the creation of man. The ungodly refuse to follow the guidance and direction that God gives. Our society today gives evidence of this rebellion through political extremes; corruption of our educational system; lack of accountability and justice for criminal acts; tax dollars funding abortions; and the breakdown of the family.

The ungodly who have this mindset know they can't actually take their disdain out against God directly, so instead they lash out against the godly—those who remind the evil-doers of their sins. This is a battle that will go on until Christ returns. So, we need to ask ourselves, "Are we willing to surrender to evil, or fight back?" God has been removed from so much in our society/world. And it will continue until we stand up and take action. It's up to us to bring Him back and make Him the cornerstone of our lives, and our nation.

*Heavenly Father, our fallen world is getting out of hand. We call upon You for strength and courage to ward off the evil that is in all aspects of our society. We pray that those who have turned their backs on You would see the error of their ways. Give us guidance and wisdom to fight the battle to return You to the center of our lives and the core of our society. We pray that You would raise up godly leaders who can enact laws and policies that focus on the good that You bring to all of us.*

**Faith Produces Love**

*"The only thing that counts is faith expressing itself through love."*
Galatians 5:6 (NIV)

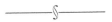

God's grace is a free gift. If we have to work for our faith, we nullify His free grace. Faith has nothing to do with works. We are not hired by God to do works in order that He will pay us with faith. Faith, through which we are justified, is not simply cognitive understanding. It is a life-changing conviction. We receive the power of the Holy Spirit by faith.

This faith produces love, which if it is genuine faith, is expressed in works and deeds that represent the love we have for God and for others. It produces love by removing certain things like; greed; guilt; and fear from the heart. Faith gives to our hearts the love, promise, forgiveness, and faithfulness of God, which move us to love. Faith is not something we merely claim, feel, think, or believe. We can't see someone's faith, but we can demonstrate the genuineness of our faith through accepting God's grace and expressing it faithfully in love.

*Father God, thank You for your abundant grace You have poured out to us. Your redemption is truly a gift, for we could never have earned this on our own. You live in our hearts through Your Holy Spirit, and for that we are tremendously blessed. May our lives, and all we do, bring honor to You. Please cultivate genuine faith in our hearts so all our actions profoundly express our love for You, and our love for others.*

# February 1          Wisdom Through Humility

*"After pride came, disgrace followed; but wisdom came with humility."*
Proverbs 11:2 (NET)

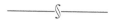

Wisdom isn't gained simply through attending formal education and perhaps earning a degree. It's not something for which you can pay money to achieve. Gaining wisdom is a daily, life-long process of growth, which we should pursue. The path a prideful person takes in order to gain wisdom is an uphill battle because pride does not allow one to admit their errors; to seek and accept advice from God; and ultimately achieve true happiness.

When we look for an example of humility, we need only look at Christ. Humility is acknowledging that God controls everything. When we submit ourselves to God and depend on Him alone, we can discard our prideful and self-righteous attitudes and bask in His grace, mercy, love, and protection. Lust, greed, and pride are evil desires of the world, that lead to disgrace. Unfortunately, we have seen leaders in our nation that have chosen pride over humility, which has brought disgrace on them and our nation as a whole. This pride leads to complete denial of their wrong-doing—despite being caught red-handed. But they have Big Tech and the left-leaning media to have their backs—all the while turning their backs on God.

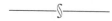

*God, we humbly come to You knowing that You are the Source of wisdom. Forgive us for the times we have allowed pride and self-centeredness to contaminate our relationships with You and others, and have prevented us from gaining true wisdom. We seek Your grace and humbly depend on Your will to prevail. We pray that our leaders will seek wisdom, as well.*

# February 2

# Spiritual Gifts

*"God has given each of you a gift from His great variety of spiritual gifts. Use them well to serve one another."*

1 Peter 4:10 (NLT)

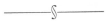

Every believer has graciously been given at least one spiritual gift. God considers each gift to be equally valuable, and expects us to use these talents for serving in His Kingdom. We are "spiritual snowflakes" in that we are individually gifted with abilities unique to us. Now, please don't confuse the term "snowflake" with the term commonly used to describe some people in a younger generation who are often offended by opinions that differ from theirs—which sometimes require "safe spaces", and/or feel entitled to special treatment. Hopefully, they find their safe space in God.

Our spiritual gifts, which God aligns with our DNA, are to used to serve. Jesus' joy came from doing the Father's will. So it stands to reason that our joy should also come from doing His will by utilizing the gifts and talents, which are empowered by the Holy Spirit, in serving others. What breaks the heart of God more than witnessing the "holes" in the world, is seeing His children doing nothing about it. Let's put our gifts to work; serve others; and experience the same joy as that of Christ.

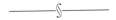

*Lord, You have opened our eyes to the condition of the world. Now it is time for us to do something about it. At the very least, we can pray. Beyond that, God we ask that Your Holy Spirit would guide us to discover our talents and abilities, with which You have graciously blessed us, and allow us see the vast number of ways that we can employ those gifts to help improve the spiritual condition of our world.*

# February 3        Heeding God's Warnings

*"God's Word warns us of danger and directs us to hidden treasure."*
Psalm 19:11 (MSG)

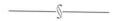

God communicates with us in numerous ways, yet none more complete than through Scripture. His Word guides; instructs; and warns us against sin, error, foolishness, and every other threat to our spiritual well-being. How we respond to His instruction and warnings is of great concern to God. Will we delay taking action through procrastination? Will we bury our head in the sand through our denial? Will we become passive and do nothing? None of these options are advisable.

The Bible is full of countless examples of people who heeded God's warnings, as well as those who chose to ignore them—like Lot's wife and Adam and Eve. They paid a heavy price for their disobedience, which should serve as warning lights to us. Instead, we can acknowledge His warnings and respond without delay by going to God with a humble and repentant heart. In doing so, we can experience the hidden treasure of wisdom found in His Word, and knowing we are acting according to God's will.

*Father God, how blessed we are that Your love, grace, and patience is unending. God, forgive us for thinking even for a moment that we can get through this life on our own. We are nothing without You. Forgive us for the times when our pride, stubbornness, laziness, or spiritual blindness results in our failure to respond to Your warnings. As Your Creation is perfect, so is the Word You have given us. Thank You for sending Your Holy Spirit to guide and protect us. May we respond to You without hesitation and find joy in Your will.*

# February 4                                    Undeserved Grace

*"For God saved us and called us to live a holy life. He did this, not because we deserved it, but because that was His plan from before the beginning of time—to show us His grace through Christ Jesus."*                                    2 Timothy 1:9 (NLT)

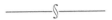

How amazing it is that we have been saved by the grace of God, despite the labels we have been assigned and the reputations we have earned, as a result of our choices and actions. Yet our past (and present) sin cannot contend with the grace of our Lord and Savior, Jesus Christ. We've done nothing to deserve this—He has done it all for us! As if this wasn't enough, God continues to bless us with the privilege of having a personal relationship with Him, whereby we can praise and worship Him directly, any time we wish. He's always with us to answer our prayers—even to the point of blessing us with an occasional miracle or two.

It is a tragedy that our nation is drifting from God's grace. Without Him in our lives, we won't acknowledge, let alone repent to correct the course. This has been happening at a greater speed in recent years, and *we the people* are suffering from destructive choices our leaders are making. Pray that God will not give up on us!

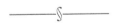

*Almighty God, You love us beyond measure, despite our unworthiness and despite our sinfulness. In Your mercy and grace, You have looked past the labels and reputations we have acquired. You have done for us what we could never do for ourselves. May we always be mindful of this truth. Please change the hearts of those who are in power, and have their decisions and actions reflect You.*

# February 5                      Atrocious Sins

*"So put all evil things out of your life: sexual sinning, doing evil, letting evil thoughts control you, wanting things that are evil, and greed. This is really serving a false god."*

Colossians 3:5 (NCV)

The carnal mind has purposes, aspirations, and desires that are hostile to God. The goal of the carnal mindset revolves around temporal things that will one day pass away. If our minds are centered in Christ and focused on the things that please God, we can begin to take on His character. Just because we are Christians does not mean we are exempt from temptations the world offers. Yet, because we have the Holy Spirit in us, we have the power and ability to focus on things that are above—not on worldly things. We all have the responsibility to investigate the areas of our life where sin could potentially destroy us.

One huge problem we have in this country is human trafficking, which is a form of modern-day slavery. This crime involves the exploitation of a person for labor and/or commercial sex. These horrendous acts are on the rise, mainly due to our open southern border. Pray that our border can be secured to reduce this evil brought upon innocent victims. Pray also that those in government responsible for these atrocities, would have a change of heart—before it's too late.

*God, thank You for the truth of Your Word. Thank You for delivering us from this world, and giving us the promise of eternal life with You. God it is so difficult when the influences of the world seem to be everywhere we turn. Yet, we find peace in knowing that You are always the One on whom we can set our mind, so that we don't need to be "of" the world. Guide us in how we can end human trafficking, and other wickedness infesting our world.*

# February 6          Godly Family

*"But as for me and my family, we will serve the Lord."*
Joshua 24:15 (NLT)

The challenges of Joshua's day are no less than those we face today. However, we can choose to live according to God's design for us in our home. Is our home His home? Do we behave at home as we do in church? Are we worshiping other things and people more than God? Is Christ the head of our household? When our physical bodies are unhealthy, we seek treatment. Treatment is also available for what spiritually ails individuals and families. Scripture is God's prescribed plan to build a healthy family.

When we exalt God in our homes; establish Godly values; instruct our children in His way; apply appropriate and consistent discipline; respect one another; utilize effective communication; encourage faithfulness; kindness and compassion; and when we love each other as our Heavenly Father loves us—our families will be truly blessed. Think of the impact this way of life has on our children. Having God be first in their lives is a shield against the ungodly propaganda they may be facing in their schools. Young minds are impressionable, and without a solid Christian foundation in the home, who knows how they will react to the evil and radical practices that are taking place in our failing education system. Guard your family—it is the best preventative medicine!

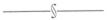

*God, we are so blessed and grateful to be part of Your family. You have also given us the opportunity to be part of our earthly family, for which Your expectations have been clearly laid out in Scripture. The truth is that there is no better place to disciple future Christians, than in the family. It is in our home that we have a chance to show how Christianity applies to every part of life. God, we ask that Your Holy Spirit would guide us in allowing our family to experience the unity of Christ each day.*

# February 7          Truth for Our Children

*"We will not hide these truths from our children; we will tell the next generation about the glorious deeds of the Lord, about His power and His mighty wonders."*

Psalm 78:4 (NLT)

Scripture teaches that children develop in four areas. Luke 2:52 tells us that Jesus grew in wisdom (mentally); stature (physically); favor with God (spiritually); and favor with mankind (socially). The development in these areas begins in the home. God has commanded that we teach our children God's Word, both by our being models of Christ-likeness, as well as our proactive and consistent commitment to family worship. The greatest gift we can give our children is to communicate our all-consuming love for Jesus Christ. Our Heavenly Father isn't interested in all the reasons, excuses, and distractions we have in our busy lives for not making this a priority. The child's relationship with God is mediated through the parents. That is how God designed it, and commanded it to be.

Our nation is facing a rapid decline of Christianity. Several factors can be attributed to this—one of them being the influence of the liberal media, social media, and policy changes have on the minds of young (and old) people. Conservatives are viewed as being "out-of-touch" and "narrow-minded." If a young person is labeled in this manner, they may be in fear of being "cancelled" by their peers. Unfortunately, they sometimes blame the church and fall away. A solid Christian foundation in the family can help to ward off children's concerns about being cancelled.

*God, we want to be faithful in communicating with our children, Your truths, Your deeds, and Your love. Help us to consistently take the responsibility to develop a generation of godly children.*

# February 8          Put God First

*"We know that we are children of God and that the world around us is under the control of the evil one... Dear children, keep away from anything that might take God's place in your hearts."*          1 John 5:19, 21 (NLT)

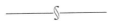

There is an intensity that is taking possession of our worldly lives, which is growing out of control. In our fervent efforts of seeking amusement; in moneymaking; in our quest for success; and in our very struggle for existence, we are crowding God out of the picture. And when we don't leave enough margin for God, we suffer as individuals, and as families. Many of us sincerely desire to do what God would have us do, but we don't have any *space* for Him, because our lives are already packed with other commitments and responsibilities. Perhaps we could expand our parameters if we would learn contentment; find rest in God; partner with Him in prayer before taking action; learn to say 'no'; and surrender to His will. Let us put God *first* in our hearts, and in our families.

We live in evil times, which has been the case ever since the original sin in the Garden of Eden. The Devil is always lurking in our midst to tempt us away from God through our interest and/or dependence on the idols in our lives. Resist and flee from the evil one!

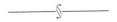

*Lord, forgive us for crowding You out of our busy lives, when You never have, and never will, do that to us. Help us to take an inventory of our life so that we can make the necessary adjustments to find balance that will allow us to connect ever closer to You, and closer to our family. Help us to remove those things that take Your place in our hearts.*

# February 9          True Contentment

*"Yet true godliness with contentment is itself great wealth. After all, we brought nothing with us when we came Into the world, and we can't take anything with us when we leave it. So if we have enough food and clothing, let us be content."* 1 Timothy 6:6-8 (NLT)

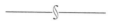

God does not put a limit on how much money we can have. But He does place a limit on what our attitude toward money can be. God's love for us is not based on if we are rich or poor. Our value to God is based on the fact that Jesus Christ came into this world to save us from our sins. None of us could live for even a second on this planet if God didn't abundantly share His wealth with us. The Bible teaches that people are poor, or people are rich because of God's purposes—His design. Compared to the rest of the world, we are considered to be rich, yet some don't feel that we are.

God has blessed us with all that we have, which is likely to be more than we need. As a result, we are to be content. Jesus has told us to be content with what we have. Our confidence and contentment should be in God because He is the Giver of all good things.

*Almighty God, we have been given so much and we understand that it all comes from You. Because You are the Provider of all, we are truly grateful. God, we ask that You would guide us as we learn how to "be" rich, versus how to "get" rich. With that, Lord, may we become responsible stewards of all of which You have provided us. May we experience a contentment like never before, and acknowledge that the use of our wealth is a spiritual issue. Our trust is in You for everything.*

# February 10                           Proper Stewardship

*"Yes, a person is a fool to store up earthly wealth but not have a rich relationship with God."*                                    Luke 12:21 (NLT)

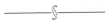

Possession of wealth is a gift from God, given to us as a stewardship to be enjoyed, as well as employed. God entrusts us with all He has given so that we may demonstrate our character; our gospel concern for others; and our willingness to invest in His Kingdom. Choosing to honor God with our money is to say 'wealth is not my master.' Yes, it is foolish to selfishly stockpile our earthly wealth and possessions because what we keep we lose, and what we invest with God we gain eternally. When Jesus walked this earth, He gave thirty-six parables, and sixteen of them had to do with our attitude toward money. It becomes a matter of perspective, priorities and personal choices: How we see things; what we hold as important; how we live. The idea of biblical stewardship is God's wonderful way of asking us to see things differently—through His eternal lens.

Don't you wish our government would be good stewards of our tax dollars? Administration after administration, regardless of party affiliation, is responsible for the reckless spending and a lack of sensible budgeting, which is ruining our nation. Lean on the Lord for help, because we need it.

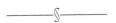

*God, we can clearly see that You knew we would have issues dealing with our attitude concerning money and possessions. Your Word is full of what You expect of us, regarding the stewardship of such. God, we pray that our government would gain biblical wisdom regarding how to properly manage the nations finances.*

*"Look at the nations and pay attention! You will be shocked and amazed! For I will do something in your lifetime that you will not believe even though you are forewarned."*

Habakkuk 1:5 (NET)

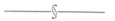

For years Habakkuk had seen Judah headed in the wrong direction and cried out to the Lord. God told His prophet, that as a result of His people's unrighteous and unfaithful ways, He was sending the evil and wicked nation of Babylon as an instrument for His purpose of punishing Judah for its rebellion against God. Habakkuk was told to look around, to observe all the ungodliness.

We too, must do the same in our own nation. It should move us to a place of holy discontent! This should drive us to share in God's vision. Faith is the food that feeds that vision. When we see what God sees, He gives us the courage, hope and passion to be used by Him to fulfill His purposes. God has been preparing us for such a time as this. God is giving us a clear warning that if we continue to shut Him out of lives and institutions, we too will suffer dire consequences. He's been giving us some subtle hints already. What are we going to do about it?

*Lord, for some time now, You have been putting all the pieces of Your divine plan into place, both physically and spiritually. God, our nation is in a spiritual crisis, with so many citizens who know nothing about Your love, Your grace, Your forgiveness, Your power, and Your promise. God, help us to all look around at this critical situation, and come to a place of holy discontent. Give us the passion to share in Your vision for how our church can help restore our nation, which was founded on Your principles. God, we need Your help!*

# February 12            Unwavering Faith

*"Abraham never wavered in believing God's promise. In fact, his faith grew stronger, and in this he brought glory to God. He was fully convinced that God is able to do whatever He promises."*          Romans 4:20-21 (NLT)

One objective of Abraham's faith was to glorify God. He whole-heartedly believed and trusted that God would do what He said He would do. Our faith is always strong or weak depending on how we perceive the object of our faith—God. Faith is an unconditional trust in what God says; strictly on the basis that He said it! The faith of Abraham was a faith in the promise of God to make him the father of many nations. Despite being in his late 90's and that his elderly wife Sarah was barren, Abraham's faith did not waver.

Faith takes a future reality and gives it present substance. It's different from hope, which is the desire for something to happen. Faith is the confidence that it *will* happen, and the acts of obedience and the promises of God are fulfilled. The Bible says that without faith, it is impossible to please God. Who doesn't want to please God? May we all develop greater faith.

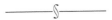

*Heavenly Father, thank You for richness of Your Word and to see the examples of those who lived with unwavering belief in Your promises. We desire the level of faith that trusts in You for the impossible; sees Your powerful hand; and sees the wonderful spiritual miracles happening through us. God, we want to live by faith and enjoy the assurance of things hoped for and the confidence of things we can't yet see, because You have promised that You will work all things to Your glory and for our good.*

# February 13          Stand Firm in Faith

*"Be on guard. Stand firm in the faith. Be courageous. Be strong."*
1 Corinthians 16:13 (NLT)

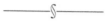

The Christian life must be a life of alertness to evaluate and be aware of what the adversary is doing. Satan is full of lies and all sorts of tricks, and if we are not alert to his shenanigans, he will fill our minds with doubts, apathy, and distortions of truth. We must remain alert to temptation to avoid falling victim to the enemy's trickery. We are also to stand firm in our faith and devotion to Christ. It is our shield of protection that we must use in order to live the life worthy of God's calling.

In light of the current state of our nation, we absolutely need to be on guard and stand firm in our faith. We may go through doubts, anxieties, fears, worries, struggles, trials, and even persecution—but as long as we believe in God's power and promise, we will remain courageous and strong. God records our faith, our love, and our sacrifice. He sees our actions in helping His church move forward by faith. The Christian life demands spiritual stamina and strength—never wavering from the truth of the Gospel.

*Almighty God, You alone are our refuge and strength in all circumstances. As individuals, as well as a church body, we have made a commitment to You to help grow Your Kingdom. May we always rest in Your truth as we courageously resist the attempts by the enemy, who tries to thwart our efforts to keep our commitments to You. May we never forget that You are in control and that You only want what is best for us. Let's finish the work we have ahead.*

# February 14                                        Love Is...

*"Love is patient and kind. Love is not jealous, it does not brag, and it is not proud. Love is not rude, is not selfish, and does not get upset with others. Love does not count up wrongs that have been done. Love takes no pleasure in evil but rejoices over the truth. Love patiently accepts all things. It always trusts, always hopes, and always endures."*

1 Corinthians 13:4-7 (NCV)

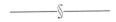

Love is always ready to allow extenuating circumstances; to give the other person the benefit of the doubt; and to believe the best about people. Yet, many of us have developed a certain distrust of people because of negative experiences. Or sometimes we form a gap between the actions of others versus what we "expect" their actions should be. When we face this kind of gap, will we choose love and trust—or will we choose suspicion, skepticism, and mistrust? What a difference it makes when husbands and wives, parents and children, teachers and students, friends and co-workers, and church members and neighbors truly believe in each other. Every relationship in life is built on trust—or destroyed for the lack of it. Without trust, there can be no real relationship.

We can't control the actions of others, but we can control how we will respond to those actions. Can we trust God enough to help us narrow the gap and believe the best about other people? God believes the best about us and others, so shouldn't we do the same? Love comes to us in Jesus Christ—through the love of others—and invites us to always trust.

*Abba Father, we are eternally grateful that you always trust us and shower us with infinite love. Despite our sinful nature, You have never treated us as our sins deserve. You have called us to always trust in You. May our relationships with each other grow stronger by allowing trust to fill the gaps we create.*

# February 15                                    Yes and Amen

*"For every one of God's promises are 'Yes' in Him; therefore also through Him the 'Amen' is spoken, to the glory we give to God."*                    2 Corinthians 1:20 (NET)

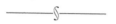

All the promises of God to us have been fulfilled in Jesus. Jesus is the fulfillment of God's promises spoken through the Old Testament prophets. Some may take this verse out of context to imply that God endorses *all* of our requests and fulfills every whim—in the timing that we expect. God is not a vending machine, where we put in our coins and receive the snack. Remember, it is the promises of God—not the snacks—that are always fulfilled with a resounding 'YES.'

How we approach God through prayer plays a role in how and when we experience to the fullest God's promises in our lives. Often times we *want* to hear 'yes' from God, but with a glass-half-full approach we anticipate hearing 'no.' A God who loves us so much that He gave us His Son for our salvation is more than willing to say "yes" to His promises, when we come to Him in faith. And when we hear 'Yes', our response should be 'AMEN!' Walk closely with God and we will see Him bring His promises to fulfillment.

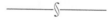

*Almighty God, every promise from You is 'Yes' and 'Amen.' Thank You for fulfilling Your promise of Jesus, Who came to deliver us from sin and death with the promise of eternal life with Him. Lord, give us patience to wait on You for answers to our prayers, and to faithfully trust in Your promises. AMEN!*

# February 16                                    Boundless Love

*"Return, O Israel, to the Lord your God, for your sins have brought you down" ...The Lord says, "Then I will heal you of your faithlessness; My love will know no bounds, for My anger will be gone forever."*                                    Hosea 14:1, 4 (NLT)

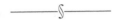

We have all been born into sin and rejection of God. Yet, He penetrates that universal rejection by pouring out the most unique kind of love to us who haven't earned it, and certainly don't deserve it. God's love is passionate; unqualified; without conditions; and everlasting, which makes it absolutely unlike the love we often show. Our love is not like God's love. Ours is often full of conditions. Yet, God's love does not come without demands for responsibility and even limits—it demands accountability and obedience.

Through his personal experience with his unfaithful wife, Hosea was led to understand how man's sin costs God more pain than anger, and came to understand the divine love and forgiveness of our heavenly Father. In a similar way, the sinfulness our nation has experienced, and our turning our backs on God, is causing Him pain and sorrow. We must return to the Lord our God and allow Him to demonstrate in amazing ways just how wide, how deep, and how great is His love for us all.

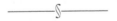

*Father God, thank You for this great and unfathomable love of which we are completely unworthy. We are humbled and truly grateful that You chose to love us even before the world was created, and that despite our sinful nature, You will continue to love us forever and ever. Thank You for providing us with the truth that forgiveness is possible, no matter the trespass. God, we want to love the way You love.*

*"There is no Jew or Gentile. There is no slave or free person. There is no male or female. That's because you are all one in Christ Jesus."*      Galatians 3:28 (NIRV)

————§————

When we have become quite conscious of the destructive power of prejudice—whether based on ethnic identity, social standing, gender, physical, emotional, or mental conditions—we should rejoice that we are all one in Christ. Yet, we so often fail to grasp that distinctions don't exist in God's eyes—we all count; we all matter; and we are precious in His sight. He loves and accepts us with full knowledge of our sinfulness, shortcomings, and flaws.

The Bible does not use the phrase *systemic racism* in any translation, and neither the word *systemic* nor *racism* is found individually. Generally, the term systemic racism suggests that race-based discrimination is ingrained or woven into rules, laws, or traditions—even if the actual text of laws makes no overt reference to race. The concept of systemic racism implies that someone or something is racist even if a person, group, or policy *doesn't* actually hold racist attitudes. And it is getting out of hand. Of course, it's possible for nations to have openly racist laws or policies. Sadly, there are some nations/societies that are clearly racist. But the United States, as a whole, is not one of them. It makes us wonder, then, if there were more believers in the world, racism would fade into the sunset. May our eyes learn to see what God sees in His children—one *Human Race*. We need to put God back in our lives as individuals, and the life of our nation, and look through His lens.

————§————

*Heavenly Father, we are all created in Your image. No race, no gender, no position in life is better than the other. We are all playing in the same orchestra, and You are our Conductor, Whom we praise. May we clear our hearts and minds of prejudice and see others as You see them and grasp the fact that everyone counts; everyone matters to You.*

# February 18　　　　　　　　　　True Confession

*"Finally, I confessed all my sins to you and stopped trying to hide my guilt. I said to myself, I will confess my rebellion to the Lord. And you forgave me! All my guilt is gone."*

Psalm 32:5 (NLT)

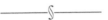

It's hardly a coincidence that God designed the Gospel so that we must acknowledge the fact that we are all sinners before we can be forgiven; before we can be saved. Why? It is because He wants us to accept responsibility for our actions. We gladly take credit for our accomplishments, but we often blame our failures and sins on other people or circumstances (i.e. genealogy, environment, government, bad luck). David was miserable due to his un-confessed sin regarding his tryst with Bathsheba and arranging the murder of her husband. He could have placed blame in several areas, including Bathsheba, but once confronted, he took full responsibility for his actions and confessed to God. Only then did he experience inward healing. His guilt was taken away, and he received God's forgiveness.

It would be great if our government officials would admit when they are wrong and when their actions have damaged our republic. One example is the illegal possession of classified documents—to which both parties are responsible. We want to see accountability for corruption in government. It is highly likely that true confession and repentance to the citizens of this country, on the part of crooked politicians, would result in forgiveness.

*You are the Almighty God of mercy and grace, yet we often fail to realize that truth. We are thankful for the indwelling of Your Holy Spirit, Who guides us to sin less. Yet, when we do commit a transgression, help us to realize that forgiveness and restoration cannot happen until we accept full responsibility for our actions. We pray that we will renew our relationship with You through faithful confession of those things that are blocking us from fully experiencing Your love.*

# Everyone Matters

*Every day they continued to meet together in the temple courts. They broke bread in their homes and ate together with glad and sincere hearts, praising God and enjoying the favor of all the people. And the Lord added to their number daily those who were being saved.*

Acts 2:46-47 (NIV)

———§———

What a beautiful description of the birth of the church. They didn't have their own building; no paid staff, no worship band, no internet website or podcasts, yet it was unified and it multiplied. Through their shared common faith in Jesus Christ, the early believers devoted themselves to communal worship; promoting caring relationships; meeting in small groups to grow spiritually and support each other's growth; praising and thanking God through prayer; generously giving of their time, talents, money and possessions to minister to those in need—all of which filled them with great joy. The early churches started in people's homes. They shared the teachings of Jesus and Old Testament Scriptures, since they didn't have the benefit of the New Testament writings. Yet, something was happening within these small gatherings that wasn't happening anywhere else. Rich, poor, old, young, Jews and Gentiles gathered to learn about the Good News of Jesus Christ. And because of that, everyone mattered.

In our nation today, we have been bombarded with false narratives that only a few of us matter, like BLM and LBGTQA+. The early church's blueprint was that everyone counts, everyone matters, and everyone is welcome. We need that same blueprint today. There seems to be much resistance to having that happen because God has been removed from the lives of many. We need to remember all people matter to God, so they must also matter to us.

———§———

*Heavenly Father, what a privilege it is to be in the family of God, where we all matter to You, and to each other. Help our nation accept Your truth and end the divisiveness. Forgive us as for the times we live like the" Lone Ranger" and fail to include others in our lives.*

# February 20        Interested vs. Interesting

*"Finally, all of you should be of one mind. Sympathize with each other. Love each other as brothers and sisters. Be tenderhearted, and keep a humble attitude."* 1 Peter 3:8 (NLT)

We live in a very proud and self-centered world. Everyone, it seems, is screaming for his or her own rights and seeking to be recognized as someone important. How then, do we expect to form meaningful relationships when we are so *full of ourselves*, that there is little room for anyone else in our life?

We will NOT find joy in our relationships if we have the attitude of self-importance! The good news is that Jesus has already given us the blueprint upon which to model our lives and our relationships. God wants us to be humble. We came into this world humble, and we really have no reason to be proud now. Only absolute humility can generate absolute love. It is the nature of love to be selfless and others-centered. Relationships thrive when we put others above ourselves. We need to show up in our relationships trying to be more *interested* than trying to be *interesting*.

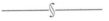

*Almighty God, none of us are worthy of all the beautiful blessings You have graciously given us. Therefore, we seek Your forgiveness for those times when we are self-centered and full of pride. God we ask that Your Holy Spirit would guide us into forming and deepening our relationships with an "others-centered" approach. May we develop unity, empathy, kindness, genuine interest, and a humble spirit in all of our relationships. Help us to humbly consider others better than ourselves. May our relationship with You, and with others, follow the example of our Savior.*

*"Remove the obstacles out of the way of My people."*
Isaiah 57:14 (NIV)

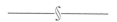

Deep within every heart is a longing to know and be known; to love and be loved; to serve and be served; and to celebrate and be celebrated. So, community isn't something we need to create. Christ has already done that—we're family. The issue is whether we are willing to remove the obstacles that we have placed in our path, in order to live the relational lives that God has intended for us.

If we have drifted from God, we need to clear the obstacles in our path for our return to Him. The obstacles we need to remove come in many forms. Too often we get caught up in the world's value system. Some of us may live our lives at such an intense pace that we don't allow time for what matters most. Or, we don't invest in connecting as much as we invest in achieving. For others, fear of rejection is at the root of our unwillingness to start and develop new relationships. Yet, that may be because we don't really understand God's love. Some of us will reject situations that don't completely cater to our likes and preferences. There's also an underlying obstacle, which is often disguised as *independence*—and that is pride. Yet, there is no joy or peace in pride or self-seeking. When we remove these obstacles, we allow ourselves to form meaningful relationships with others, and we experience God in brand new ways.

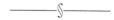

*Heavenly Father, it's amazing that You put no obstacles in the way of connecting with us. You are always available. Help us to acknowledge and break through those barriers that keep us from having deep and meaningful relationships with You and others.*

# February 22　　　　　　　　　　　　Spiritual Mirrors

*"A truly good friend will openly correct you."*
Proverbs 27:5 (CEV)

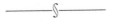

The Christian life is a journey, and at times the road becomes difficult when we veer off the path God would like us to take. One of the true riches we can have in this life is friendship. Authentic friends are those who encourage us and lovingly provide us with much needed feedback and correction. Friendship is a two-way relationship. There are times when we must be willing to display courage as we lovingly offer truths and observations to our friend(s) regarding their conduct or actions. And there are times when, in return, we need to exercise humility and vulnerability, as we invite accountability and readily receive the feedback from a concerned friend. If we want to reap a life of personal integrity and purpose, we must cultivate relationships that will keep us on track.

Be careful, because in our attempt to maintain peace with our friends, instead of speaking truth about your concerns for them, we can cause more harm. God will hold us accountable for our silence. A good friend can serve as a spiritual mirror—you reflect in them, and they reflect you.

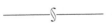

*God, we are thankful that Your design is that we may have the kind of friends in our life that help us to become more like Christ. Through these invaluable relationships, it is Your desire that we use friendships to counsel, encourage, and even rebuke each other. The most challenging times are those when situations call for us to offer correction or a loving rebuke to a friend. We ask for strength, courage and willingness to 'say what we need to say' to our friends, as well as the humility to 'hear what we need to hear' from our friends.*

*"They aren't connected anymore to the head, who is Christ. But the whole body grows from the head. The muscles and tendons hold the body together. And God causes it to grow."*

Colossians 2:19 (NIV)

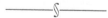

The Apostle Paul was warning the Christians in Colossae about false teachers that were promoting angel-worship, through which spiritual growth would be hampered. In doing so, he used the metaphor of the head and body relationship.

Through God's amazing and intricate design and purpose, the human body is comprised of systems totally dependent upon various muscles, organs, nerves and other components. But, without a skeletal system a body has no structural support; is unprotected and immobile. The muscles and tendons are what hold the bones together. Take away these parts, and the human body cannot stand. Just as the human body receives all of its direction from the head, the Lord Jesus Christ, directs the church body. The spiritual support, or backbone of the church body, is its core values. Take away a church's core values and beliefs, and the church loses its strength. Yet, our core values can't simply be something we put on paper; they must be put into action. Jesus says that what we do is the overflow of who we are on the inside. Our nation's moral compass no longer points north to God. Do we genuinely value, follow, and apply the things that are most important to Christ? We used to—the question is, can we return to those things?

*God, You are the source of all our strength for us as individuals, for the church body, and for our nation. May that same strength be the centerpiece of the morals, values and principles upon which we function. May we always be aligned with Your purposes as we strive to make a positive and lasting impact for Your Kingdom.*

# February 24                                    Don't Drift from Truth

*"For this reason we must pay closer attention to what we have heard. Then we won't drift away from the truth."*                                    Hebrews 2:1 (GW)

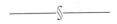

This verse is not an isolated command in the Book of Hebrews. For example, Hebrews 3:1 says to *"consider Jesus"* and Hebrews 12:1-2 says, *"Let us run with endurance the race that is set before us, fixing our eyes on Jesus."* Listen! Consider! Focus!—These are not difficult commands, unless we choose not to do them. Everything else in the Christian life grows out of these.

God does not force His attentions upon us. He waits patiently, reaching out to us in love—eager for us to discover His character, His truths, His ways, and His will for our lives. One way we can become more attentive to God is to focus on what He is doing in and through us—rather than what we are doing for Him. Every day, we can invite God to transform us to become more like Jesus by pursuing His will, and basing our decisions on His guidance. Let's abide in Him daily, so that we will not slowly drift away from the powerful truth He has provided.

As a nation, we have drifted from God on so many levels. He is truth, but some in our country are hell-bent on distorting or ignoring His truth—and that's why we are in the mess we are today. Stay firm in your faith, and firm in His truth.

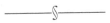

*Heavenly Father, it is truly magnificent that it is Your desire to have a deep and personal relationship with each one of us. Forgive us that we often fail to put You first in our lives. We ask that Your Spirit would guide us and that we would abide in Christ; that every day we would be completely present and attentive to You, and that we would willingly respond in loving obedience. May we completely trust that You are always available to us.*

*"Since we are receiving a Kingdom that is unshakable, let us be thankful and please God by worshiping Him with holy fear and awe."*

Hebrews 12:28 (NLT)

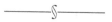

True worship is drawing near to God with our hearts, minds, and bodies in response to what Christ has done for us. True worship is the delight of the believer generated by the work of God in our heart. So when we come to worship Christ in spirit and in truth, we become self-denying, obedient, and confessing Jesus as Lord with reverence and awe.

That is why we love to sing praises to Him, and why we love to serve Him—this is the fruit of worshiping God in our heart. Worship is what we know to be true about Who God is, and what He has done. Ministry or service is that which comes *down* to us from the Father through the Son by the Spirit in the believer. Worship is that which goes *up* by the Spirit through the Son to the Father. Yet, worship is the priority. Worship is first—and ministry follows. We are so privileged to engage in this worship throughout eternity.

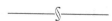

*Lord God, the greatest command is to worship, and to love You with all our heart, soul, mind, and strength. That's the essence of worship. Anything less than that falls way short of giving You the worship You deserve. May we worship You in ways that please You at all times and in all situations, for You are worthy beyond our comprehension. Thank You for creating in us the life that is eternal and divine that enables us to worship You with faithfulness and awe. May songs of thanks and gratitude, and prayers of praise flow from our hearts at all times. We love and worship You.*

# February 26                    Use Every Opportunity

*"Be wise in the way you act with people who are not believers, making the most of every opportunity."*
                                                        Colossians 4:5 (NCV)

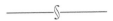

From the beginning, Christianity has been characterized as being evangelistic—for the sake of everyone's eternal life. In Matthew 28:19, Jesus commanded it as His parting passion for the church: *"Therefore go and make disciples of all nations..."* God's sovereign plan is to use ordinary people, like you and me, to season the world with the Christian message. Every encounter is a chance to walk boldly through an open door into the heart of an unbeliever—and then let God do the rest. We should not let fear, hesitation, or lack of preparation steal those opportunities from us. And, we should especially drop any notion that someone is not deserving of salvation—that is for God to decide. This can be a difficult challenge when we encounter people, especially those we have elected to lead, who appear so far from God by their actions and decisions.

The Bible is very clear that there are only two choices regarding where we will spend eternity. It would be wrong to have a cure for cancer and not share it with everyone. Yet we have something more important to share than that. Christians are to be a bridge, not a wall.

*Father God, Your mercy and grace are so above our full understanding. Please forgive us when we hold on to our constraining concept of mercy, and instead fail to share the same concerns that You have. God, help us rid ourselves of bias as we view each day as an opportunity to be used by You, to help spread the truth about Who You are to the lost.*

*"He was in the world, and the world was made through Him, and the world did not know Him. He came to His own, and His own did not receive Him."*   John 1:10-11 (NKJV)

In chapter 2 of Matthew's Gospel, we are shown three different ways in which the birth of our Savior was received. The first was with "hostility." King Herod, who was a Jew by birth—not by faith. As a Governor in Judea he was given the title King of the Jews by the Roman Senate. He reacted to the news of the birth of the real King of the Jews by using his familiar murderous tactics. The second method of receiving news of the Messiah's birth was "indifference" or "unbelief" on the part of the religious leaders and scribes. They were well aware of the many prophecies outlined in the Scriptures, yet didn't even make an effort to travel the short distance from Jerusalem to Bethlehem to investigate for themselves. The three Magi, on the other hand, were on a quest to find baby Jesus for the sole purpose of "worshiping" Him and bringing Him gifts. How ironic that these Gentile foreigners recognized and received Jesus for Who He really was, whereas Herod tried to kill Him, and the scribes ignored Him.

Have we truly received Jesus? Our nation seems to push Him farther and farther away—we've removed Him from our schools; we say, *"Happy Holidays"* instead of *"Merry Christmas;"* and we've turned Christmas into a marketing exploitation of His birth. We need to *receive* Him back—immediately!

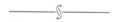

*Heavenly Father, You gave us the greatest gift—Your Son Jesus Christ. He came into the world He created, and was not received as Lord and Savior. God, help us to do what we can to restore Him into the foundation of our nation and receive Him fully.*

# More or Less?

*"He must become greater; I must become less."*
John 3:30 (NIV)

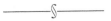

The entire objective of the ministry of John the Baptizer is summarized in this verse. His mission was purely to point men and women to the Lord. John realized that his success came only from God, not from his own efforts. John knew his role, his ministry, and his purpose in God's Kingdom. He saw himself as "the best man" and Jesus as the "Bridegroom." John was not the least bit jealous of Jesus' and His ministry. Instead, John was filled with JOY to see Jesus become greater, as he became less. John understood that he must keep himself in the background.

For a servant of Christ to seek to attract attention to himself is really a form of disloyalty to the One we are to serve. Having goals, having visions, and having a mission statement are great. In fact, the Bible has given us one—it's called the Great Commission. However, in fulfilling this command from Jesus, we *must* embrace a "less of me and more of Jesus" attitude.

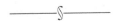

*Father God, we thank You that You have sought to save sinners, and that You sent Your Son to go to the cross to make that possible. We pray that Your Holy Spirit will do Your work through each one of us, as we offer You our faithful service in humble gratitude for what You have given us. May we follow the example of Your servant, John the Baptist, and make You greater, as we become less. May Christ be the center of our service and ministry through everything we do.*

*"The thief comes only to steal and kill and destroy; I have come so that they may have life, and may have it abundantly."*
John 10:10 (NET)

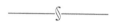

Even as believers, we are sometimes vulnerable to the antics of Satan—the thief; the enemy. As our Good Shephard, Jesus wants to provide us with full protection from what could destroy us. Think about it. Satan comes to steal, kill, and destroy, while Jesus comes to give us the fullest life we could ever imagine.

Jesus came into this world to fill a void (spiritually), which nothing in this world can satisfy. To some, an abundant life means wealth and prosperity, or successes in the endeavors of life. Yet, abundance isn't an abundance of things—it's an abundance of Jesus. It isn't that God has changed the world we live in; but He has changed us. The abundant life is about relationships—our relationship to God; to our Savior Jesus; and our relationships with others—especially those God has yet to place in our paths. An abundant life is one that is fully yielded to God and His plans for us. It is a life of service and it is a Spirit-filled life of joy, love, peace, and faithfulness. Let us live life to the fullest now, as we prepare for an abundant eternal life.

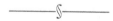

*Almighty God, we're so grateful for Your grace that has been poured out upon us as individuals, and collectively as a church family. We give You thanks and praise for every good gift and blessing that You've given to us. Thank You for Your protection against the evil one. Thank You for sending Your Son to fill our empty lives with the abundance of Your love.*

# We've Turned Our Backs

*He was despised and rejected—a man of sorrows, acquainted with deepest grief. We turned our backs on Him and looked the other way. He was despised, and we did not care.*
Isaiah 53:3 (NLT)

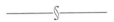

God spoke through the prophet Isaiah and foretold of how Jesus would be rejected, and how mankind would fail to see God in the life and ministry of Jesus because of their willful ignorance and spiritual blindness. No wonder Jesus wept as he entered Jerusalem during His final week on earth. The people were expecting a different kind of King, one who would rid them of Roman rule and return them to being an independent nation—they wanted this, of course, without addressing the need for their own spiritual change. While His followers praised Him by yelling "Hosanna," it would be just days later that the spiritually blind would yell "Crucify Him!" The One who shed His tears for them, would also shed His blood.

Just as He wept over Jerusalem, Jesus weeps today over every lost soul, who continues to reject the salvation and eternal life He is offering. Jesus also weeps for the evil and corruption that is taking place in our education system, and at all levels of our government. As a nation, we have turned our backs on Him—will He turn His on us? We have looked away far too long. If we don't do something fast, we might experience what it is like to have God completely turn His back on us—and that will *not* be pretty!

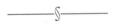

*God, our hearts are heavy as we see how the people in Jesus' day despised Him and turned their backs on Him. Regrettably, we have done the same in our time. God, give us the strength to fight back against those who have tossed You aside. Help us to rid the evil and corruption that is destroying our nation.*

*"Yet there are some of you who do not believe." For Jesus had known from the beginning which of them did not believe and who would betray Him.*     John 6:64 (NIV)

Betrayal is something only a friend or loved one can do. To betray, one must first secure the trust or loyalty of another. An enemy may plan for our destruction and attack us. Our competition may deceive us. Yet betrayal is a grievous act committed by one who has pledged support. Rejection may cause a wound, but betrayal pours in salt to make it sting. Criticism and insult may hurt our pride, but betrayal breaks our heart.

Scripture refers to Judas as "the betrayer," and his betrayal was a kiss of death. Judas is a real-life illustration of the danger of being religious, but lost. Being aware of Jesus' ministry is not the same thing as embracing Him as the Son of Man, Who gave His life to redeem us from our sin. Judas knew that Jesus claimed to be the Savior of the world, but Jesus was not *his* Savior. He walked with Jesus for three years, but never allowed the power of Christ to transform his life. Judas chose betrayal over accepting God's amazing grace. Let's pray we have all chosen correctly.

*God, the power of Satan, the greed and betrayal of Judas, the hypocrisy and rejection by the leaders of Israel were just players in Your divine plan. May we all look at our own lives and ask the question, "where am I in this whole scene?" Our prayer is that we all discard our own agendas and fully devote ourselves to Your calling, Your purpose, and Your plan. May the life and light of Christ shine brightly through us always.*

# March 3                      Get Out of the Boat

*They had rowed three or four miles when suddenly they saw Jesus walking on the water toward the boat. They were terrified, but He called out to them, "Don't be afraid. I am here!"*             John 6:19-20 (NLT)

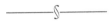

Why would Jesus come walking on the water? Why not suddenly appear in the boat? Perhaps He wanted to show His disciples that the very thing they feared—the wind and the sea—were a walkway He would use to come to them. Why did the disciples become so terrified when they saw Jesus approaching them? It was because they were not looking for Him. Had they been waiting in faith, they would have recognized Jesus immediately.

*Peter said, "Lord, if it is really you, then command me to come to you on the water." Jesus said, "Come."* (Matthew 14:28-29) There's no way Peter would have gotten out of the boat on his own. He only did so in response to Jesus order to *"Come."* When God appears on the scene, new possibilities open before us if we will trust Him. And if God says it's okay, that's all we need to hear. We are not called to be reckless, but we are called to trust. God calls us to set sail, and once we're out on the raging sea, we see God ready and able to deliver us. Faith recognizes fear as a price of growth. God doesn't call the *equipped*, He *equips the called*. The greatest reason we have to get out of the boat is because that is where Jesus is!

*God, we do our best to manage our lives on our own in an attempt to avoid the storms of life. That doesn't work. Help us to realize the fact that without putting our complete trust and faith in You, our fear will only increase. Help us to see that if we respond to life's storms in fear, we will lose the opportunities to fully experience You. Help us to faithfully get out of the boat and come to You.*

# March 4                                        Sin in Our Religion?

*Jesus replied, "You hypocrites! Isaiah was right when he prophesied about you, for he wrote, 'These people honor Me with their lips, but their hearts are far from Me.'"*

Mark 7:6 (NLT)

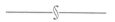

The Bible reveals that the Jewish religious leaders came to honor their own traditions far above the Word of God. However, before we criticize them, perhaps we should examine our own hearts. We, too, may be guilty of replacing God's truth with religious exercises. Are the teachings of Jesus making a home only in our minds, while bypassing our hearts? Are we filling our heads with religious information and knowledge, yet failing to transform our lives?

What was one of the first messages that Jesus delivered after He emerged from the temptation in the wilderness? It was for us to repent. (Matt. 4:17) True repentance starts with desire in our hearts to change. It is not a one-time experience. Our sorrow for sin should be our constant teacher. All true worship comes from the heart because we love God; love His Word; and we love to obey His Word. He knows our heart. He knows if, or not, we truly love Him with all our heart, soul, mind, and strength. Let us all be authentic Christ followers by truly believing in the Word of God through repentant hearts. In doing so, may we all experience the glory of Jesus Christ.

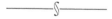

*Almighty God, we are so thankful for Your love, patience, mercy and grace. Lord, we ask that Your Holy Spirit would reveal if we have any sin in our 'religion.' Help us to understand that there is sin in our religion when it is false, superficial, shallow, ritual, legalistic, and self-righteous. If that's the case, may we have truly repentant hearts and embrace the salvation that comes only through loving Christ.*

# March 5                    Forgiven—So Forgive!

*"Get rid of all bitterness, rage, anger, harsh words, and slander, as well as all types of evil behavior. Instead, be kind to each other, tenderhearted, forgiving one another, just as God through Christ has forgiven you."*     Ephesians 4:31-32 (NLT)

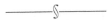

Unforgiveness consumes the heart with bitterness, anger, hostility and other damaging emotions that often lead to evil actions. The root of bitterness will keep us from being the person God wants us to be. This only robs us of the joys of our salvation and the fullness of the Holy Spirit's blessings. More importantly, it grieves God when we are not willing to forgive. God does not love us; choose us; and redeem us because we are deserving—but purely because He is gracious.

If God is so gracious to us, how much more, then, should we be kind and tender-hearted to each other and forgive our fellow sinners? If God reacted to us the way we react to one another, He would have washed His hands of us long ago. Instead, He reached out to save us by forgiving all of our sins. Forgiveness takes place when we can show compassion and try to gain some understanding into what is going on inside the person(s) who have wronged us. God blesses us when we choose to forgive others. He removes the baggage of bitterness, resentment, and malice that weighs us down, and replaces it with peace and joy. It's a challenge when we have animosity in our hearts about the current state of our nation and its leaders. But this animosity is not pleasing to God. Instead, we need to pray for His intervention.

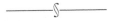

*Heavenly Father, it should be clear to us that forgiveness is paramount in Your eyes. May we be reminded that forgiveness was part of the final words Jesus uttered while He was nailed to the cross. (Luke 23:34) Your forgiveness in Christ has set the standard for our forgiveness of others. May this truth penetrate our heart.*

*"For I am not ashamed of this Good News about Christ. It is the power of God at work, saving everyone who believes—the Jew first and also the Gentile."*    Romans 1:16 (NLT)

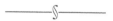

The Gospel message began in Jerusalem, a Jewish city, then spread to the rest of Judea, Samaria, and to the ends of the earth.  It is for everyone.  There is no racial barrier; no gender barrier; no social barrier; no age barrier; no moral barrier; no economic barrier; and no national barrier; to hinder anyone from accepting this truth of salvation.  God uses us as a human channel through which this good news is shared with the various "audiences" we face each day, throughout our lives.  Unfortunately, our fear of man, and not being able to handle their arguments, is often times the greatest snare in witnessing.  That coupled with the godless state of our nation, it is challenging.

Whether we are alone, or among many, the Gospel message is simple to share:  Jesus Christ came into the world—fully God and fully man.  He perfectly obeyed God's law and perfectly fulfilled His will.  He died in our place; and as our substitute He paid for all of our sins.  He was crucified on a cross, buried and was resurrected from the dead.  He was seen by many before ascending into heaven.  He will one day return to earth to establish His Kingdom.  We are commissioned to share this Good News to all people, now more than ever.  Oh, and it is always helpful to add what impact His salvation has had on our own life.

*God we seek courage to share the greatest gift You have provided—our eternal salvation. How is it that we are so willing to share our material possessions, our accomplishments, and other worldly aspects of our lives with others, and fail to jump at the chance to share what is most important—the Good News?  Help us to be like Paul and not be ashamed, or afraid to share this gift.*

*"Truly my soul finds rest in God; my salvation comes from Him."*
Psalm 62:1 (NIV)

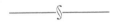

There are times in all our lives when our soul becomes exhausted, perhaps because of the trials we are experiencing or temptations we are resisting. The persecution we may face or the burdens we are carrying for others may be wearing us down. Perhaps the constant reports of evil and corruption in our cities, our schools, our border, and our government are draining us. In the same way that we are filled with sin and worries of the world, so we must find rest and replenishment for our soul.

To do that, we must first stop from the busyness of our lives; be still and empty ourselves so that we can feel God's presence. Despite what we may think, we can't recover on our own. Only God knows how to provide rest and rejuvenation for our soul. There are many ways in which He can do this; but first we must fully trust Him; be still; and patiently wait for Him to act. He can strengthen us through His Word, through prayer, through others, or through our circumstances. Unless we are willing to be still; wait for Him; and reflect on His goodness; we will not be able to fully experience those intimate moments of finding rest in God and restoration for our soul.

*Almighty God, You are the Source of all that is good to sustain us through this life. Please forgive us when we fail to lean on You for strength, comfort, guidance, and rest for our soul. And forgive us when we fail to give You even five minutes a day where we can ignore everything else in our lives and just be still in Your presence, and rejuvenate our soul. We give control of our lives to You.*

*"So now, those who are in Christ Jesus are not judged guilty. Through Christ Jesus the law of the Spirit that brings life made you free from the law that brings sin and death."*

Romans 8:1-2 (NCV)

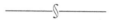

We are all burdened with the curse of sinfulness, and there's no getting rid of it on our own. It is a defiling disease that cripples and degrades every person; agitates every soul; and steals peace and joy from the heart; and replaces it with trouble and pain. Yet, this thrilling promise from God fills every heart with hope. God sent Jesus into the world not to condemn us, but to save us. Because of our faith in Christ, and the regenerating work of the Spirit of God, we have been set free from sin's power, authority, dominion, and ultimate penalty.

However, the Christian has two natures: We've been born from Adam and are stuck with his sinful nature until we die. But, we've also been born again from Christ and by His Spirit, and we want to go God's way. Therein lies the struggle. We may stumble, we may go astray, we may sin—and we do. Yes, we may struggle, but God will not condemn those who are in Christ Jesus. This struggle will be life-long, yet we'll never pay the penalty because 'Jesus paid it all.'

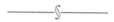

*Glorious Father, how amazing is Your love for us—a love that is certainly undeserved. It is difficult for us to truly grasp Your promise that because we are in Christ, no condemnation awaits us for our seemingly endless sins. That level of forgiveness and withholding of judgment is the ultimate example that we could and should use when it comes to judging ourselves and others. Thank You for sending Your Son to pay our penalty. May we worship with sincere hearts and obey the voice of Your Spirit, Who leads us to righteousness.*

# March 9                                         Fault-Finding

*"Stop judging by outward appearance! Instead, judge correctly."* John 7:24 (GW)

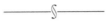

Scripture teaches us that we are not to judge those outside the faith, yet we are responsible for judging the visible, unrepentant sin of those within the church. However, some take this responsibility to a whole new level—one of abuse. This occurs when we go on a fault-finding mission by being ultra-critical regarding the pettiest things. And, this often occurs without valid and sufficient reasons, forming unfavorable opinions about another person's qualities, appearance, words, actions, or motives. In simple terms, it means looking for the worst in others. The real problem in criticizing and judging others in this way, is that it binds us to our own sin by keeping us focused on others' shortcomings. This ultimately prevents us from experiencing a right relationship with Christ. Fault-finding is the venom of the soul. It destroys our joy; drains our happiness; and prevents us from having close friendships. This sin comes partly from spiritual pride and sometimes from disguised envy. We must ask ourselves each time we start to have critical or judgmental thoughts about insignificant or petty issues concerning another person; "Is it necessary to judge them?" "Will my criticism encourage them?" "Is it true?" "Does it really matter?" All too often the answer is, "No."

Our society today is littered with accusations of racism—mainly from the minority community claiming many Americans are "white supremacists" or have "white privilege (whatever that is). In fact, the next time you hear someone throw out those terms, just ask them to give you an example. Chances are, they will not be able to come up with one.

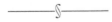

*God, forgive us when we have overstepped our bounds by becoming overly critical when it comes to those gray areas of others. Help us to withhold judgment of others when it simply boils down to our own personal opinions and preferences. You look at the heart of individuals—help us to do the same.*

# March 10                         Sow in the Spirit

*"Do not be deceived: God cannot be mocked. A man reaps what he sows."*
                                                        Galatians 6:7 (NIV)

God doesn't always intrude upon our *planting*, yet He has let us know that we will have consequences for whatever we choose to sow. Inevitably, those consequences impact others, as well as ourselves. God never plays favorites with the law of sowing and reaping—none of us can elude the dreadful consequences that happen when we choose to sow in the field of the flesh, instead of sowing in the field of the Spirit. Sowing to please our sinful nature will always result in a harvest of destruction regarding relationships with others and with God. When we plant godly seeds, we will reap quality things—such as peace, integrity, and healthy relationships—things that have permanent value.

The farmer never stops believing that his labors will be rewarded. From the beginning, he anticipates a bountiful harvest. And that's how we should live. We should always be ready to receive God's blessings when we obey His Word and sow ourselves; our service; and our resources; toward His purposes. We must conduct a self-examination to see in what field we are sowing. God already knows, despite our efforts to try to fool Him. He's just waiting for us to take responsibility to sow in the Spirit, and reap holiness.

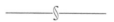

*Our Father in Heaven, You know every aspect of our being. Therefore, it is futile to even consider that our thoughts and actions could somehow slip past your notice. You are a loving God Who has given us freedom of choice. You have not set boundaries and guidelines to suppress us into a place of misery. Instead, they are to teach us to recognize that You are God Almighty, Who desires for us to reap blessings for sowing in the Spirit.*

*Then they heard the Lord God walking in the garden during the cool part of the day, and the man and his wife hid from the Lord God among the trees in the garden. But the Lord God called to the man and said, "Where are you?" The man answered, "I heard you walking in the garden, and I was afraid because I was naked, so I hid." God asked, "Who told you that you were naked? Did you eat fruit from the tree from which I commanded you not to eat?"*        Genesis 3:8-11(NCV)

The way Adam and Eve attempted to deal with their sin is the pattern with which we attempt to deal with it today. And the way that God dealt with Adam and Eve is the way He deals with us. So there the first couple were— in their ridiculous fig leaves—hiding from God in paradise lost. What the couple heard was the rustle of God's step. It was the sacred sound that they had heard before and that had so filled them with joy; but now brought dread. God's *"Where are you?"* was remedial—in a graciously gentle manner was like a father's question to a naughty child hiding behind a door to avoid his face.

Their disobedience had serious consequences, to which we face today. Yet even when the shame of that disobedience drove them (and us) to hide from God, He still searches us out with a, *'Where are you?'* Maybe God is asking us the same question for us to do some soul-searching on the health of our relationship with Him—So, *"Where are you?"*

*Our Father in Heaven, we are eternally grateful that, despite our sinfulness which separates us, you seek us to be in relationship with You. Thank You for the sacrifice of Your Son to allow that to be. May we seek You, like You seek us. We love and praise You.*

*"Do not merely listen to the word, and so deceive yourselves. Do what it says. Anyone who listens to the word but does not do what it says is like someone who looks at his face in a mirror and, after looking at himself, goes away and immediately forgets what he looks like."*

James 1:22-24(NIV)

How is it that listening to God's Word can be deceiving? Just listening to God's Word and never applying it to our everyday lives is like owning a treadmill and never using it. We would be deceived into thinking we were getting more physically fit simply by having it in our home. Too often, we attend Sunday service and/or read our Bible and feel *closer to God* as a result. Yet, once we exit the church building and/or close our Bible, we fail or *forget* to put into practice those nuggets of truth, principles and expectations from God so we can live the life He intended for us to live.

We not only have to take it in, we've got to put it back out again in our living. The laws and commands of God are an expression of Who He is. The Bible then becomes a mirror that reveals who we really are—on the inside. A sermon is not merely intended to inspire us. God holds us accountable for each and every word that we read or hear from the Bible. We can either forget what we've heard, or choose to apply what we've heard (or read) in order to be transformed closer to the image of Jesus Christ.

*God, we cannot begin to describe the power and the richness of Your living Word. Help us to listen with a pure and humble heart. More importantly, help us to see that we need to continually put Your Word into action. Your Word is our food, our drink, our light, and our path to righteous living. We pray in Jesus' name, that we'd have a new willingness to do more than merely listen; that we would, instead, always apply Your Word.*

# March 13        Do You Want to Get Well?

*One who was there had been an invalid for thirty-eight years. When Jesus saw him lying there and learned that he had been in this condition for a long time, He asked him, "Do you want to get well?" "Sir," the invalid replied, "I have no one to help me into the pool when the water is stirred. While I am trying to get in, someone else goes down ahead of me."*        John 5:5-7(NIV)

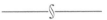

*'Do you want to get well?'* seems like a ridiculous question to ask a person who has been sick or disabled for thirty-eight years, but not when it comes from the lips of our Lord. It is the question that Jesus asks all of us—believers and non-believers. Yet, notice the man did not respond with a resounding 'of course I want to get well!' It's a risky invitation that Jesus makes. If he (or we) say, 'yes' to His question, things will change, life will be less predictable. Being well again will take a lot of adjustment, responsibility, and accountability. There is comfort in the familiar. We often choose to stay in our debilitating condition, craving to be healed, yet resisting any change to do anything about it. In his self-pity, the man had shut out the possibility of healing. Instead, he focused on the injustice all around him and blamed others for his situation. But, Jesus crashes his pity-party by healing him and commanding him to *'Stand up, pick up your mat, and walk!'* The man needs to decide to take action.

God is inviting us to break the paralysis of inaction in our lives. He is offering the opportunity to have some real power to change our patterns of behavior. God is offering us freedom from whatever it is that has us paralyzed. Let's step out of our comfort zone and say 'yes' to His invitation to live the abundant life He intends for each one of us.

*Father God, we ask You to guide and encourage us to move toward spiritual, physical, and emotional healing. We can't do it on our own and rely on You for strength.*

*But the Lord said to Samuel, "Don't look at how handsome Eliab is or how tall he is, because I have not chosen him. God does not see the same way people see. People look at the outside of a person, but the Lord looks at the heart."*      1 Samuel 16:7 (NCV)

God does not place us on the planet without purpose; He has a divine plan for each of us. Three thousand years ago, God chose a young lad named David to be the future king of Israel. Samuel expected God to select Eliab, the eldest son of Jesse, not the youngest. David was not perfect. In fact he failed, and failed big, yet God looked past that. He sinned, but he was quick to confess and he manifested a genuine heart of repentance.

And that's the point—God is not nearly as impressed with people's achievements and physical characteristics as we are. He is caught up in the condition of our heart! He looks at what we can become. God is not looking for the most impressive people. His measuring stick is the heart. When we are characterized by our willingness; our availability; our humility; and our commitment to serving Him, He can do amazing work through us.

It would be wonderful if our elected representatives would have a humble heart and a willingness to serve *we the people* with honesty and integrity. Can they be men after God's own heart? We can only pray for such.

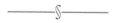

*Heavenly Father, how amazing is Your love for us! You not only see those things in our hearts that are ugly and shameful, but You also see the hidden talents, the special gifts and the virtues that make us unique creations that are precious to You. We pray that you would place people in leadership positions who have a heart for You.*

*"Those who long to be rich, however, stumble into temptation and a trap and many senseless and harmful desires that plunge people into ruin and destruction. For the love of money is the root of all evils."*                                     1 Timothy 6:9-11 (NET)

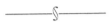

Jesus has to be our only Source of security. Yet, sadly for many of us, we cherish another master—riches. The source of our security determines the direction of our life. Money is not the root of all evil, but the *love of money* is. Money can poison our lives either by its presence, or its absence. Money has the power to blind us. A truly godly person is not motivated by the love of money, but by the love of God. He/she seeks the greatest riches, which are spiritual contentment and complete trust in the ever-present and ever-able God.

Sadly, this is often the case with politicians we elect to serve us. They may have good intentions during a campaign, but once in office, the pressures to conform to questionable practices, and the evidence of financial gain for succumbing to a persuasive influence—a bribe in disguise—politicians surrender their integrity. They fold like a rusty old lawn chair. Once the ill-gotten money starts flowing in, the love of power and control are manifested—which just adds to the vast amount of government corruption that exits. Pray that God will expose these wrongs *before* we vote.

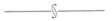

*Lord, we pray that the convicting work of Your Holy Spirit will help us divorce ourselves from our unhealthy attitude regarding money and possessions. Help us to be righteous stewards of all that You provide for us, by trusting You completely, and by following the Scriptural principles. Please root out the evil practices in our government.*

# March 16                              God's Purposeful Timing

*"Lord, if only you had been here, my brother would not have died."*
John 11:21 (NLT)

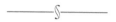

Have you ever felt that way?  Where were You, Lord?  You showed up too late?  Where were You when....?  Our human nature can make waiting for God's perfect timing a difficult thing to do.  In fact, in the hustle and bustle of our frenzied lives, we often find it difficult to wait for anything or anyone.  We want what we want now!  As a result, we not only lose our patience, but also find it increasingly difficult to discern God's timing.  The truth is, that God's timing is never early; and it's never late.  No event in history has put so much as a wrinkle in the timing of God's eternal plan, which He designed before the foundation of the world.

When news reached Jesus that his friend Lazarus was critically ill, everyone expected Jesus to rush to Lazarus's side.  Instead, Jesus waited—an act of love misunderstood by many of His disciples, as well as Martha and Mary.  But Christ's delay of love had a purpose:  that God might be glorified through it all. Another key to understanding God's timing is trust.  Martha's greeting to Jesus, though filled with grief, still contained some evidence of faith.  She trusted that *if* Jesus had not been late, He could have healed her brother.  Yet, did she trust Him with all of her heart?  Martha wanted a *resuscitation*—but Jesus wanted a *resurrection*.

*God, help us to grow in knowledge and confidence of our identity and purpose in You. May our faith be stretched that we might be able to see the fullness of what You can do in our lives, not only in the future, but also in the present.  May we come to understand that You are with us in every move we make and every breath we take.*

# March 17                  Blessedness in Christ

*"But may the righteous be glad and rejoice before God; may they be happy and joyful."*
Psalm 68:3 (NIV)

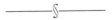

What is the source of our happiness? We will never experience true happiness unless we realize God's path to find it. Jesus came and cleared up a fundamental error in our understanding of happiness when He gave the Sermon on the Mount, as He gave us the true notion of blessedness. The *world's* beatitude is: "Blessed are those who are rich and honorable in the world, whose possessions and circumstances give them pleasure." Is this a promise from God? Did He really say this is how we should attain happiness?

While it is true that God wants to bless us and has great plans for us, we venture into extremely dangerous waters when we begin to believe that His ultimate plan for us is our *worldly* happiness. True happiness is found only in the Lord. True joy and gladness come only as we continually seek God's presence and walk in His paths of holiness. Worldly happiness is temporary, but blessedness in Christ is eternal. All of the blessings that God gives us in this life as we pursue Him are just samples to whet our appetite for the eternal blessings that await us still.

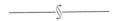

*Heavenly Father, we thank You for revealing Yourself to us. We thank You that we have the privilege of being Your children. That is the ultimate blessing. Help us to restructure our priorities so that we will always seek You and Your Kingdom first, rather than things of this world. When we do, our joy and happiness overflow! We love You and praise You.*

*"But the Holy Spirit produces this kind of fruit in our lives: LOVE"*

Galatians 5:22 (NLT)

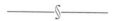

In so many ways, we could regard the entire Bible as a love story—from the creation of the world; to the protection of the Israelites; and finally, to God sending a Savior, Jesus Christ. The Bible sends a simple, but powerful message: God loves us and expects us to love Him and others. There are four types of love, with the first three being the kind of love we generally exhibit: *"Eros"* is a passionate, romantic love; *"Storge"* is love for family members; *"Phileo"* is love for friends; *"Agape"* is divine, unconditional love. Agape love is the first quality listed as a *Fruit of the Spirit*, because it most clearly reflects the character of God. This kind of love allows the other fruits to be cultivated and flourish within our soul. Jesus commanded us to love, as He loves. And where God commands, God always equips. Only by knowing God can we have this *agape* love, and only by loving can we know Him! We are to imitate Christ. God's Holy Spirit moves us to be more loving, less egocentric, and allows us to be fruitful through agape love.

The way Jesus spoke of and demonstrated this kind of love was counter cultural. He told His followers to love in a way that no one else did—humbly; unconditionally; equally; sacrificially; and generously. These are too often in direct contrast to the way we love. Our responsibility is to bear the fruit of our connection to God by showing agape love to *all* of God's creation.

*Heavenly Father, we praise You as the only true, pure, and eternal Source of love. We are so thankful and blessed that You loved us first. Fill us with Your Holy Spirit to the point where it becomes abundantly clear to the world that You are love! May we imitate You through agape love for others.*

*"But the Holy Spirit produces this kind of fruit in our lives: JOY"*
Galatians 5:22 (NLT)

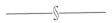

God's Spirit is a tree of life, producing life-giving fruit. That fruit includes joy that is beyond description. More than happiness, which is contingent on favorable external conditions, joy is internal. It is not dependent on outside circumstances, but can be abundant despite negative or opposing conditions. In fact, as we mature in our faith, joy will become more evident in our life. Joy is celebration in the heart of a believer for what God has done. Joy is not an emotion, but rather an inner appreciation and sense of satisfaction due to a spiritual reality. Joy is the delight expressed when God is victorious over evil; when Godly works are done; and when the will of God is accomplished.

Interestingly, the Bible never *recommends* we rejoice—it commands us to do so. We certainly have reason to rejoice. We've been given something precious; priceless, and beyond what we can imagine or hope for, through our Savior. Joy, the fruit of God's Spirit, has its roots in the realization of God's purpose, and produces the outworking that transforms us into His image. It is a discipline we must cultivate and practice: Joy reads! Joy sings! Joy meditates! Joy encourages! Joy thanks! Joy communes! Joy gives! and joy serves! Joy is the by-product of God's immeasurable gift, and it is the outward expression of His inexhaustible love.

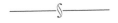

*Precious Jesus, thank You for the abundant joy You graciously pour out through Your Holy Spirit, when we are abiding in You. May Your gift of joy become so fruitful in our lives.*

*"But the Holy Spirit produces this kind of fruit in our lives: PEACE"*
Galatians 5:22 (NLT)

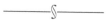

The fruit of the Spirit is the by-product; the result; and the overflow of the Spirit of Jesus Himself living in and working through us. Peace, is one of these attributes of Christ that we receive as a gift, when we surrender our lives to Him. The *world* doesn't understand peace as a positive concept, but instead, views peace as merely the absence of trouble. It is shallow and temporary, and it is a peace apart from God. The peace Jesus spoke of the night before His crucifixion enabled Him, and can enable us, to remain calm, tranquil, and secure despite difficult circumstances. We can only experience this peace that surpasses our comprehension when we abide in Christ—and stay connected to the Vine.

When the risen Christ first appeared to the disciples following His resurrection, His first words were *"Peace be with you..."* (John 20:19) The message these disciples would carry would be the Gospel of peace, now that they had both peace *with* God, as well as the peace *of* God. Before Jesus said anything about power or purpose, He wanted to establish peace—the kind of peace He embodied during His earthly ministry. Since we are created in the image of Christ, we have no excuse for not cultivating the fruit of peace in our relationship with God and with others.

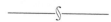

*Heavenly Father, we are grateful that You sent to us the Prince of Peace, through Whom peace was accomplished on the cross. May Your Holy Spirit guide us to receive Your gift of peace, and lead us to a place where we can bear the fruit of peace in all of our relationships.*

*"But the Holy Spirit produces this kind of fruit in our lives: PATIENCE"*
Galatians 5:22 (NLT)

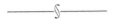

Of all the fruit of God's Holy Spirit, patience may be the most challenging for us to display in our lives. We certainly don't have a shortage of occasions for patience. One occasion for cultivating the fruit of patience is when we must endure some kind of mistreatment or abuse. Some translations refer to patience as "longsuffering." This aspect of patience is the ability to suffer a long time while being mistreated, without growing resentful, angry, or bitter. 1 Peter 2:23 describes how Christ reacted to the suffering and mistreatment He received from others, and is our recipe to follow. Like Jesus, we must faithfully leave those situations fully in the hands of God to handle. Another occasion requiring patience is in responding to provocation. Provocation denotes those actions of others that tend to arouse our anger or cause us to lose our temper.

A more common occasion for cultivating patience is in tolerating the shortcomings of others. In our lives we encounter people who behave in ways that (though not aimed directly against us) affect us; irritate us; or disappoint us. We must have the same level of tolerance of others, that God has for us. And lastly, patience with God is perhaps the toughest occasion to exercise the fruit of patience. We need to have patience—faithfully waiting on God for His solution to our problems and His answers to our prayers.

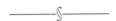

*God, we understand that it is Your desire that we live fruitful lives by having Your virtues, characteristics, and qualities become evident in our lives. May the fruit of patience grow in special ways through endurance, through suffering, through forbearance, through perseverance, and mostly through our waiting on You.*

*"But the Holy Spirit produces this kind of fruit in our lives: KINDNESS"*

Galatians 5:22 (NLT)

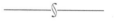

When we study the Fruit of the Spirit, we are painting a picture of Jesus, through Whom every single quality of the Spirit-filled life was expressed during His time on earth. When we describe Jesus, we are quick to think of His power and devotion—but the Gospels record the fact that those closest to Him described His kindness. His first miracle was an act of kindness—turning water into wine to save the newlyweds and wedding host the embarrassment of running out of wine at their reception. There is no other quality so beautifully expressed in the life of Jesus as the quality of loving kindness. We see Him curing a woman on the Sabbath day, even though the Jewish law forbade it. Jesus' act of kindness elevated her well-being above the Jewish law and healed her anyway. We see him feeding 5,000 hungry people by His miracle of the loaves and fishes. We see Him reaching out to a man at the Pool of Bethsaida, touching his life and making him well. We see him talking with Mary and Martha in the gentlest terms. Even in His words of correction to Martha, there is kindness.

Kindness starts with caring—being tender-hearted and compassionate toward others. It's an action of love done for the well-being of another, regardless of whether the other person deserves such action, or not. Kindness is a universal action—everyone understands it and desires it.

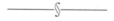

*Heavenly Father, we are reminded of Your loving grace and kindness You always show to us, for which we are forever grateful. Help us to embrace this aspect of Your character and freely share it with our family, friends, community and world.*

# March 23                                           Goodness

*"But the Holy Spirit produces this kind of fruit in our lives:  GOODNESS"*
Galatians 5:22 (NLT)

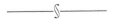

Goodness is a character trait. It is God's goodness, evidenced through His love, mercy, grace, and holiness that is offered to us as a Fruit of the Spirit. Character is what we are doing when no one else is looking. The character of goodness must be present all the time, not just when we feel like it. Goodness is an action that comes from a place of selflessness.

Developing goodness comes from the growth of our faith. Goodness is encouraging and helping others—*kindness* in action. It is pure, holy, generous, and righteous. Goodness comes from the inside out—from God's Holy Spirit. In a world filled with lies, hypocrisy, evil and corruption, it's tough to show kindness.

We can have thoughts of kindness and intentions to be good to others, but you must have goodness to *follow through* with those kind thoughts and intentions. Our goodness can reflect Jesus to those who have yet to put their faith in Him. Choose goodness.

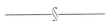

*Father God, goodness defines Your entire nature. Who You are, what You create, give, and command is good! Lord, help us to see that goodness is the essence of seeking You for the benefit of others, and not a focus on self. Help us also to see that goodness is not a single act, but instead it is a development of character that can only grow through Your Holy Spirit within us. May we emulate Jesus through our empathy, encouragement, selflessness, generosity, grace, and mercy toward others.*

# March 24                                Faithfulness

*"But the Holy Spirit produces this kind of fruit in our lives: FAITHFULNESS"*
Galatians 5:22 (NLT)

———§———

In our reflections of the Fruit of the Spirit, we have seen how these virtues are rooted in the character of God, and it assures us that producing this fruit is ultimately God's work. The Old Testament resounds with examples of God's faithfulness, despite His people's unfaithfulness to Him. Today, God remains one hundred percent reliable, trustworthy, and truthful—one hundred percent of the time. He never ceases to be faithful. God is steadfastly devoted to us and to our eternal salvation. In today's world, commitment, dependability, and trustworthiness are traits that are hard to come by. Yet, God longs for us, His children, to be faithful to His call on our lives.

The Apostle Paul was a great example of putting faithfulness to God above all else. Paul was so committed to the path of submission and obedience unto God, that he considered himself as a man who was literally bound by the Holy Spirit's direction, and a slave unto the perfect will of God. He was completely undeterred by the external influences and circumstances he faced. Paul was committed, trustworthy, loyal, devoted, and constant as he persevered to reach the goal set before him—to finish his spiritual marathon and feel the joy from hearing, *"Well done, good and faithful servant!"* (Matt. 25:23) Will we be able to hear the same?

———§———

*Almighty God, we thank You that You are completely and utterly faithful. Forgive us for those times when our faith wavers and our devotion and dependence on You lessens. We pray for strength, guidance, and resolve to grow our faithfulness in You and others.*

*"But the Holy Spirit produces this kind of fruit in our lives: GENTLENESS"*

Galatians 5:23 (NLT)

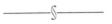

As we continue to more fully understand the Fruit of the Spirit, we find that "gentleness" (or "meekness" as it is referred to in other Bible translations) is often misunderstood and undervalued in today's society. Contrary to what many may think, someone displaying the qualities of gentleness is *not* someone who is weak, spiritless, or lacking in strength and courage. Gentleness is never false modesty or humility; self-depreciation; or a spineless refusal to stand up for anything. Jesus, the Savior of the world, went so far as to identify Himself as "gentle" and "humble" (Matt. 11:29), a description that certainly did not capture the essence of the Messiah His followers had anticipated. He wanted to be very clear that He cared passionately about man and his sin, and would fight to the death for our salvation, albeit from a position of gentleness, humility, and love.

Through the work of the Holy Spirit, the fruit of gentleness can be seen in our attitude; in our behavior; and in our conversation. Gentleness enables us to bear patiently with those insults and injuries we might receive from others. It makes us ready to accept and offer correction from, and to, others. With gentleness, revenge is never part of the equation. Without gentleness, kindness has no works, patience cannot wait, and love is not present.

*Heavenly Father, how blessed we are that You have always treated us with the utmost gentleness, in every step we take in our spiritual walk. May Your Holy Spirit continue to cultivate gentleness for our every thought, action, and spoken word. Lord, our prayer is that the more we display a gentle heart, the more the world will take notice and come to know our Source of gentleness.*

*"But the Holy Spirit produces this kind of fruit in our lives: SELF-CONTROL*

Galatians 5:23 (NLT)

§

It was very wise that the Bible listed "self-control" at the end of the list of the Fruit of God's Holy Spirit. Think of how disheartening it would be if it had been listed first? Yet, perhaps it is the most important characteristic because if we don't have self-control, we will never be able to implement the means of grace that will cultivate and bear all the other godly characteristics in our lives. According to Scripture, living under our own control is precisely the problem. More often than teaching us how to develop self-control, the Bible instructs us to deny ourselves; to put off our *old self*, in order to bring ourselves under the power and influence of the Spirit of Christ. When the Holy Spirit is at work in us, these wonderful results flourish: *Love, Joy*, and *Peace* reign in our hearts. *Patience, Kindness, Goodness, Faithfulness*, and *Gentleness* demonstrate themselves in our relationships. And *Self-Control* governs our actions, which otherwise would look only to satisfy the flesh.

Being filled with the Holy Spirit doesn't mean we have more of God's Spirit, it means God's Spirit has more of us. We are filled with the Holy Spirit when we abide in Christ—the Vine. Only then can we bear much godly fruit that will benefit others and glorify God.

§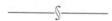

*Heavenly Father, words cannot describe how amazing it is that Your Spirit dwells inside each of us. As with all of Your characteristics, self-control is also a gift—one that we must receive actively. We submit to the guidance of Your Spirit to strengthen our "new self" and control the direction and activity of our lives, through the choices and decisions we make, to reflect the fruits of Your Spirit in us.*

# March 27               Secret Disciples

*They intended to bury him with criminals, but He ended up in a rich man's tomb, because he had committed no violent deeds, nor had He spoken deceitfully.*      Isaiah 53:9 (NET)

By bringing about the fulfillment of Isaiah's prophecy in the way He did, God gave compelling proof of the resurrection of the Lord Jesus. Since Christ was crucified as a criminal—and with criminals—His dead body was to be thrown on a garbage heap. But God had other plans. God used *secret disciples* of Jesus in ways we would not have thought. How ironic that among the Sanhedrin, such disciples (Nicodemus and Joseph of Arimathea) would emerge. They took action when the public disciples, who had spent time with Jesus, lost heart, and temporarily abandoned Him.

The cross was the turning point for Nic and Joe when they bravely took possession of Christ's crucified body; lovingly prepared it for burial; and laid Him in Joseph's unused tomb. It was an act of love and an act of worship. Yet they never expected what would happen next. The cross is the turning point of all history when our Lord laid down His life only to be raised on the third day.

*Almighty God, we are in the midst of Holy Week—the most special time of year when we can truly honor our Lord and Savior. We are grateful that You moved in the hearts of Nicodemus and Joseph who, at great personal cost, showed Jesus love, respect, and honor even following the shame of His death. We are grateful that they did not desert Him. God, we want to be counted as followers who will stand up to declare and defend our faith in Christ, even when we face adversity.*

# March 28                                He Is Risen, Indeed!

*"Praise be to the God and Father of our Lord Jesus Christ. In God's great mercy He has caused us to be born again into a living hope, because Jesus Christ rose from the dead.'*

1 Peter 1:3 (NCV)

———§———

Resurrection from the dead is the cornerstone of Christian doctrine. It is mentioned over one hundred times in the New Testament. The crucifixion of Christ loses its meaning without the resurrection. Without the resurrection, the death of Christ becomes simply the heroic death of a gifted teacher and a noble martyr. The truth is, Jesus was resurrected. and that fact, which was witnessed by hundreds of people, is a harbinger or precursor of our own resurrection—and that is our living hope. It is one thing for claims to be made about Who Jesus was. But God set His own seal upon Him at the resurrection validating those claims. The resurrection proclaims the deity of Christ. His death on the cross may have accomplished our redemption as He paid for the sins of the world, but it did not prove to the world that Christ was God in the flesh. But the resurrection did!

The resurrection of Jesus gives us proof that God has completed our salvation, and provides us with encouragement, hope, and confidence in an eternal life in God's Kingdom because we, too, will be resurrected from death. Living hope is hope that has power and produces changes in life. Jesus is indeed alive in believers.

———§———

*Heavenly Father, we thank You for our triumphant Savior and His glorious victory over death. Thank You for the joyous assurance and hope we have because of this amazing gift. God we pray for those who are still skeptical of Who Jesus is, and what He has done, and that You would awaken their hearts to the truth of the Gospel.*

*That afternoon, the whole earth was covered with darkness for three hours, from noon until three o'clock. About three o'clock, Jesus shouted, "Eli, Eli, lama sabachthani?" which means, "My God, My God, why have You forsaken Me?"*   Matthew 27:45-46 (TLB)

Out of the darkness came a cry from our Lord. It must have been an eerie moment when out of the black atmosphere of darkness came the voice of Jesus fulfilling the great Messianic Psalm 22. He gave full expression to the feelings of abandonment, and yet all the while had complete confidence, patience, and trust in the sovereignty of God the Father. In the midst of the darkness, God is dealing with His Son in a way that is beyond our human comprehension. Because God is holy, He cannot overlook sin and must punish it. God doesn't want any part of sin. He won't look at it; smell it; taste it; hear it; feel it; or think about it. He must destroy it. Jesus, the Lamb of God, had no sin of His own and could offer Himself as the perfect Atonement for our sins, and endure the temporary and agonizing *separation* from God.

From the beginning of time, Jesus knew this day would come and that this separation from God would be hell for Him, so it would never be hell for us. In the midst of the darkness of the cross we must see the light of grace. We must see that there was a reason for His excruciating physical, emotional, and spiritual pain—It was to set us free. Jesus endured God's wrath so we would not have to.

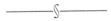

*Father God, help us to be both willing and able to comprehend and embrace the costliness of real love as You do. Thank You for sending Your precious Light into this dark world. We trust that You will never forsake us, and for that we are eternally grateful.*

# March 30                    Father, Forgive Them

*Jesus said, "Father, forgive them, for they do not know what they are doing."*
                                                        Luke 23:34 (NIV)

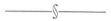

As Jesus was about to take His final breath—His tortured body hung between earth and heaven—He spoke His first words from the cross. Jesus had been betrayed, denied, mocked, tortured, and unjustly convicted prior to having nails pounded into His hands and feet, and lifted into a position where breathing was painful and difficult. Yet, His first words were a prayer—not for Himself, but for others. It was a prayer for our forgiveness, offered up to His Father in His most humiliating and agonizing state. Before Jesus placed Himself in God's hands one last time, He placed everyone else in God's hands. Who are *they* for whom He prays? They are the Roman soldiers; Pilate; the Chief Priests and Scribes; the Pharisees and Sadducees; His followers who deserted Him; and the mob of gawkers witnessing this heinous act. Yet, we need to be truthful and admit that *we* are part of the *they* for whom Jesus prayed!

As we meditate on this verse, perhaps we will see that many times our willingness to forgive is directly tied to the other person's ability to know what they've done. We're not willing to forgive until we see that this person truly knows how badly they've messed up. We're willing to forgive as long as we see the sorrow and remorse from them, but not before then! If that were the way God viewed forgiveness, would there be any salvation for us? For all of the suffering He endured on the cross for our forgiveness, His prayer was that we would forgive others.

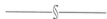

*Heavenly Father, soften our hearts so we can hear Your voice speaking to us. Forgive us for failing to always be mindful of the most amazing sacrifice made on the cross, when Jesus, while undergoing unimaginable suffering, forgave us when we were (and are) unforgiveable. Thank You for this unimaginable sacrifice.*

# March 31                                    He's Alive!

*During the forty days after He suffered and died, He appeared to the apostles from time to time, and He proved to them in many ways that He was actually alive. And He talked to them about the Kingdom of God.*                                    Acts 1:3 (NLT)

The resurrection of Jesus is the single greatest event ever! If He had merely died on the cross, He would have been considered a great teacher and moral leader. However, He would not have proven Himself as the Son of God. By His resurrection from the grave, He triumphed over death and gave the hope of eternal life to everyone who puts their trust in Him, our Lord and Savior. Every other deceased religious leader, such as Mohammed or Buddha, remain buried in the earth. A Messiah left in the grave would be no Messiah at all. It was the resurrection that proclaimed Him to be the Son of God with power. There's no power demonstrated on the cross—the power is demonstrated in the resurrection.

Whether it was the Apostles, or the associates of the Apostles; whether it was Paul who authored the majority of the New Testament books; or whether it was the men and women who made up the 500 witnesses, the message was the same—their eyewitness accounts or our risen Lord established that the resurrection is a valid reality. With all the historical evidence, we still, by faith, must choose to believe.

*Heavenly Father, we're so very grateful for the resurrection of Christ—our living Savior. Use us to spread this glorious Gospel to others, so that when we are called home, that home will be in Your glorious presence. May we share the truth that You live and have prepared a resurrection for those who love You.*

# April 1                    Foolish Leadership

*"Fools find no pleasure in understanding but delight in airing their own opinions."*
Proverbs 18:2 (NIV)

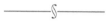

There are probably a few times in our life when we have played the fool. I'm referring to those occasions where we have displayed a know-it-all persona. It is foolish because this attitude completely reveals that we are not receptive to hearing, discussing, or understanding another's opinion or point-of-view.

If this sounds like several of our government officials, you would be correct. For example, it is absolutely foolish and corrupt to pass a bill in Congress without giving the members an opportunity to read it in its entirety—let alone have debate on the floor about the bill. Well, this is what we've had to endure for far too long—which has resulted in the passage of bills that have raised our nation's debt beyond recovery, and burdened taxpayers to the limit. Perhaps if they were truly committed to having a devoted relationship with God, that the Holy Spirit would tug on their conscious when they're tempted to perform this kind of foolishness.

The Bible has numerous verses about money and our stewardship of such. As long as money is being handled wisely and the debt payments are manageable, a government can take on the burden of financial debt *only if* it is absolutely necessary. We must push back and speak up about this, and do our best to elect representatives who will not act like fools. Pray that they change their foolish ways.

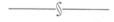

*God, we need You to save this nation. We pray that You have not given up on us to the point of allowing foolishness to overcome wisdom. Please enlighten the fools in charge of our governments, and let Your wisdom seep into their hearts.*

# April 2                                    Sinful Nature

*"Those who are dominated by the sinful nature think about sinful things, but those who are controlled by the Holy Spirit think about things that please the Spirit."*

Romans 8:5 (NLT)

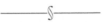

Because we are born descendants of Adam and Eve, we will always be battling our sinful nature, and that is why our loving God gave us the gift of His Spirit. Our sinful nature creates in us a penchant for disobedience, and a drive to rebel against the will of God. No one has to teach a child to lie or be selfish—rather, we go to great lengths to teach children to tell the truth and put others first. Sinful behavior comes naturally. We don't lose our sin nature once we receive Christ. The Bible says that sin remains in us and that a struggle with that old nature will continue as long as we are in this world.

Yet, a life lived honoring God, is the life that God will honor. Desiring the way of the Spirit of God and living according to His leading is the course that God upholds over and above the way of sin. The Spirit of God takes up residence in each believer and supplies the power we need to overcome the pull of the sin nature within us. So we love Jesus by loving His way for us. We step apart from the acts of the sinful nature that Paul outlined in Galatians 5, and step into the fruit of the Spirit—not because these things come naturally, but because they come supernaturally. These truths have been preserved and passed down for centuries ever since the advent of the Christian Church. Just imagine what our nation and our world would be like without the church. Yes, the church does matter today. We must do our part to ensure it remains.

*God, we thank You for the gift of Your Holy Spirit, and that He continually intercedes for us lives 24/7. May we live under the influence of Your Spirit and keep the church alive in our nation.*

# April 3 Be Still and Know

*"Be still, and know that I am God" Psalm* 46:10 (ESV)

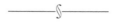

It is not in the noise of our busy lives that we grow spiritually, but in those times when we are finally quiet before the Lord. The stillness leads to knowing. In silence we learn. In silence we begin to understand. In silence we know that He is God. Some of us may think, "I don't hear God speaking to me." "Does He really do that?" Perhaps we have never devoted each day to spending uninterrupted periods of stillness where we can totally be tuned in to God. Perhaps He is just waiting for us to turn down the volume of our preoccupied minds so that we may hear Him. Acknowledging God implies that we can trust Him and surrender to His plan because we understand who He is.

Jesus was extremely busy with preaching, teaching, healing, and traveling miles and miles. Yet, He devoted time every day to be alone with His Father; to clarify His mission and priorities; to listen for His Father to speak to Him; and to meditate with gratitude on the awesomeness of His Heavenly Father. The place of stillness is the place of God's presence. Perhaps we don't hear God's voice because we've never taken the time to be still. It can't hurt to give it a try.

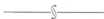

*Heavenly Father, thank You for creating in us the life that is eternal and divine that enables us to worship You. As our Creator, You know every detail of our lives, yet we often go about our day without realizing that truth. Forgive us, God, when we fail to put You first, when we fail to appreciate Your greatness and power. Help us to see that we are missing out on the amazing opportunities to know You in ways we can only imagine. May we commit a portion of time each day when we can be still and meditate on You.*

*"Love each other with genuine affection, and take delight in honoring each other."*
Romans 12:10 (NLT)

Genuine divine love is never indifferent to the needs of others, but is always looking for ways to meet another's needs with specific actions and words. God always appreciates the little—the very little—things we do for Him. So it is no surprise that He also delights when we honor others by acting in ways that let them know they are precious, respected, and special. When we do so, it gives us a break from seeking our own honor and glory. *Agape* love happens when there is a heartfelt commitment to do what is good and honoring to others.

When we elevate others, we are painting a picture of the Good News. To love and honor others it is a reflection of God's love for us. By nature we like to honor the successful, talented, attractive, and intelligent ones. Yet, Scripture teaches that regardless of a person's status or strength, we are to place their value above our own. This involves letting go of our selfishness and pride. It really comes down to the *Golden Rule* of treating others in the manner that we want to be treated. We are all uniquely created by God— no better or worse than anyone else. This should help us to recognize the wondrous hand of Almighty God.

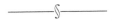

*Almighty God, when we look at all that Jesus did, and the core of His teaching, we can't ignore the fact that to be Christ-like is to be others-centered. Help us to follow His example and take delight in honoring each other.*

*"Keep your roots deep in Him and have your lives built on Him. Be strong in the faith, just as you were taught, and always be thankful."*      Colossians 2:7 (NCV)

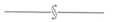

Getting to know Jesus at a deep level is not a flash-in-the-pan experience. It's not simply conversion; it is a process that takes a lifetime. To walk with Jesus, we need to get to know Who He is. We do this by immersing ourselves in His Word—especially the Gospels. The Bible teaches us that most Jews poured their hearts and minds into memorizing the Torah. We should also be firmly rooted in the Word of God so we may truly know Him and become more Christ-like.

Roots are one of the components that sustain our plants and trees. They draw nourishment and water from the soil, which makes them firm. Christ is where we should be rooted—through prayer, as well as through reading and meditating on His Word. It is His Word that lights our path in life. Isn't that the whole purpose of the Bible—to meet and intimately know Jesus? It is here that He comes to meet us, enlighten us, instruct us, correct us, comfort us, and guide us safely home. It's not a book *about* life, but a book that *gives* life. Why wouldn't we want to walk with Jesus?

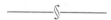

*Lord, we come to You thankful for the revelation of Your Son, the Lord Jesus Christ. We thank You for the Word in Scriptures. We thank You that the Bible has stood the test of time; that it is the anvil that has worn out many hammers; and that its truth—though endlessly assaulted—has been untouched. We thank You that it reveals Jesus Christ as the Savior, the eternal One,*

*"He who says he abides in Him ought himself also to walk just as He walked."*
1 John 2:6 (NKJV)

A disciple is one who learns from his master with the intention of becoming like the master. God's design is to make us like Christ; and His way is to fill us with His Holy Spirit. Jesus, Who is the Way, shows us His way to live so we may come to share His love; His hope; His peace; and His methods. The amazing truth is that Jesus believes in us enough that we may take His yoke upon us. He wants us to follow so closely behind Him that we are covered by the dust from His sandals. We cannot truly abide in Him if we are following Him from a distance. Every step we take should be patterned after His walk.

So how did Jesus walk? He placed God's will ahead of all things. He loved all men equally. He always did the things that pleased His Heavenly Father. He was the perfect revelation of God to man. We are to stay so connected to Jesus that we become more like Him every day. We are to walk just as He walked and become a reflection of Christ to the rest of the world. When they see us, the world should also see Him.

*Almighty God, You have called us to follow You at any price; be Your servants; be Your subjects; and be Your pupils. Make us faithful, first of all, to be marked by the hallmark of discipleship. It is a privilege and joy to learn more about You from Your Word. We humbly ask that You would reveal Yourself even more to us as we walk closely with You. May we continue to be transformed into Your image as we share Your good news with others.*

*"Love the Lord your God with all your heart, all your soul, and all your strength. Always remember these commands I give you today. Teach them to your children."*

Deuteronomy 6:5-7 (NCV)

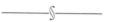

These verses are known as the *Shema* (Hebrew for *hear* or *listen*) and were recited twice daily as a creed or pledge of allegiance to God by devout Jews. In the gospels of Mark and Matthew when asked to identify the greatest commandment in the Old Testament law, Jesus directly quoted the Shema. Therefore, the Shema is as relevant to the Christian, as it is to the Jew. God is not looking for people who go through religious ritual. He wants people (us) to love Him with our whole being—a willing love; an obedient love; and an active love. We could never love God as much as He loves us. Yet, He expects us to love Him as wide as all our capabilities and capacities.

Like Israel, we would be wise to listen, remember, obey and share with others—especially with our children—that He is the One and Only true God Who is deserving of our constant love. The Shema was recited in the morning as a reminder to keep God the focus of their lives throughout the day, and at night as a way of reflection on how they did at keeping God as the center of their lives and teaching their children the importance of belonging and surrendering to Him. Let us hear it; obey it; walk it; and share it each day of our life.

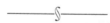

*Heavenly Father, we strive every day to live in Your Word and to share that it with others, especially our children who really need You in today's world. We thank You for Your loving grace and guidance, which is ever-present. We pray this in the Name of Your Son Jesus Christ, Your Word and love that was made flesh among us.*

*"This, then, is how you should pray: Our Father in heaven, hallowed be Your name."*
                                                                    Matthew 6:9 (NIV)

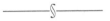

What does the name of God mean? It means all that He is and all that He stands for—His nature; His attributes; His character; His personality; His will; His authority; His power; and His glory. When we pray *"Our Father Who art in heaven, hallowed be Thy name..."* we are saying that God is holy, supremely separate or set apart from everything common, earthly, human, temporal, and spatial. In hallowing His name—or reputation—we acknowledge His glory and the fullness of Who He is. The good news is that God also views us as holy because He has united us with Christ, the One Who is holy.

No one likes to have his or her name forgotten; misspelled; or mispronounced. Our names are part of our identity and individual worth. We value having a *good name*—that is a blameless reputation. In a similar way, God's name speaks of His identity, His character, and His actions. We give God the glory and help to expand His reputation—His Name—throughout the world, through our words and actions. When we pray *"hallowed be Your name"* we are asking God to help us see Him as pure and holy, and then to help us show to others His purity and holiness in the world around us. God demonstrates His holiness everywhere by creating a holy people who will call on His name, proclaim the gospel, and accomplish good works. After all, it isn't about us—it's about Him!

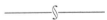

*Lord, we offer this prayer in Your name, that it may be glorified: Our Father in heaven, hallowed be Your name, Your kingdom come, Your will be done, on earth as it is in heaven. Give us today our daily bread. And forgive us our debts, as we also have forgiven our debtors. And lead us not into temptation, but deliver us from the evil one. Amen*

*A wild storm came up. Waves crashed over the boat. It was about to sink. Jesus was in the back, sleeping on a cushion. The disciples woke Him up. They said, "Teacher! Don't you care if we drown?" He got up and ordered the wind to stop. He said to the waves, "Quiet! Be still!" Then the wind died down. And it was completely calm.*

Mark 4:37-39 (NIV)

Haven't we all been in a situation where we are in the middle of a crisis and it seems like God is off somewhere taking a nap? He doesn't seem very responsive to our need—at least not in our timing or understanding of how God works. God is never in a hurry because He knows exactly what to do at exactly the right time. We must remind ourselves that when we feel we have lost the battle with our storm, that just as surely as the Lord is in control of our blessings, He is also in charge of our storms. When things look most disastrous, just look around, Jesus is about to show up! He may not keep us from going *through* the storm, but we can trust that He will be with us *in the midst* of the storm.

If we allow them to, the storms of life flourish our faith. God can use the difficult days to teach us more about Himself, and to help us grow in the Him. The storms of life serve to remind us of Who is in control. Fear and faith are incompatible. So first Jesus had to calm the storm; then He had to calm His disciples. We will find our omnipotent, omniscient, and omnipresent God in every storm we experience.

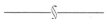

*Heavenly Father, May we take comfort in the fact that You will never leave us, even when we are in the midst of a tumultuous situation. May our faith grow stronger with the knowledge and understanding that You are our Protector and Comforter. You will always be in our boat whether the seas are rough or calm, and we can hear You say, "Be quiet! Be still!"*

*"The demon has often tried to kill him by throwing him into a fire or into water. Please have pity and help us if you can!" Jesus replied, "Why do you say, 'if you can'? Anything is possible for someone who has faith!" At once the boy's father shouted, "I do have faith! Please help me to have even more."*
Mark 9:22-24 (CEV)

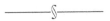

Here was a father with a son possessed by an evil spirit since childhood. When he brought his son to Jesus' disciples, they could not help him. So he asked Jesus *if* He could help. The little word *if* expresses both faith and doubt intermingled in this father's tortured soul. When we limit God in our faith through doubt, we limit the possibilities of God to move on our behalf.

From this father's heart comes truth. First he admitted his need to have even more faith. Secondly, he admitted it to the right person—Jesus. Even though this father's faith was mixed with doubt, Jesus saw his faith was *enough* to heal the boy once and for all. Jesus has taught us that even if we have faith the size of a mustard seed, we can move mountains. Faith is building our lives on the fact that God is in control, and that He will fulfill His promises even when we don't yet see those promises materialize. Our faith grows as our relationship with Jesus and His Word grows.

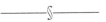

*Precious Lord, we thank You that Your love and compassion for us never ceases, and that You are so willing to demonstrate that love in miraculous ways. We ask that You teach us to live by faith; to translate that faith into persistent prayer; to have our relationship with You grow immeasurably; and to then see Your power unleashed in our lives in ways that only bring You glory. Thank You for Your many blessings.*

*Jesus saw His mother and the disciple He loved standing near her. He said to his mother, "Woman, here is your son." Then to the disciple, "Here is your mother." From that moment the disciple accepted her as his own mother.*     John 19:26-27 (MSG)

The tender instructions from Jesus during His final moments as He hung from the cross, reveal the depth of His love and care for His own. Both John (the only disciple who was present) and Mary, the mother of Jesus, loved Jesus with all their hearts. Both were full of sorrow as they their beloved Savior endured unspeakable suffering. For John, He was given this responsibility instead of Jesus' half-brothers because they did not yet believe Jesus was the Messiah. For Mary, she must have recalled the prophetic words of Simeon thirty-three years earlier when he said that her own soul would experience piercing pain. She watched her first-born in the full agony of the cross—the One she had nursed, comforted, and raised to adulthood—compassionately focus on the needs of His mother and His best friend. She stood at the foot of the cross pouring out her motherly love for her Son, suffering with Him to the end.

Now the level of love and commitment that Jesus calls them to have for one another is the deepest there can be because He calls them to actually care for each other as a mother and son—a parent and child. Can we grasp the depth of love Jesus has for every one of us?

*God, we see the finest example of the selfless love that Jesus demonstrated as He hung from the cross, bearing the sins of a fallen world. We are made in Your image, which means that we too have the ability to unite our hearts with the hearts of others, by offering compassion, love, mercy, and grace. May we take time each day to stand at the foot of the cross and immerse ourselves in Your love— an unconditional love that never runs out.*

# April 12                                    End of the Age

*As He was sitting on the Mount of Olives, His disciples came to Him privately and said, "Tell us, when will these things happen? And what will be the sign of your coming and of the end of the age?"*                                    Matthew 24:3 (NET)

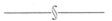

Based on Old Testament teachings and prophecy, Jews in Jesus' day believed that the Messiah would come *one* time to establish His Kingdom. The disciples' idea of the "end of the age" was the Lord's final judgment against sinners, which they believed would take place during Christ's time on earth. In no way did they envision a *second coming*, some two thousand plus years in the future, when He would return, in power and glory, to destroy His enemies and establish His eternal Kingdom. Jesus had just informed them that the Holy Temple would be destroyed, which did not fit into the eschatological theme they anticipated. Out of confusion and curiosity, they asked Jesus when these events would take place, and what sign they might see to prepare them. Jesus would later correct their faulty understanding, which averted discouragement and despair on their part.

We have the privilege of having New Testament Scriptures to give us a fuller understanding of God's Word, which had not yet been written when Jesus was on earth. So, before we cast judgment on the disciples and other Jews in that day for their inaccurate eschatology, may we be reminded to have our thinking be in sync with the Scriptures. This especially applies to our thinking and understanding of the last days.

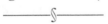

*Jesus, as we are experiencing much chaos and evil in our world today, we eagerly await Your second coming, which will bring us into Your presence. Until then, may we be motivated to study Your Word to gain deeper understanding of the impact of our Savior's first advent, as well as Your future return. May we continue to exhibit grace, grow in the knowledge of our You, and serve in Your Kingdom.*

*Jesus answered: "Watch out that no one deceives you. For many will come in My name claiming, 'I am the Messiah,' and will deceive many."*          Matthew 24:4-5 (NIV)

The followers of Jesus wanted to know when the end of the age would be and what signs would trigger it. Jesus would answer their questions, but His primary concern is that they (and us) would not be deceived. Deception is a frequent topic throughout Scriptures. It began as early as the Garden of Eden, but Jesus strongly warns His disciples about spiritual deception three times in the Olivet Discourse. These warnings from Jesus should be etched on our hearts as well. While we must always be on the alert for false teachings and false messiahs, here Jesus declares that we must be especially watchful for spiritual deceit as the day of His return approaches. Just because we are believers doesn't mean we are completely immune from demonic deceptions that could turn our hearts away from the One true God. That is why we must remain vigilant. We must thoroughly evaluate new materials to ensure that they will not move us away from the core truths of God's Word.

Jesus made it clear what would happen in the world before His return, i.e. wars; earthquake; famine; diseases; persecution of Christians; deserting the faith; increase in evil activity; and an increased spread of the Gospel throughout the world. Yet, this prophetic message is underscored with the warning to not be deceived by false messiahs and false teachings. Through various parables, Jesus provided us with a prescription that calls us to faithfulness; preparedness; expectancy; stewardship; Kingdom service; and evangelism. Are we ready for His return?

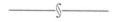

*Lord, we pray for discernment for what we experience on a daily basis. May we always remain immersed in Your Word and use Your Holy Spirit as our Guide and Protector— knowing that Your purpose is not to frighten us, but to prepare us.*

# April 14                                    Abomination

*"So when you see standing in the holy place 'the abomination that causes desolation,' spoken of through the prophet Daniel—let the reader understand—then let those who are in Judea flee to the mountains."*                                    Matthew 24:15-16 (NIV)

An *abomination* means something that is usually associated with idolatry, which is detestable; an atrocity; or something that is utterly repulsive to God. Jesus speaks of an abomination that will take place during the midway point of the Tribulation, when the Antichrist enters the rebuilt temple in Jerusalem; proclaims himself as God; and demands that the entire world worship him. This outrageous act of sacrilege will be done deliberately and publicly, and will cause the godly to desert the temple and flee Jerusalem. This heinous event is more than an act directed merely against a rebuilt temple—it will reach out and infect humanity, which will cause one to become desolate.

How should these amazing truths impact us? First, they should cause us to rejoice that we serve and worship a sovereign God, Who is orchestrating all things for our good and His glory. He has been gracious enough to reveal some of His eternal purposes, and these truths should strengthen our faith. Lastly, we should be even more motivated to share the Gospel with those who do not yet know our Lord and Savior—BEFORE these events unfold.

*Heavenly Father, we thank You for the gift of Your Word, given many centuries ago. We thank You for opening our eyes and ears to see and hear all the lines of history converging in the same direction of the last days. We believe that what is not yet fulfilled, will come to pass in Your own time, according to Your good plan. As our nation heads into darkness, if sometimes feels like the "spirit" of Antichrist that is already in the world. Strengthen our faith and make us bold for Jesus Christ. Give us a spirit of encouragement and deep joy that comes from knowing that You are in control of all things.*

*"For the Lord himself will come down from heaven with a commanding shout, with the voice of the archangel, and with the trumpet call of God. First, the believers who have died will rise from their graves. Then, together with them, we who are still alive and remain on the earth will be caught up in the clouds to meet the Lord in the air. Then we will be with the Lord forever. So encourage each other with these words."*

1 Thessalonians 4:16-18 (NLT)

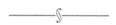

   Scripture teaches us that our resurrected Lord and Savior, Jesus Christ, will one day return to gather all believers from earth and into His presence. This is called *The Rapture*. The believers in the church in Thessalonica were concerned about those who had already died—would they be included in this glorious event? Paul reassures them that God will treat dead believers the same way He treated Jesus by raising them from the dead. That's His promise—bodily resurrection. And when Christ Himself returns to rapture His church, both those living at the time, as well as those who have died, will be united in the air to meet Jesus face-to-face.

   This truth should greatly comfort all believers as we anticipate Christ coming for His *bride*—the church. He is the Bridegroom coming to take His bride. Since *any* day might be the eve of *that* day, we should be prepared by standing firmly in our faith; keeping ourselves pure and holy; and encouraging each other as we patiently await His return.

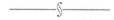

*Thank You, Father, for such a promise that fills us with hope. We ache for those in our world who do not have eternal hope, and who live with the frightening despair of final partings and hopelessness. May we find comfort in knowing that one day we will be reunited with believers we have "temporarily" lost, (whose bodies sleep while their souls are with You) until our Savior calls us into His presence. May we remain always strong in our faith and be moved to share Your gift of the resurrection with those Who do not yet believe.*

*"I will make Jerusalem like a cup of poison to the nations around her. They will come and attack Jerusalem and Judah. One day all the nations on earth will come together to attack Jerusalem, but I will make it like a heavy rock; anyone who tries to move it will get hurt."*
Zechariah 12:2-3 (NCV)

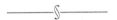

As with everything else, the land of Israel belongs to God. Three times in history God allowed Israel to fall into exile—to the Assyrians, Babylonians, and the Romans. In 1900, there were only 40,000 Jews in Palestine. God re-gathered His people and re-established the nation of Israel in 1948, and re-occupied Jerusalem following the miraculous six-day war in 1967. Today, Israel's population is over eight million, with over seventy-four percent being Jewish. The Bible prophesies that all nations of the world will come together against Israel in the last days. But God, Himself, will see to it that Jerusalem will be undisturbed, secure, and shielded by God. It is God Who made it all, and Who will end it all. Satan has his purpose—the destruction of Israel. Yet God has His purposes—the purging of unbelieving rebels; then to save the remnant; to save the nation; and to save the city of Jerusalem.

The Bible clearly teaches that God never pours out His wrath without warning, for He is a just and loving God, Who does not wish that any should perish. That's why He has provided so many signs to alert us to the fact that we are living on the threshold of the last days. Therefore, the crucial question is: "Are we ready?"

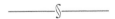

*Heavenly Father, we acknowledge that Your Word is powerful and divine. And, despite being written thousands of years ago, it is truly accurate, as we are witnessing Your prophetic truths come to fruition. We pray that there will be many more Jews and Gentiles who will come to embrace Christ as their Savior. May Your Spirit of grace and mercy come upon them, and that You would powerfully work in this day, as You will one day in the future for Your beloved nation.*

*"Then, the Arrival of the Son of Man! It will fill the skies—no one will miss it. Unready people all over the world, outsiders to the splendor and power, will raise a huge lament as they watch the Son of Man blazing out of heaven."*    Matthew 24:30 (MSG)

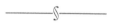

Prophecy occupies one-fifth of the Bible, with half of the prophetic verses concerning Jesus Christ. Of these, over two-thirds refer to Christ's second coming, which have yet to be fulfilled. Jesus, Himself, refers to His return at least twenty-one times in the New Testament. At His first coming, Jesus was rejected; humiliated; crucified; and resurrected—fulfilled prophecy. Yet God has promised His Son will return to rule in glory and power, as He brings unimaginable peace and redemption to the remnant of Jews—and to all who accept Jesus—and an "Eden-like" environment in which to live.

It is sad to think of the millions of people who will lament, wail, and moan because they ignored the predictions and promises made by God that this glorious event would take place. If we have people in our lives that fall into this category, pray for them. In Matthew 24:42, Jesus warns us to *"keep watch."* Yet, simply watching world events is not about what Jesus was speaking—He wants us to watch our hearts, and more importantly, He wants us to watch our relationship with our loving God.

*Almighty God, we are so thankful for Jesus' promise: "When everything is ready, I will come and get you, so that you will always be where I am." (John 14:3) In our excitement and anticipation of Your glorious return, we pray that You will speak to the hearts of those who have not yet surrendered their lives to You, so they will have the privilege of experiencing Your splendor and power. Lord, we trust You completely that Your promises to Your beloved children of Israel, to the Church, and to the nations will be fulfilled.*

*"Why do you look at the speck of sawdust in your brother's eye and pay no attention to the plank in your own eye?"*         Luke 6:41 (NIV)

It's a destructive tendency that we all have demonstrated, at one time or another—to exaggerate the faults of others and minimize our own. Here, Jesus is teaching us to stop criticizing; stop condemning; and stop being self-righteous every time others don't do something the way we think it ought to be done. When we do judge others in this way, we manifest an erroneous view of ourselves. In Romans 2:1, Paul warns that the problem with judging others is that we are often guilty of the same or worse sins ourselves. We shouldn't misunderstand this verse to mean that we should never offer help when we perceive when a fellow believer is struggling with sin in their life. But, we should first take a look in the mirror and present ourselves to God for His examination, and ask Him to reveal the truth to ourselves.

We cannot help one another as long as we are blinded by our own delusions about ourselves—in other words, the "plank" in our own eye. We can't overlook the fact that Jesus said both the speck *and* the plank were to be removed. Jesus treats the removal of a judgmental spirit from our own lives as a higher priority than our critical efforts to remove the sins of others. If we fail to consider this, we are simply behaving as hypocrites.

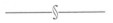

*God, we ask for Your forgiveness for our many judgments, and our many criticisms we have formed about others. You have been far more merciful with us, than we are with each other. This has been a difficult challenge because of the fallen and failing nature of our nation. When we see the wrong direction our nation is headed, give us discernment to speak out with methods to correct those wrongs, instead of merely being critical and judgmental.*

# April 19      Shed Some Light

*"Take no part in the worthless deeds of evil and darkness; instead, expose them."*
Ephesians 5:11 (NLT)

If there was any a time in our nation when evil deeds and darkness should be exposed, it is now. As our nation has moved further and further away from God, these acts of deceit and corruption are happening much more frequently, especially in our government and schools. Because the liberal media is in cahoots with the liberal, power-hungry and greedy people in government, these destructive acts are not exposed to the average citizen. Light and darkness cannot coexist. When the light is turned on—exposing the evil—the darkness goes away. The best way to cleanse our government of evil and corruption is to drag it into the light. We are more concerned with exposing the sin, more so than the sinner. It is the sin that is having a devastating effect on all of us.

There have been countless examples of lies and corruption in the past several years, such as: agencies like the FBI and CIA involved in cover-ups of the Russia collusion hoax; concealing the truth about corruption with foreign nations on the part of a presidential candidate and his family; false statements about the southern border; our energy disaster; COVID; big pharma; the economy etc. We're challenged to expose and shed light on this darkness to the masses because of the media. Yet, we must not give up trying. As more light flows in, darkness cannot stand.

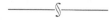

*Heavenly Father, this is the result of our nation throwing You aside. Please give us the discernment, courage, and means by which we can do our part to expose the evil and corruption in our government to all Americans, so that darkness will vanish.*

# April 20                     Lazy and Entitled

*"When we were with you, we gave you this rule: Anyone who refuses to work should not eat."*                    2 Thessalonians 3:10 (NCV)

The Bible has plenty to say about laziness and idleness. When the Apostle Paul was on his mission trips, he did not expect to get paid or take food for free. In fact, in various cities where Paul was spreading the Gospel, he and his companions were willing to take side jobs to pay for their provisions. They didn't want to be a burden on the communities they visited. When Paul had heard that some people were *unwilling* to work and were being disorderly in the church, he reminded them of this rule.

Well, this *rule* should be in place today. In the past few decades, we have allowed a generation of entitlement believers to flourish—able-bodied individuals who are unwilling and refuse to work because they are receiving *unwarranted money* not to work. This is not beneficial to anyone! This mindset has evolved into an entitlement culture that teaches, some individuals *deserve* benefits and special privileges be given to them, "just because"—such as unemployment benefits; health care; education; promotions; etc. This culture believes the whole world revolves around their *perceived* rights and wants. Entitlement is not recognized as a God-given unalienable right. The effects of this type of culture have made our nation less productive; more divided; and has provided our nation with a bleak future. If we had godly leaders in our government, this could all change, and the lazy will be forced to work—or starve.

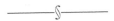

*Heavenly Father, we pray that our nation will wake up and elect leaders who will change the destructive laws and practices currently in place and restore us to a God-loving, God-fearing nation and rid the mindset of entitlement and laziness.*

# April 21        Idol Re-Arrangement

*"Dear children, keep away from anything that might take God's place in your hearts."*
1 John 5:21 (NLT)

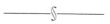

Humans are made to worship. We will worship something created, whether it is a sports team, person, possession, achievement, activity, or even ourselves. We might think, "I don't do anything like bowing down to a golden calf, so how could I be an idol-worshiper?" Idolatry lies in the worshiper, not the thing worshiped. A golden calf is just a golden calf. It becomes an idol only when it becomes too important to us; when we allow it to rob God of His proper place in ourselves. If it walks like an idol, and quacks like an idol, it is an idol. We can fall into the trap of worshiping the created thing, instead of the Creator. When we do, it steals our peace, and we falsely believe it will satisfy us beyond our relationship with God.

While discernment and wisdom from God can help us to identify and break down idols in our lives, this is clearly a problem of the human heart. So, it becomes an on-going challenge to prevent created things from becoming a priority of our worship, rather than fixing our eyes—our emotions, dreams, desires, hopes, and determination—on Jesus. Money, family, career, children, performance, relationships, etc. can all be idols. This calls for an *idol rearrangement* to take place in our hearts. The idea is not to love good things less, but to love our awesome God more.

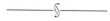

*Almighty God, Your greatest command is a command to worship; to love You with all our heart, soul, mind, and strength. Anything less than that is a failure to give You the worship You deserve. Forgive us for when we allow anything to knock You out of first place in our hearts. Thank You for creating in us the life that is eternal and divine that enables us to worship You. We give You the praise and the glory for all You've done.*

# Devoted to Prayer

*"Devote yourselves to prayer with an alert mind and a thankful heart."*
Colossians 4:2 (NLT)

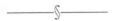

Prayer is our Spiritual Union with God. Prayer submits our will to the Lord's; aligns our desires with His purposes; and cements His truth in our heart. Prayer is the highest form of worship in which we can participate. Through prayer, we acknowledge His sovereign will and our utter dependence; we confess His glory and our sin; we affirm our reliance on His wisdom, grace, power, preservation, protection; and admit our weakness. Prayer is not about getting our way or convincing God to change His mind. It is about glorifying Him through declaration of His position and nature; acknowledging our dependence upon Him; and uniting our will with His will so that we might be used by Him. Jesus' life on earth was characterized by both public and private prayer. So, as believers how much more do we need to pray for ourselves, and for one another, as well as for spreading of the Gospel? Paul says we are to devote ourselves to prayer.

Prayer should be a priority on which we spend effort, energy, and time each and every day. Prayer begins in our hearts. It is an outpouring of our thankful and grateful hearts towards God, and is a direct reflection of our loving relationship with Him.

*Heavenly Father, we thank You that You have called us to prayer, and that our prayers are used as part of the means by which You accomplish Your great purpose. Glorify Yourself! Glorify Your Son! God, we pray that You will do Your work in a great way in all of our hearts and draw us to You in a righteous way. May we pray the way that Jesus instructed us to pray, and know the joy and blessing that comes from that. May we devote ourselves to prayer each day with thankful hearts, and know that each prayer is centered on Your Name, Your Kingdom, and Your will.*

*"This same Good News that came to you is going out all over the world. It is bearing fruit everywhere by changing lives, just as it changed your lives from the day you first heard and understood the truth about God's wonderful grace."*          Colossians 1:6 (NLT)

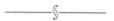

The early church knew why they existed. Jesus had enlisted these followers not to a life of leisure, but to a life of service. While each had a different task, they all had the same calling: to fulfill the Great Commission. These men and women functioned as one body of Christ—the church—whose objective was reaching the world for Christ. It's not just the job of the pastor or the staff to be missionaries for Christ to reach the lost; serve the needy; or start churches in new places. It's a responsibility and a command for the entire body of Christ. Whether we *go* or *give*—or both—we play a significant role in carrying out Christ's mission.

The New Testament draws its breath in missions—the work of the church body. The Gospels are living recordings of missionary preaching, and the Epistles are teachings and encouraging words concerning Christ's expectation of the church body. The missionary enterprise did not originate in the brain of any man—its originating source was in the heart of God Himself. Let's step up and step out through going and/or giving, so we can help the church body bear fruit—fruit that will last eternally.

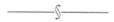

*Father, we continue to thank You for Your never-ending love. You "so loved the world" that You gave us Your Son—the ultimate Missionary. Your field is the world, and You have asked each of us to participate in Your divine work, and to be part of Your church. May our joy be abundant as we spread the Good News to the ends of the earth, and bear much fruit in Your name.*

*Then Jesus said to them, "Follow Me, and I will make you become fishers of men."*
Mark 1:17 (NKJV)

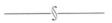

When Jesus called the Twelve, He was inviting them to make a personal investment, and to become learners in the context of relationship. As they shared life together, Jesus spoke truth to them; revealed sin in them; modeled His Father's ways for them; and later challenged them to make disciples of all nations. By concentrating His life in a few, He multiplied His life exponentially. Jesus chose this type of shoulder-to-shoulder, life-to-life approach as His strategy for evangelization of the world. Discipleship is essential to our personal growth in Christ, as well as our individual and collective impact on the world. Discipleship is truth transferred through relationship.

Jesus preached to and reached crowds, but He focused most of His time and energy on His twelve closest followers. He invited them into that relationship to follow Him in order to challenge them to become *fishers of people*. They accepted His challenges because they had been invited into a relationship with Him. And we have been invited into that same relationship with Him.

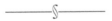

*Precious Jesus, we have all been invited to follow You and become fishers of people. We know that to follow You, it will require forming meaningful relationships with others and sharing Your truth—be it local or global. We must remind ourselves that You never intended for us to walk our spiritual path alone, or to be silent believers. May we embrace Your design for us to develop relationships with others, in which honesty, vulnerability, accountability, encouragement, joy, and grace abound. May we be willing to become disciples, as well as willing to be discipled.*

*"Teach these new disciples to obey all the commands I have given you. And be sure of this,*
*I am with you always, even to the end of the age."* Matthew 28:20 (NLT)

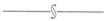

A genuine Christian is one who is willing to learn the practices, postures, and principles that Jesus taught and commanded us to follow. Discipleship is not merely an opportunity to give our advice, it is an opportunity to seek God with a fellow believer and grow in the wisdom that comes from Christ's commands. Jesus had twelve disciples, yet His core discipleship focused on three of the twelve—John, James, and Peter. In these settings, the disciples could confess their sins to one another; pray for one another; encourage one another; and hold one another accountable. We cannot make disciples without accountability—that would be like raising a child without discipline. Jesus trained them, equipped them, sent them out, and had them report back. Jesus used accountability to instill spiritual growth in the lives of His disciples. God desires for us to have mentoring relationships in our lives to provide us with loving direction on our spiritual path.

Accountability enables us to share our lives with another in a meaningful, introspective way, which helps us to get to know God, ourselves, and others on a much deeper level. Accountability is also vital in any community and nation as a whole. Sadly, we are lacking in this area. Discipleship could produce more godly leaders.

*Father God, thank You for sending Your Son to live the perfect life and model how to become like Him. God, we know that for us to experience the kind of spiritual transformation You desire from us, that we need to do more than simply attend church and read Your Word. May we all grow to become fully devoted disciples of Christ through these powerful relationships.*

*"We must focus on Jesus, the source and goal of our faith. He saw the joy ahead of Him, so He endured death on the cross and ignored the disgrace it brought Him. Now He holds the honored position—the one next to God the Father on the heavenly throne. Think about Jesus, Who endured opposition from sinners, so that you don't become tired and give up."*                                Hebrews 12:2-3 (GW)

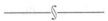

As we go through this life, we often skip over the fact that God has a plan and purpose for each of us. When we do, our faith in God begins to erode because we feel that God has somehow let us down because He hasn't done what *we* expected Him to do in the timeframe in which we had hoped. Too often, we allow circumstances and worldly influences to govern our loyalty and fidelity to God. This is *circumstantial faith*—when our level of trust in God is based on our life situations. However, we are not God! His plans and methods are beyond our comprehension, and too often, our assessment of what He's doing, or not doing, is completely inaccurate. This passage reminds us that Jesus is the *Perfecter of our faith* and that His entire earthly ministry was the very embodiment of complete trust in God. During those times when our faith is shallow, or when we feel that God is silent, we must lean on His promises that He will never leave us or forsake us.

Even though we don't understand His ways, we must keep our focus on Jesus. God wants us to find Him through the lens of faith. The irony is that God is everywhere. To search for Him is like hunting for our eyeglasses while we are actually wearing them!

*Almighty God, we confess that too often our faith wavers because we have relied on ourselves, or the world, instead of on You. Help us to keep our focus on You.*

*"Faith makes us sure of what we hope for and gives us proof of what we cannot see. It was their faith that made our ancestors pleasing to God."*          Hebrews 11:1-2 (CEV)

Faith is absolute confidence in the trustworthiness of God. It is the conviction that what God says is true, and that what He promises will come to pass. Biblical faith is confident obedience to God's Word, in spite of our circumstances and consequences. If we get real with ourselves, we want God to be like us, and to want the same things we want. Yet, God's purposes so dwarf our *in-the-moment* wishes, that we are staggered by His wisdom and foresight on our behalf. The Bible is full of examples of Old Testament promises from God, and how people of faith gave substance to what was yet in the future. One of the best examples was Job. Despite all that Job had experienced through loss and suffering, his faith did not waver. Although Job mourned his losses and struggled with questions, he didn't stop loving God and believing that God would bring him through. This verse sums up Job's trust and faith in God's will and promise: *"I know that my Savior lives, and at the end He will stand on this earth. My flesh may be destroyed, yet from this body I will see God."* (Job 19:25-26)

For Christians, our faith rests in the truth and promise from God, that we will live eternally in His presence. If we can be certain of this declaration from God, despite having not yet experienced it, how much can our faith grow in all other areas of our spiritual walk. Faith is the affirmative response to the will and the Word of God.

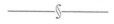

*Heavenly Father, You are the Promise Maker and Promise Keeper. So great is Your faithfulness! Grant us ever-growing faith and ever-strengthened faith. We have faith that You will save our nation, which is in desperate need of You.*

# April 28          Divine Empathy an Understanding

*"For our high priest is able to understand our weaknesses. He was tempted in every way that we are, but he did not sin. Let us, then, feel very sure that we can come before God's throne where there is grace. There we can receive mercy and grace to help us when we need it."*                                                                 Hebrews 4:15-16 (NCV)

————§————

It is a truth told by Jesus, and experienced by every person, that we will have pain and problems in our life. John 16:33 states, *"In the world you will have tribulation."* When troubles do come, they seem to concentrate their power against our faith in the Lord. Satan wants to do all that he can to make Christians doubt that God will go through those trials with us. Jesus, our perfect and sinless High Priest, has a phenomenal proficiency for empathy. It goes far beyond the intellectual, because it is truly experiential. Jesus does not *imagine* how we feel—He truly *feels* it! Jesus came in the flesh so He could experience the weaknesses and the temptations that come with the flesh. He experienced hunger, pain, rejection, hatred, injustice, thirst, need, temptation, betrayal, ridicule, love, warmth, cold, exhaustion, elation, and sadness.

The throne of our gracious God is available to us 24/7 to which we have an open invitation. When we accept, we can receive two of the greatest gifts that He has promised—mercy and grace. We receive mercy for our past failures, and grace to meet our present and future needs. It is comforting to know that we will never be alone in our times of trouble because He is with us.

————§————

*Heavenly Father, our faith is based on the knowledge that Jesus died to save us and that He lives to keep us. He has an unequaled capacity to understand our every situation because He's been there. It is comforting to know that we can freely and confidently come to Your throne to receive Your promised mercy and grace.*

**April 29**                    **Strength Through Weakness**

*"Three different times I begged the Lord to take it away. Each time He said, My grace is all you need. My power works best in weakness. So now I am glad to boast about my weaknesses, so that the power of Christ can work through me. For when I am weak, then I am strong."*                    2 Corinthians 12:8-10 (NLT)

————§————

It's likely that very few of us are able to value the onset and/or endurance of anything unpleasant or difficult, and we usually grasp its value or purpose in retrospect.  Everything comes to us from God by His grace.  Even suffering is a tool God uses for building godly character; growing our faith; and ensuring our total dependence on Him for everything.  Paul knew a thing or two about suffering.  Paul told the church in Corinth that he was *"given a thorn in his flesh."*  God did not allow this to *punish* Paul, or keep him weak for the sake of weakness.  All of us have some type of thorn in our flesh and spend a lot of our time in complaint or pleading to God, "why me?"  God allows, and uses suffering to *humble* us; to reveal our spiritual character; to draw us to Him in intimate communion; to shower us with His grace; and to perfect His power. Paul passionately and repeatedly prayed for God to relieve him of his suffering.  God's answer was that He would supply Paul with enough grace and strength to endure the load he bore.  Instead of taking away the thorn, God would strengthen Paul under it, and show His strength through Paul's weakness.

We can't receive God's strength until we know our weakness. The ultimate purpose of God in our weakness is to glorify the kind of power that moved Christ to the cross and kept Him there until His amazing work of love was completed.

————§————

*God, we can't receive Your strength until we know our weakness.  Help us to joyfully embrace the suffering because it has such great spiritual benefit.*

# No Regret of Surrender

*"For I have come down from heaven to do the will of God Who sent Me, not to do My own will."* John 6:38 (NLT)

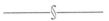

Our Lord Jesus Christ voluntarily took the place of a servant in order to carry out the will of His Father. This does not mean that He did not have a will of His own, but rather that His own will was in perfect agreement with the will of God. Jesus endured all the wickedness, persecution, and suffering this world threw at Him all to fulfill a greater purpose. To understand the will of God doesn't mean we always know *why* God is doing a certain thing. Nor does it mean that we always know *what* God is doing. It means we understand that God has a will for us and that it is always best for us. Yet, pride and fear become our stumbling blocks—we are either too prideful or too afraid to totally surrender to God. His plans for us are so full, so complete, and so perfect, that we have every reason to trust Him; to depend on Him for everything; and to seek His guidance in all things.

Trust is an essential ingredient to surrender. We won't surrender to God unless we trust Him, but we can't trust Him until we know Him better. Fear keeps us from surrendering, but perfect love casts out all fear. The more we realize how much God loves us, the easier surrender becomes. That is great faith! No one has ever surrendered his or her life to God and lived to regret doing so.

———§———

*Heavenly Father, our confidence grows each day knowing that You are Who You say You are, and that You will do what You have promised. You have given us the power of choice for us to exercise. Our prayer is that we would make the right choice to totally surrender our will to Yours. Guide us to live by Your every Word; trusting You in trial and darkness, as well as in the light; walking by faith and not by sight; relying on You with unquestioning confidence; and resting in Your perfect love.*

# May 1                                    Stewardship and Governance

*"Everything under heaven is Mine!"* Job 41:11 (NKJV)

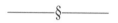

A steward is someone entrusted with another's wealth or property and charged with the responsibility of managing it in the owner's best interest. Stewardship is faithfully using whatever God gives us—opportunities; interests; skills; employment; family; talents; spiritual gifts; land; money etc.—for His glory. The real issue of stewardship is whether we are administrating our affairs and possessions as though they are ours, or as though they are God's. We will openly *admit* that God owns everything, yet in our daily lives we *live* like *we* are the owners. We choose our house; our cars; our clothes; where we will invest; how we will spend our time etc., like we are the owners of it all—never even thinking to ask the real Owner what He wants us to do with it all.

Don't you wish that our government officials would manage our tax dollars to produce balanced budgets and stop reckless, pork-filled bills that are passed without any consideration to seek the Lord's guidance—let alone have floor debate. But how can they when they have removed God from the way they govern and the decisions they make, as well as personally profiting at the expense of those they represent? We need more stewardship in governance.

*Almighty God, we are so grateful that You have placed in our trust a measure of time, a unique set of talents, and a sufficient treasure to carry out Your will for our lives. We pray that those who have been elected to represent us, would have the same mindset, and seek Your wisdom and guidance to properly manage that which You have entrusted them to do. God we pray for wise stewards with integrity to be our representatives.*

*"So be careful how you live. Don't live like fools, but like those who are wise. Make the most of every opportunity in these evil days."*                    Ephesians 5:15-16 (NLT)

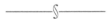

Time is the capital that God has given us to invest. We can't delay it; speed it up; save it; or lose it. The challenge is not to manage time, but to manage ourselves. We tend to squander this gift from God by doing too little, or doing too much in areas that are of little or no service to God's Kingdom. The way we use our time reveals where our values and priorities in life exist. The Bible teaches that we are to use our time and our talents in ways that bring glory and honor to God. This verse in particular teaches us that we are to make the most of every opportunity by utilizing every situation as the perfect occasion to do God's will and influence others for Him, by investing our time in our families, friends, fellowship, and service. We are accountable to God for how we spend our time.

We are gifted by God to do many things, but none more important than to serve others in the name of Christ. One of those things is to work hard at bringing God back into our personal and national lives. Perhaps God is tired of hearing all of our excuses: "I've served my time" "I don't know enough" "I'm too busy" "I don't want to get involved." What if God had that attitude with us? Thankfully, He doesn't—yet!

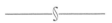

*Heavenly Father, Thank You for giving us the gift of life. You invite us to discover how precious each moment can be. Your presence and activity in our lives gives us the confidence to face each occasion with hope. You invite and challenge us to participate in making this world a blessed place. Guide us to use our time wisely as your faithful servants. Help us to fulfill Your work in the way that brings glory to the name of Christ Jesus.*

# May 3             Godly Budgeting

*"Honor the Lord from your wealth and from the first fruits of all your crops; then your barns will be filled completely, and your vats will overflow with new wine."*

Proverbs 3:9-10 (NET)

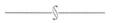

When we financially honor God with our first fruits, we are saying that "we love You;" "we thank You for Your all that You have given to us;" and that "we trust You for Your continued provision." Our giving is an expression of who we are. It is an act of faith, and an unwavering declaration that God is our main priority—He's number One in our life! In order to more fully understand the principle of giving, we need to recognize that managing money is a spiritual issue. True financial success comes not from accumulating a large surplus in our bank account, but from following God's plan for our finances—His three-step plan: 1. Give to God first! The truth is there will never be "enough" to give. If we wait until all of our needs and desires are met before we start to give, it will never happen. 2. Set aside funds for regular savings. We must plan our savings *before* we plan our spending. 3. Spend the rest on what we need. The key is to develop a good budget, which is basically is a *spending plan.*

The point of this Proverb is that, in God's providence, He so often appoints that when we are generous through having a consistent and systematic giving plan, we will be generously supplied so that we can generously give—our generosity will not make us poor! Give, save, and live on the rest.

*Father God, we long to be faithful givers, modeling ourselves after You, Who has given everything to us. Because we trust You as our Provider, we will freely give as we have freely received. We pray that our faith will deepen so that we can be better stewards of our finances, which will allow us to willingly, joyfully, and consistently give to You our first fruits.*

*When Jesus had received the sour wine, He said, "It is finished!" Then bowing His head, He gave up His spirit.*                                                  John 19:30 (HCSB)

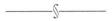

As Jesus was about to give up His spirit through death on the cross, He declared to His Father—and to us—that He had finished the work that the Father had commissioned Him to fulfill from the very beginning. Jesus had accomplished His mission; announced and inaugurated the Kingdom of God; and revealed the love and grace of God by saying, *"Tetelestai."* This statement of triumph is a Greek word which was commonly used in various situations in everyday life in those days. Tetelestai means to finish, complete, or accomplish. Perhaps the most familiar use of tetelestai was from merchants when a debt or bill was paid in full. When Jesus said *"Tetelestai,"* He proclaimed that the debt owed to God by each and every one of us for our sins, was victoriously cancelled through the shed blood of the Lamb of God.

Through His finished and perfected work, we now have the assurance of having an eternal and direct relationship with our Creator and Savior. *"Tetelestai"* is Jesus' powerful cry of victory! His work is finished. There is no back-up plan, because His death and resurrection for our salvation is all that is necessary.

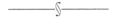

*Lord Jesus, we can never find the words to express our gratitude to You, our Savior. You finished all for which You had been sent—faithful in life; faithful in death. You accomplished what no one else could do—taking the sin of the world upon Your sinless shoulders; taking our sin so we might receive Your forgiveness and a new life. All praise be to You, gracious Lord, for finishing the work of salvation. Hallelujah!*

*"I thank my God every time I remember you, always praying with joy for all of you."*
Philippians 1:3-4(NCV)

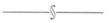

Joy is the supernatural delight and deep satisfaction in God for the utter beauty and worth of Who He is. We find the theme of joy resonating in Paul's letter to the church in Philippi. The joy captured in his words was an absolute joy that he experienced as a result of his obedience to the Lord. Paul penned these words to the church in Philippi while in captivity, but we wouldn't know it by the spirit of joy he expressed. Paul truly understood that having joy did not depend on his circumstances. Paul was not only conveying his thankfulness to them, but he was making it clear that he thanked God for all of them. Paul knew genuine joy because he was faithful in praying for others. It was an act he always did with joy. His joy was not tied to pleasures on earth; possessions; freedom; prestige; outward success; or a good reputation.

Like for Paul, these worldly things will not bring us the extraordinary joy that we can only find in our relationship to God and with those He places in our lives. When we are bitter, resentful, and critical, we lack joy. On the flip side, when we appreciate others and prayerfully thank God for them, we will experience the level of joy about which Paul so often shared with us.

*Heavenly Father, we are eternally thankful for Your love and allowing us the privilege of having a deep and personal relationship with You. You are the Source of our joy, and from that joy is where we find our strength. May we follow the example of Your servant Paul, by delighting in Your gift of joy that Your Holy Spirit produces in us. May we always be grateful to You for those You have placed in our lives, and faithfully keep them in prayer with unending joy. We love You and praise You.*

*"Are you strong because you belong to Christ? Does His love comfort you? Do you have joy by being as one in sharing the Holy Spirit? Do you have loving-kindness and pity for each other? Then give me true joy by thinking the same thoughts. Keep having the same love. Be as one in thoughts and actions."*        Philippians 2:1-2(NLV)

Paul's goal was not to make us question these things, but to remind us that they are present. Unity is a precious gift of the Spirit. It is to be prized; to be sought; and to be guarded at all costs. When it is lost, it is hard to regain. Joy comes from living in harmony, humility and helpfulness. Paul is saying that whatever we have received from Jesus—encouragement, comfort, fellowship, tenderness and compassion—shouldn't we then also express such experiences to others? So, what prevents us from doing so? The answer is sin expressed through pride and selfishness/self-centeredness. The key to a life of joy is a God-centered; Gospel-based; and grace-enabled shifting of our attention away from ourselves and onto others. A misconception of Christian unity is that we Christians must all unanimously agree. But if everyone in the room always agrees, then someone is not using their God-given brain.

It is Jesus' desire that we have unity in the church. Additionally, it is also His desire that we have *unity* and *civility* in our nation. After all, it is called the *United* States for a reason. Again, we can have different views, opinions, and plans, but at the same time we can have a unity of spirit in our loving God.

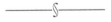

*God, we thank You for all that You have given us through Your Son and Holy Spirit. We pray for unity in the church, as well as all aspects of our life in this nation—from which joy can abound. Our prayer is for unity and civility.*

*"Have the same attitude that Christ Jesus had. Although He was in the form of God and equal with God, He did not take advantage of this equality. Instead, he emptied himself by taking on the form of a servant, by becoming like other humans, by having human appearance. He humbled himself by becoming obedient to the point of death, death on a cross."*      Philippians 2:5-8 (GW)

———§———

Our fallen nature is not interested in being emptied, but in being filled. We are more interested in becoming something or someone, than in becoming nothing and no one. It runs contrary to our fallen sinful nature to become less, so others can become more. And yet, if we are going to be like Jesus, we must become servants, allowing others to become more, at our expense. Attitude is equivalent to our mindset—the underlying disposition that shapes our thoughts and actions. Paul's letter draws upon Christ as the model of humility, which is the means of unity. We cannot copy His deity; His incarnation; His perfection; His miracles; or His redemptive work. Yet, we are called upon to pattern our lives after His humility.

Jesus never displayed an attitude of entitlement, which is so prevalent in our world today. Instead, He emptied Himself and put us first. To imitate His attitude, we must turn from using people and possessions for our own advantage, and instead, use our gifts, resources, and time to love and serve others to the glory of God. We must put the interests of others ahead of our own. This is vital if we are to maintain unity within the church. That is how we can express and experience true joy: J (Jesus) O (others) Y (yourself). When we try to reverse this formula, joy cannot be obtained; we cannot find joy by putting ourselves first. We must be others-centered.

———§———

*Precious Jesus, thank You for how You humbly emptied Yourself to redeem us on the cross. We pray that Your Holy Spirit would pervade our souls to influence our daily life to reflect the attitude of service, obedience, and sacrifice that You exemplified.*

*"Rejoice in the Lord always. I will say it again: Rejoice! Let your gentleness be evident to all. The Lord is near. Do not be anxious about anything, but in every situation, by prayer and petition, with thanksgiving, present your requests to God. And the peace of God, which transcends all understanding, will guard your hearts and your minds in Christ Jesus."*  Philippians 4:4-7(NIV)

———§———

Paul is not asking us to deny the pain and trials in our lives. Instead, he is commanding us to focus our attention on Jesus even in the midst of our stress and troubles. Rejoicing is not a function of grit; it is the result of grace—God's grace! God does not promise us a trouble-free journey to the Kingdom of Heaven. But He does offer to fill our hearts with joy and peace, as we stay focused on Him. Christian joy is the emotion springing from the deep-down confidence that God is in complete and perfect control of everything, and eventually will bring from it our good, and our glory in eternity. When we become anxious, we are actually saying, "God, I really can't trust You with this one...I have to take this inside myself and be worried and anxious." Yet, the prescription for a troubled heart is prayer. There is no problem that is too big, or too small, that God cannot manage.

Prayer carries the components of adoration, devotion, worship, and thankfulness. When we devote ourselves to spending time in prayer with God, we are filled with a peace—His peace, which rests in unlimited measure in the heart of God. It is a peace that comes from total dependence upon Him. And having joy in the Lord becomes a lasting joy. Rejoice in the Lord always!

———§———

*Almighty God, we are comforted to know that in the face of trial and hardship, that we have Your promises to re-awaken our hope, and fill our hearts with Your loving peace. Help us to use our anxiety as an alarm to remind us it is time to come to You in prayer with our worries and anxieties. May we always be full of joy in You.*

*'Now, my God, may you be attentive and responsive to the prayers offered in this place.'*
2 Chronicles 6:40 (NET)

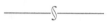

Under the leadership of King Solomon, construction of the first temple of the Lord was completed, and now was the time for the dedication. God's promise to King David was fulfilled. Solomon dedicatory prayer consisted of his request for God's continuing presence and power, and that God would be attentive to the prayers made in His dwelling place.

What is prayer? It is an intimate two-way communication with our Creator, which can draw us into a deeper relationship with Him. Prayer is relational, not simply a regimented, religious formula. It's not memorization—it is simply talking to God about anything.

When we commune with God, it has to be where *He* dwells—a place or temple we have made for His presence. That place is more than a place of concrete and pews—that *place* is the human heart. We can't expect God to listen and respond to our prayers if we haven't willingly and continually established a place for Him in our hearts.

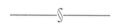

*Heavenly Father, it is hard to have this truth sink in that You, with all Your glory and power, would choose to dwell in our hearts. We have all experienced frustration when our prayers feel like they are not being heard. Yet, we have also experienced joy in those times when it is undeniable that You have listened to and responded to our prayers. The truth is, You are always in our presence regardless of how, what, and when Your response will be. We love You and praise You.*

*"Bring up a child by teaching him the way he should go, and when he is old he will not turn away from it."*                                             Proverbs 22:6 (NLV)

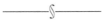

First and foremost, this begins in the home. Children raised and taught to love God, often continue to do so as adults. Parents are the key to ensuring this happens. Sadly, this is not often the case. In this day and age, some parents toss that responsibility for all aspects of teaching their children over to so-called teaching professionals. Yet in many public schools today, it's hard to define some teachers as *professionals.*

Many government-run public schools are indoctrinating the minds of children in Critical Race Theory—which is misinformation about the truth of our nation's history—and gender identity studies—which is completely inappropriate in the school curriculum. Instead of focusing on true academics, public schools today are encroaching upon parental authority; defining everything as racist; dumbing down curricula; and becoming hostile to beliefs and values expressed in the Bible. Even public, taxpayer funded libraries routinely conduct *drag queen story hour* to young children. These clown shows are pedophilia with wigs. It is vital, then, that parents teach their children at the earliest age about God, so that a strong foundation can be built, and that once exposed to this secular heresy, the child can resist and communicate the goings-on in the schools, with their parents. We need to stand up for our children and fight back against this evil. Write countless letters/emails to elected representatives and shine the light on this evil.

*Heavenly Father, in the past several generations, government has removed prayer in schools and tried to remove You from everything. Give us courage to fight back against this evil nonsense and return our schools and nation to the tenets of our founding.*

# May 11           Truth from Godly Thought

*"Be careful what you think, because your thoughts run your life."*
Proverbs 4:23 (NCV)

———§———

Our thoughts determine our actions, our self-image, our attitudes, and our destiny. For example, Moses could not fulfill his destiny until he adjusted his thinking. God thought of Moses as the deliverer. Yet, Moses thought of himself as insignificant. We know how the story went. Once Moses adjusted his thinking in line with God's truth, he became the great deliverer that he was destined to be. Of the thousands and thousands of thoughts we have each day, how many of them are rooted in truth? God, the Creator of all, and His Word are the source of absolute truth. So, it makes sense that if our thoughts are to be truthful, we should discipline ourselves—with the guidance of the Holy Spirit—to transform our thought-life to be like that of Christ. If we get real with ourselves, how often do we discover that when we are not grounded in God's truth, our thoughts turn out to be completely flawed?

Abraham Lincoln once used a clever ploy to teach some people about truth. They had come to him with a decision that was based on supposition, rather than truth. After hearing their logic, Lincoln asked, *How many legs would a sheep have if you called its tail a leg?* They quickly answered, *"Five!"* Lincoln then said, *"No, it would only have four legs. Calling a tail a leg doesn't make it one."* Taking control of our thoughts by the power of God leads to a victorious, joyful life.

———§———

*Almighty God, we know that temptation and sin begin in our mind. You have created us in such a way that our actions follow our thoughts. God, You have provided us with all the truth we need. Our prayer is that we would immerse ourselves in Your Word so that our thoughts would always be influenced by Your truths. May that be the only filter we use for our thought process.*

*"She is clothed with strength and dignity, and she laughs without fear of the future. When she speaks, her words are wise, and she gives instructions with kindness. She carefully watches everything in her household and suffers nothing from laziness. Her children stand and bless her. Her husband praises her."*       Proverbs 31:25-28 (NLT)

God's divine purpose for women is extraordinary. Proverbs 31 describes the "virtuous woman" from which our model of faith can come. Her character is God-centered, giving her confidence to face a future of unexpected challenges. The instruction she gives her family is done with a balance of godly wisdom and kindness. She is very engaged with the affairs of her household, church, and community. She has earned the love, respect and praise of her family for her role as a devoted wife and mother. Her physical qualities are not mentioned because it's not about physical beauty, but the beauty of her heart that matters.

She knows in Whom she trusts, so she operates absent any fear. When she speaks, it is without slander, gossip, or mistruths. She is diligent in ensuring the household operates in a godly fashion, as she performs her duties with grace. Her children and husband, as well as her community as a whole all benefit from these virtues and praise her for such. This is all a result of her own commitment to God, which underlies her productive and godly life.

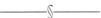

*Heavenly Father, we are so grateful for all the mothers who have joined with You in the wonder of bringing forth new life. God, we ask You to give them the wisdom and strength necessary to care for the physical, emotional, and spiritual growth of their children. May they honor their husbands with grace. May they always know that nothing they teach their children matters if it does not point them to Jesus' saving grace. May they adopt the model of faith You designed to influence their loved ones.*

*The Lord says, "Forget what happened before, and do not think about the past. Look at the new thing I am going to do. It is already happening. Don't you see it? I will make a road in the desert and rivers in the dry land."*                    Isaiah 43:18-19 (NCV)

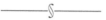

As long as we are bound by the grievances, hurts, failures, and sins of the past, we will never be able to move forward in a hopeful and positive way. We will not have the privilege of experiencing the future plans that God has for our lives. God wants us to bring our hopes, dreams, and faith—not our fear, sorrow, and pet-peeves. The same can be said about our past victories and accomplishments. The past has many great testimonies of God and His mighty acts, but our lives can't stop there. If we are continually looking behind, we cannot see to where God wants to lead us. Our faith is often limited by what we have experienced in the past. God is not saying that our past events are unimportant. Instead, He does not want us to limit His greatness simply to what He's already done. God wants us to have a *future focus* that is eager and prepared to experience the new thing He has set in motion for each of us.

To help us prepare, we can ask ourselves the following God-centered questions: "What is one thing I desire from God?" "What is one thing I lack in my spiritual relationship with God?" "What is one thing I need to let go of from my past?" "What is one promise from God that I need trust with all my heart?" We may not see the *new thing* God has planned for us, yet we can trust that it will happen because God has promised it will.

*Father God, open our hearts to truthfully answer the "one thing" questions, as we completely surrender to You so You will fulfill Your plans and promises for us. The one thing we can always count on is the fact that You love us, and will always be with us. God, we praise You and thank You for that comforting truth.*

*"But you will receive power when the Holy Spirit comes into your life. You will tell about Me in the city of Jerusalem and over all the countries of Judea and Samaria and to the ends of the earth."*            Acts 1:8 (NLV)

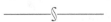

The mandate of the Great Commission is to *go*. This is a word of action! Most of us will never go to the *"ends of the earth;"* but we can witness to our families, our co-workers, our neighbors, total strangers; to anyone we meet; anywhere we go. A witness for Jesus Christ is simply someone who tells the truth about Him. Everyone has a personal sphere of influence with whom we interact. Odds are, we know at least one person who isn't a believer. Voila! An opportunity! As we are saved by the grace of God, believers are gathered into the flock—or church body—where we grow in the Gospel together. But, we are also a flock of ambassadors who are sent on a mission into the world.

We are expected to *scatter* in order to *gather* the lost, who are outside the confines of the gathered church. It is a command—not a suggestion or a favor—that Jesus is asking of us. The first disciples were given the same instruction—the mission hasn't changed. We are to do the same. Therefore, we must ask ourselves: "Will we be obedient and faithful to our Good Shepherd and go to the ends of the earth to gather the lost?"

————§————

*Heavenly Father, thank You for sending Your Son as our Good Shepherd, Who sacrificed His life for us. Through Your Holy Spirit, guide us, protect us, and fill us with the desire and courage to go where You send us to reach the lost. We pray that we will become much more aware of the opportunities we have each day to become effective witnesses to Your glory and to all You have done in our lives. Give us a passion to be instruments to accomplish Your will. We love You and praise You.*

*"Those who love their life in this world will lose it. Those who care nothing for their life in this world will keep it for eternity. Anyone who wants to serve Me must follow Me, because My servants must be where I am. And the Father will honor anyone who serves Me."*
John 12:25-26 (NLT)

———§———

The Bible says we are saved to serve. Have you ever thought why, at the moment we surrender our lives to Christ, God doesn't just zap us and we instantly go to heaven? Why did God leave us here on earth when we became a Christian? It's because He has something for us to do. His plan for us involves serving others in this life, until we eventually have the privilege of serving in His eternal Kingdom. By looking at the example of Jesus, a life of service is made possible; and that life of service constitutes giving our life away—dying in order to live. The truth is, we all give our lives away. It comes down to a question of *to what* do we give it? If we spend or invest our lives on money, power, amusement, adventure, and worldly pleasure, Jesus taught that these things don't give life in return. Conversely, giving ourselves away to God; serving others; laboring for justice; loving sacrificially the things Jesus commanded us, give life back.

A true disciple of Jesus is to serve—not be served! Service is not a common attribute of humanity. More often than not, we are more interested in *serve-us* than we are *service*. It doesn't do any good if we serve out of duty, fear, guilt, or anger. Instead, it pleases God when we serve others out of love, gratitude, and with humility.

———§———

*Lord Jesus, You poured out Your love to the world because You desired us to see our Savior in the flesh. As You walked this earth, You ministered with a heart-filled love and compassion. Lord, help us feel it a privilege to serve in Your Kingdom. May those we serve see Your light in us.*

*Elisha told her, "Ask your neighbors for their empty jars. And after you've borrowed as many as you can, go home and shut the door behind you and your sons. Then begin filling the jars with oil and set each one aside as you fill it."*     2 Kings 4:3-4 (CEV)

An impoverished widow was in danger of losing her sons to slavery because of unpaid debt. In desperation, she cried out to Elisha the prophet. Elisha took action by first asking how he could help her, followed by asking her what she already had in her house? Elisha doesn't start by giving her something, but by telling this widow to consider her own resources. God's plan for our lives always begins with what we have. The widow didn't have much—only a little oil. Yet, she offered it to Elisha, hoping he could use it to help her. Elisha instructed her to go to her neighbors and gather as many empty jars as they would give her. God wanted the woman—and us—to actively cooperate with Him and depend on Him. Elijah's instruction required faith, obedience, and submission to God and His promise to her through the prophet. Next, Elisha told her to go into her house with her sons and 'shut the door' behind her. The miracle that was about to take place was not to be a public spectacle. This was going to be a very private miracle to show God's personal love for this widow and her sons. As she poured her small flask of oil into those borrowed jars, the oil kept on flowing until all the jars were filled. There was enough to pay off her debt and have plenty to spare.

The way God generally meets our needs is to take what He has already given us—our talents, abilities, possessions, etc.—surrender them to Him, and have enough faith to trust Him to take what we have and to multiply it. God only fills the empty jars we bring to Him.

*God we thank You for the various "flasks of oil" with which You have provided for us. We pray for extraordinary faith to utilize what You have provided, for Your glory, and trust that You will bless us with those things we need, just when they are needed.*

*"If you are pleased with me, teach me your ways so I may know you and continue to find favor with you. Remember that this nation is your people."*          Exodus 33:13 (NIV)

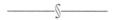

Finding favor in God's sight is the unconditional ground of knowing God, through knowing His ways.  One definition of "favor" is: kindness beyond what is due or usual.  Moses' prayer was to know God at the deepest level.  Yet, God offered Moses something even better.  God promised Moses His presence.  He offered to be Moses' Guide. Guidance for a Christian comes from our ongoing relationship with God.  He wants us to know Him, and to walk with us each step of our journey.  Walking with God is about friendship. It was the friendship with God that empowered Moses to bring the testimony of God's covenant to God's people.  It was friendship with God that allowed Moses to know God's ways, and not just His works. When God became flesh in the man Christ Jesus, He revealed His desire to be our friend.  He was a friend of sinners and He made known to His disciples that friendship was precious.

Yes, it is important that we serve God; yet it is more important that we know Who He is.  When we favor someone, we want to be with him or her. We delight in him or her.  We connect in a way we don't connect with everyone.  We usually favor those who also favor us.  In the same way, God shows favor to the ones who delight in; connect with; and give honor to Him.  Finding favor with the Lord keeps our thoughts and actions pure, because we desire to please Him, more than we desire to please ourselves.

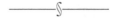

*Lord, we thank You for the immeasurable gift of Your all-providing favor of Your unconditional grace.  Our prayer is that the magnitude of our communion with You would grow deeper and deeper all the days of our lives.*

*The Lord was with Joseph and made him successful.*
Genesis 39:2 (GNT)

———§———

From the story of Joseph in the Book of Genesis, we might ask: "Was it that the faithfulness of Joseph resulted in the favor of God?" Or, "Was it that the favor of God gave rise to the faithfulness of Joseph?" Or, "Was it both?" When we see Joseph in chapter 37, he was a cocky teenage boy, who lacked diplomacy when dealing with his half-brothers, who already had envy and hatred in their hearts toward Joseph. But later we read that, *"the Lord was with Joseph."* God's initial favor towards Joseph was not a result of goodness in Joseph—for he had shown very little of that—but of the grace of God! And it was only then that we begin to see Joseph act as though he truly was walking with God through his obedience and faithfulness. The favor of God is for a purpose, and Joseph responded to the opportunities that God put in front of him. God's favor leads to our faithfulness. Even in slavery and imprisonment, Joseph set his heart to trust God, and even found favor in the eyes of those held him captive.

Favor is the current that moves us from our present situation into the destiny that God has for us. Will we open our eyes to see it? Will we respond in obedience to His instruction and calling? So, which came first: our faithfulness or God's favor? If we look carefully at this story of Joseph, and the Bible in general, we discover that the answer is "both." In both cases, however, the final credit always belongs to God! After all, *"We are His workmanship..."* (Eph. 2:10)

———§———

*God, when we endure trials, may we be like Joseph, who chose not to become discouraged and rebellious, or engage in self-pity, but instead saw the opportunities You presented to him, and obediently completed the work You had for him. May we walk in Your favor.*

*"How wonderful and pleasant it is when brothers live together in harmony!"*
Psalm 133:1 (NLT)

While this psalm refers to the people of God in general, it can also apply to the family unit. But Jacob's family didn't enjoy the blessings of harmony because, from its inception, the home was divided. Jacob's first two wives were rivals, and the addition of two concubines didn't diminish the tension. When you have in a home one father, four different mothers, and twelve sons, you have the ingredients for multiple problems. Unfortunately, Jacob came from a divided home and brought the infection with him. Why did the brothers hate Joseph so much? Because Joseph was Jacob's favorite son. The love and favoritism Jacob had for Joseph was expressed by Jacob's giving Joseph a distinctive tunic. We can't be sure what the famous *coat of many colors* really looked like, but needless to say, young Joseph's sudden appearance in the distinctive robe ignited his brothers' hatred. This is an interesting and sad portrait of human nature; they hated Joseph, not his father. Those who are envious often turn their hatred on the one favored, not on the one who shows favoritism.

Harmony is vital for families, communities, and nations to succeed. Perhaps if we accept and respect that God has uniquely wired each of us—and embrace those differences, while overlooking the short-comings of others—we would experience more harmony.

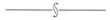

*Heavenly Father, it must break your heart when families, and our nation, have unhealthy times that are absent of harmony. May all our families experience the peace and harmony by loving the way that You do.*

*Joseph had a dream, and when he told it to his brothers, they hated him all the more.*
Genesis 37:5 (NIV)

Joseph was a dreamer—literally.   He experienced extremely vivid, meaningful visions.  Joseph told his family about two of his dreams, both of which strained his tenuous relationship with his brothers.  In the first dream, Joseph binds sheaves of grain with his brothers.  His sheaf stands tall, while his brothers' bundles gather around and bow before his.  There's no mystery about the meaning of this dream, and the brothers fire back, "Will you really rule over us?"   Their hate toward Joseph intensified.  But Joseph didn't hesitate to tell them about his second dream, sharing this one with his father as well.  This time the sun, moon, and eleven stars clustered around him to bow down.  Jacob echoed his sons.  Would *he*—the patriarch and head of the household—also bow down to Joseph?   Perhaps Joseph might have been more diplomatic in the way he reported his dreams, but surely he was right in sharing them with the family.   This wasn't *adolescent enthusiasm*; it was the will of God.  Not only did Joseph experience dreams, he would later prove to possess the God-given ability to interpret them, as well.

God uses dreams to communicate with us.  We often long to hear from Him, and this is one of the means by which He speaks.  Through dreams, God can calm the present, or guide us into future events———the key is to *tune in* to Him.

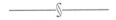

*God, it is our prayer that when we hear from You, by whatever method You choose, that we can truly digest the meaning.  And if shared with others, that jealousy, unbelief, or hatred to not enter the picture—those are feelings from the enemy.  Thank You for Your love.*

*So when the Midianite merchants came by, his brothers pulled Joseph up out of the cistern and sold him for twenty shekels of silver to the Ishmaelites, who took him to Egypt.*

Genesis 37:28 (NIV)

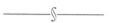

It must have given them great pleasure to strip Joseph of his special robe and then drop him into the empty cistern. But let's not give the brothers a free pass. Their plan of revenge was even more despicable than was Joseph's conceit. Even though they had just dumped their brother in a pit and thought about killing him, they had the callousness of heart to be able to sit down and enjoy a nice meal! Then seeing the Midianite merchants, gave his brother Judah an idea. Why not sell Joseph to them as a slave, whom they in turn could sell in Egypt? That way, Joseph would be removed from any further influence in the family—which was what the brothers wanted most—and still his life would be spared and they would not be guilty of murder.

Starting with Cain's murder of Abel, man's inhumanity to man is painfully recorded in both biblical and secular history. We're made in the image of God, and we belong to the same human family, and yet we can't seem to get along with one another. Everything from differing opinions on current events, to civil wars blamed on ancient boundary lines, it is evident that the world desperately needs a Savior who can make hearts new. Envy, unforgiveness, bitterness, and hatred can result in unthinkable consequences if we remove God from the picture. Thankfully, *God was with Joseph* through all of this.

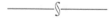

*Almighty God, what a glorious truth that the One who created the world, who's omnipotent, omniscient, sovereign ruler over the universe, that You're with us right now. We may never be thrown in a cistern or sold into slavery, but in our own trials, we know that You are with us, and that gives us great peace and comfort.*

*Pharaoh said to Joseph, "I hereby put you in charge of the entire land of Egypt."*
                                              Genesis 41:41 (NLT)

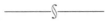

God's people are never promised a life free from suffering.  Joseph endured many difficulties, from being sold into slavery by his brothers to being falsely accused of rape by his master's wife.  One incident landed him in a pit, the other in a jail cell.  But Joseph's trust in God never faltered.  He believed God would remain faithful to His promises.  In spite of repeated hardships, Joseph did not allow his heart to become bitter or resentful.  Instead, he persevered.    Then he was summoned to interpret two unexplainable dreams of Egypt's Pharaoh—all the while declaring that God had sent the dream. God had given the interpretation to Joseph; and God would bring it all to pass.  Pharoah followed Joseph's advice about how to deal with the future famine that his dream foretold.

Pharaoh and his advisors were amazed and impressed, not only with Joseph's ability to interpret the dreams, but also with his wise counsel, as well as his whole manner and character. They also recognized that he was a man of unique spiritual attributes—and indeed, this was the real reason for his other abilities. With all his brilliant insights, he was deeply humble by giving complete credit to God.  Those who are faithful in little things are blessed with greater responsibilities.  Joseph was faithful as a mere slave, so God made him the personal assistant of Potiphar.  He was faithful in the prison, so God made the warden put him charge of the other prisoners.  He was faithful at that job so God made hm second in command to Pharaoh.  Our faithfulness is rewarded with God's favor.

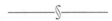

*Heavenly Father, we are so grateful that You gift each of us with unique abilities to work in Your Kingdom. We thank You for times when You have placed wise and godly leaders who—operate with discernment, honesty, and integrity—into leadership roles.*

*Then Joseph added, "Look! You can see for yourselves, and so can my brother Benjamin, that I really am Joseph! Go tell my father of my honored position here in Egypt. Describe for him everything you have seen, and then bring my father here quickly." Weeping with joy, he embraced Benjamin, and Benjamin did the same. Then Joseph kissed each of his brothers and wept over them, and after that they began talking freely with him.*

Genesis 45:12-15 (NLT)

The predicted famine of Egypt arrived and affected other lands, including Canaan, where Joseph's father and brothers still lived. Because of Joseph's leadership, he was able to stockpile enough grain to have Egypt and other nations survive the famine. His brothers heard that grain was available to be purchased in Egypt so they set out to get it. Joseph was amazed when he recognized his brothers yet did not disclose his identity at that time. Through some testing to see if his brothers had changed from their ways, so that restoration of the family could take place, he could see signs of repentance. Joseph was more concerned about *reconciliation* with his brothers than for *vengeance*.

When Joseph finally disclosed who he was to his brothers, he not only told them he was Joseph, but also reminded them what they had done to him over twenty years prior. The shock and awe of the moment brought mixed responses of fear and bewilderment. Yet, Joseph displayed compassion and mercy, and true reconciliation took place.

*Heavenly Father, we all must be brought to a place of confession and repentance when we sin. And, thank You for this wonderful example of how we can graciously and maturely forgive others when we are in a position to do so.*

*But Joseph replied, "Don't be afraid of me. Am I God, that I can punish you? You intended to harm me, but God intended it all for good. He brought me to this position so I could save the lives of many people. No, don't be afraid. I will continue to take care of you and your children."*      Genesis 50:19-21 (NLT)

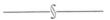

How does God assure His children that He has indeed forgiven them and forgotten their sins? The same way Joseph assured his frightened brothers— He comforted them and spoke kindly to them—as God does to us from His Word. Twice Joseph said, "Don't be afraid!" God says the same to us; we just need receive it into our hearts, and trust it completely. God often brings good out of evil and seemingly unbearable situations. He promotes the designs of His *Providence* even through the sins of men.

Joseph didn't minimize their sins, for he said, *"You intended to harm me"* (Gen. 50:20). He knew that there had been evil in their hearts, but he also knew that God had overruled their evil deeds to accomplish His good purposes. This reminds us of what happened on the cross. Out of the greatest sin ever committed by humankind, God brought the greatest blessing that ever came to humankind. Although Christ suffered much more evil in His life on earth than did Joseph, God used the evil and suffering of both of them for the good of all of us. We love an amazing God.

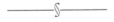

*Almighty God, when we look back on all the ways You have blessed us, we are truly grateful. Even when we have found ourselves in situations—regardless if they were of our own choosing or not—we can rest in the truth that You have always been there to deliver us. You continue to lift us out of any pit, and use us for Your good. Thank You for the example and lessons from the life of Joseph.*

*Many tax collectors and sinners came to listen to Jesus. Then the Pharisees and the teachers of the law began to complain, Look, this man welcomes sinners and even eats with them!*

Luke 15:1-2 (ERV)

Thieves, thugs, addicts, cons, prostitutes, pimps, homeless, and diseased—this was Jesus' mission field. John 3:16 doesn't say: "For God so loved *some* of us..." It says: *"For God so loved the world."* That's right, each and every one of us. We are all created in God's image. So, if we are worthy of love, so is everyone else because of Who made them. Jesus demonstrated time and time again that He came not for those who are well, but for those who are sick—physically and spiritually! Jesus actually chose to hang out with outcasts, instead of the self-righteous religious. The very people who should have welcomed Him with open arms, actually shunned Him. And the very people who were shunned, welcomed Jesus with open arms. Christ's example is a great challenge to us as Christians if we examine the kinds of people to whom He ministered. Why? Because it will call us to reach out too, to those who make us uncomfortable; to those we would rather not have to deal with; to those we would dismiss as ever deserving God's love and favor—the lost and the outcasts.

How easily we forget the kind of love it took God to accept us! Let us remember when the Good Shepherd found us hanging over the edge of the cliff at eternal doom, He rescued us. Christianity is the only religion in which God comes seeking man. He diligently searches like the shepherd, and never gives up until all His lost sheep are found.

*Father God, how wonderful it is to know that there is not one person You do not love—there are only people who haven't yet accepted Your love. Help us to willingly help the lost get found, by seeing them as Jesus did—children of God. We love You and praise You.*

*The jailer woke up, and when he saw the prison doors open, he drew his sword and was about to kill himself because he thought the prisoners had escaped. But Paul shouted, "Don't harm yourself! We are all here!"*            Acts 16:27-28 (NIV)

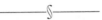

Paul and Silas had been beaten and thrown in jail. But that didn't stop them from praying and singing hymns to God. Just so happens that God was in there with them. God caused the earth to quake; the cell doors to swing open; and the chains to break loose from the prisoners legs. Instead of fleeing from the jail, Paul and Silas stayed where they were. Why would they do something like that? Well, it was a golden opportunity for freedom for Paul and Silas, it was also an opportunity to *free* or save the soul of the jailer and any of the other prisoners.

The jailer was so distraught that he might be responsible for having prisoners escape that he was considering doing harm to himself. Keep in mind, he had been listening to the singing and prayers coming from Paul and Silas before God intervened. Through the providence of God, the jailer fell to his knees in front of Paul and Silas and asked what he needed to do to be saved. Paul and Silas shared the Gospel truth with him, and the jailer ended up taking them home with him. As it turned out, the jailer and his whole family were saved and baptized that very evening. Now, that's what you call a Divine *Get-out-of Jail Free* pass!

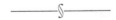

*Heavenly Father, that is such a beautiful example of how you intervene in our lives. We all have our own story of how we surrendered our lives to Christ, and each one has Your fingerprints all over it. We thank You for Your grace, mercy and divine intervention. We thank You for giving each of us a get-out-of jail free pass.*

*"And what does the LORD require of you? To act justly and to love mercy and to walk humbly with your God."*

                                                    Micah 6:8 (NIV)

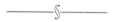

Some of us may experience bouts of anxiety when we seek to know God's *personal* will for our life. Therefore, it might be helpful to understand the nature of God's will. First, there is God's *providential* will—the means through which our Creator sovereignly governs and controls all things in the universe. From the beginning, this was God's plan, and His promised plans always come to pass. There is nothing we can do to change them. For example, it is God's providential plan that Jesus will one day return. Now, that is something in which we can delight. The other facet of God's will is His *moral* will—this is what God has already revealed to us through Scripture. God has purposed to lead His people through our obedience to the only authoritative and infallible guide—His Word. It is simply the *dos* and *don'ts* that God has commanded. Understanding this aspect of God's will acknowledges that, while we have the *choice* to disobey God's commands, we do not have the *right* to do so. It really comes down to obedience.

When we fully grasp the understanding of the unchanging sovereignty of God (His providential will) and are obedient to His revealed will (His moral will) then we might be freed from our anxious search for His personal will for each of us. Obeying what is already the known will of God is the path to His unknown will. Again, this happens when we receive what He already revealed, and when we act justly, love mercy, and walk in humble obedience with God.

*Heavenly Father, thank You for this simple, straightforward passage of Scripture that starts, and ends, with our heart. May this serve as the foundation upon which to more clearly see Your personal will for our life—to do justice, love mercy, and walk humbly with You.*

# May 28                                    Befriending Fools

*"Walk with wise people and become wise; befriend fools and get in trouble."*
Proverbs 13:20 (CEB)

People who hang out with, and/or seek worldly advice from the ungodly have their minds set on the evil things of this world—power; greed; corruption; and lies. We see this every day in communities, nation, and world. And sadly, it often comes from those who are placed in positions of leadership to legislate and govern the jurisdictions for which they represent. Sometimes it is done overtly and blatantly revealed—often times without consequence or accountability applied. Other times, is covertly committed, which can be more dangerous. At times, the covert evil is discovered by those who actually investigate the actions of those in power; but again, accountability is rare.

When people have been in politics for a long time, their once godly attitude and behavior dissipates because they have befriended by, and/or sought advice from ungodly fools. This is a result of hardening their heart to God. This is unfortunate because when ungodly advice is applied from leaders, those being led suffer. Perhaps *term-limits* might be in order. It won't eliminate evil and corruption in government, but it could somewhat curb it.

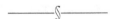

*God, we know that You are in control of all things, including our government and those elected to serve in it. We pray that the people we elect would hold on to You, Your Word, and Your wisdom in how they lead. We pray they will stand strong in their faith to resist the temptation, influence and advice from the ungodly fools. God, we need You so much to return to the hearts of all of us.*

*But Rehoboam did not listen to the advisors' recommendation. Instead, he asked the opinions of his childhood friends who were more likely to give him the advice that he wanted to hear.*
         2 Chronicles 10:8 (VOICE)

———§———

How do we discover God's will when we are faced with a decision we need to make? As Christians, we desire to live our lives in a way that is pleasing to the Lord. Our first course of action is to seek the advice of God and what He has said in His Word—the truest source where we may obtain guidance, instruction, and important principles that can assist us in becoming wise decision-makers. God has also given us another resource to aide in our effort to make wise and godly decisions—His people. So often we neglect or ignore the wise counsel that is available to us from those in our lives who have walked through the season in which we now find ourselves. Advice doesn't mean we have to follow it, just listen and weigh it carefully. Rehoboam received advice from two sources. However, he should have taken the advice of the godly elders instead of listening to young, inexperienced men like himself.

We will always have decisions to make in our lives, both big and small ones. Yet, for each one we should ask ourselves: "What are the values by which I want to make my decision?" "Will my decision glorify God?" "Will it be beneficial to others?" "Will it strengthen my spiritual maturity?" "Would Jesus make the same decision?" Then we can make our decision and put our trust in God.

———§———

*God, our hearts' desire is that all of our decisions would be godly and honoring to You. We are grateful that You place godly men and women in our lives to offer wise counsel to help in our decision-making. We pray that our leaders in government would do the same when faced with decisions that impact those they serve.*

# May 30             Take Our Doubts to God

*Then give him this message, "Blessed are those who don't doubt Me."*
Matthew 11:6 (TLB)

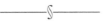

This was Jesus' response to His cousin, John the Baptist, who had been sitting in a prison cell for several months. The man who had baptized for the forgiveness of sins, and publicly announced Jesus as the One promised from Scripture was starting to doubt. Was it because he was swayed by the popular expectations of the promised Messiah—Who would come to rescue Israel from political oppression, or because he felt God was inattentive to his circumstance. God was M.I.A in John's eyes. We have all gone through seasons in our life where our struggles and challenges become too much to bear. When we feel God seems silent, absent, or indifferent to our situation we begin to shrink our faith. We question God, because He could have done something about our circumstance, and yet He hasn't. We become perplexed by the plan of God—or what we think His plan should be! Despite John's doubt and disappointment that Jesus had not rescued him from prison, he did the right thing by taking his concern to the Lord. Jesus' message to John was for him to reflect on His works—His miraculous works that prove He cares for people in difficulty.

We, too, should remind ourselves of the countless victories we've experienced from the hands of God. Our difficult circumstances do not reflect how God feels about us. Jesus' death on the cross exemplifies His love for us. Let God be God! Accepting His sovereignty means trusting Him, even when it appears He is inattentive.

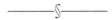

*God, we know that everyone's faith has weak moments, and no single event or circumstance is the full story of our life. In our times of doubt, may we follow the approach that John the Baptist took and bring those doubts and concerns directly to You.*

*The disciple who had reached the tomb first also went inside. He saw and believed. They still did not understand from Scripture that Jesus had to rise from the dead.*

John 20:8-9 (NIV)

There is no greater event in human history than the resurrection of Jesus Christ. The resurrection of Christ is the pivot upon which all of Christianity turns. If we erase the resurrection, we erase everything. We eliminate salvation; the deity of Christ; and eternal life with our Lord and Savior. The entire destiny of man hinges on whether Jesus Christ is simply a crucified rabbi, Whose remains lie in some tomb, or whether in fact He is the living Son of God, as proven by His resurrection. Amazingly, eyewitnesses found His tomb to be empty! However, the tombs of Mohammed, Buddha, Confucius, and every other religious founders and/or philosophical gurus still hold the remains of their occupants.

Christianity has at its foundation not just in philosophical doctrines, but is founded and nourished in a person—the One we know as Jesus the Christ. What is not found in other religions is a devoted relationship and faith in the Person of Christ—Who is alive! As far as the disciples could discern, it was all over! They had not yet associated Christ's death with all that was foretold through the Laws of Moses, the books of the Prophets, and the Psalms concerning His ultimate resurrection. Jesus, Himself, had told them repeatedly, but they did not take it in until they either saw the empty tomb and/or saw the resurrected Jesus. The rock of the tomb was rolled back not to let Jesus *out*, but to let the disciples—and the world—*in* to see that He is risen and alive!

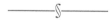

*Jesus, You defeated death through the power of Your resurrection, and have blessed those who believe in You with Your Holy Spirit, Who gives an amazing relationship and hope for our own resurrection and eternal life with You. Jesus has given us a new way to be human. You are risen, indeed!*

# June 1                                         Dark Times

*There was no king in Israel at that time; everyone did whatever they wanted.*
Judges 17:6 (GNT)

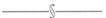

Life was not easy during the period of the Judges. The Book of Judges is the story of Israel at one of its lowest points in history and is a record of division, cruelty, apostasy, civil war, and national disgrace. God was their King, but the Israelites weren't satisfied with that—they wanted a worldly king like their surrounding nations. God would give them what they wanted in the years to come. They eventually found out that replacing God didn't work out so well.

Spiritually speaking, we are living *today* in the Book of Judges. Like Israel in the past, many of God's people today are living in unbelief and disobedience and are not enjoying the blessings of God. We have removed God from almost every aspect of our lives, that our leaders are ruling our nation without His influence. We're divided on so many fronts. We are experiencing the cruelty of crime and violence in our cities; lethal drugs and illegal migrants are pouring into our unsecured borders without consequence; our young people are getting their minds poisoned by mistruths and disgusting indoctrination that is completely inappropriate in our schools. To top it off, our elected leaders either are in denial about these atrocities or are out-and-out lying to Americans. This is what happens when we have no King—God—and everyone does whatever they want.

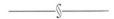

*Heavenly Father, we plead for your mercy in our nation. We pray our leaders, and all of us would renew focus on what is right in your eyes, not our eyes. God, we see in the book of Judges the horrifying effects of sin, rebellion, and disobedience to You and ask for Your healing and guidance.*

# June 2                    Leaving Without Seeking God

*In the days when the judges ruled, there was a famine in the land. So a man from Bethlehem in Judah, together with his wife and two sons, went to live for a while in the country of Moab.*
Ruth 1:1 (NIV)

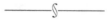

It seems incredible that this beautiful love story should take place at such a calamitous period in the Israel's history, but is this not true today? Today we experience national and international perplexities, moral decay, and difficulties of every kind, and yet God still loves this lost world. In spite of alarms in the headlines and dangers on the streets, we can be sure that God still loves the world and wants to save lost sinners.

The Book of Ruth opens at a time when the land of Judah experienced a famine. Although famines were common in the days of the Patriarchs some eight hundred years earlier, this is the first recorded famine encountered by Israel since entering the land of Canaan. The man's name was Elimelech. It was a great name for an Israelite. It means 'God is King' or 'God is my King'. It expressed the right attitude God's people should have—living in submission to God's rule. The tragedy of these verses, however, is that Elimelech did not live up to his name—he made the wrong decision when he decided to leave home and go to Moab with his wife Naomi, and their two sons. What made this decision so wrong? He failed to seek the will of God. A husband and father certainly wants to provide for his wife and family, but he must not do it at the expense of losing the blessing of God. By going fifty miles to the neighboring land of Moab, Elimelech and his family abandoned God's land and God's people for the land and people of the enemy.

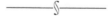

*Heavenly Father, forgive us when we, too, have failed to seek Your guidance before we make decisions on our own. Yet, in Your providence and grace, You still do not abandon us.*

*Then Elimelech died, and Naomi was left with her two sons. The two sons married Moabite women. One married a woman named Orpah, and the other a woman named Ruth. But about ten years later, both Mahlon and Kilion died. This left Naomi alone, without her two sons or her husband.*                     Ruth 1:3-4 (NLT)

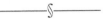

The Moabites were descendants of Lot from his incestuous union with his firstborn daughter, and they were enemies of the Jews because of the way they had treated Israel during their pilgrim journey from Egypt to Canaan. When Elimelech and his family came to Moab, they did not find life easier. Elimelech soon died, and his wife Naomi [which means "pleasant"] was left to care for their two boys, Mahlon and Kilion. We sometimes think we can move away from our problems, but find we just bring them with us. No matter where we go, we bring ourselves with us— so the same problems can continue in a different place.

Elimelech's death left his family in Moab, with the result that his sons married Moabite women, one named Orpah, and the other, Ruth. Given the past history with Moab and the way Moabite women had led Israelite men astray to worship other gods, this could not have been a wise thing to do. Throughout Scripture the Lord's people are commanded repeatedly not to marry outside His people. For about ten years the Israelite men and their wives Orpah and Ruth lived in Moab. They had apparently given up all thought of returning to Bethlehem. The widow Naomi remained with her sons. In those days a widow was almost totally dependent upon her sons for support. As fate would have it, however, Naomi was shortly left destitute. Her two sons both died.

*God, as we journey through the story of Ruth, open our hearts and minds to the valuable lessons and revelations of You that are ever-present for us to apply in our lives. We love and praise You.*

*Then Naomi heard in Moab that the Lord had blessed His people in Judah by giving them good crops again. So Naomi and her daughters-in-law got ready to leave Moab to return to her homeland... "No, my daughters, return to your parents' homes. Things are far more bitter for me than for you, because the Lord Himself has raised His fist against me."*          Ruth 1:6,12-13 (NLT)

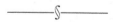

At some point along the road Naomi urged her two daughters-in-law each to return to their mother's house—encouraging these Moabite women to return and go back to their homes in the hope of finding another marriage. Knowing that she must be deprived of the companionship of these two fine daughters-in-law made Naomi's burden even harder to bear. She had lost both her husband and sons to death. Now she was about to lose the last dear ones she had on earth through separation. All of this misfortune Naomi attributed to the actions of God.

As Naomi considered her sad circumstances, she understood rightly that the Lord was in control. The bitter pill she was tasting was from Him. But how does this fit with His transforming kindness? As we carefully trace the Lord's dealings with men and women in the Bible, we see how the different aspects of His character always fit together. This means that tasting His bitter pill is never inconsistent with His kindness. The Lord can and does use bitter experiences to prepare the way for experiences of His undeserved kindness.

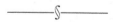

*Almighty God, when we experience the consequences of our decisions and actions it can leave us bitter. Yet, we know that the responsibility lies with us, not You. May we find comfort that You are with us through all of our good times, as well as those that are difficult.*

*"Look," Naomi said to her, "your sister-in-law has gone back to her people and to her gods. You should do the same." But Ruth replied, "Don't ask me to leave you and turn back. Wherever you go, I will go; wherever you live, I will live. Your people will be my people, and your God will be my God."*          Ruth 1:15-16 (NLT)

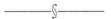

Orpah [not Oprah] went back to Moab, and perhaps idolatry. Nothing more is said of her. No word of commendation or condemnation is spoken about her. The very silence of Scripture is sufficiently eloquent to suggest a life of tragedy. Yet, when Ruth *chose* to follow Naomi, she made a momentous decision for the One true God and the true worship of Him.

Ruth chose God, and He chose her in the greatest plan of the ages: namely the bringing of Jesus Christ into the world. Ruth made a choice for God when she elected to go with Naomi. She never stood again at the crossroads of life to make a decision for eternity. After that moment, she had only to walk the ordinary path of His leading. Ruth chose the God of Israel and took her place of trust under His wings. All she knew of the Lord must have come from Naomi. Orpah went backward to darkness, paganism, superstition, and gloom. Ruth went onward to the light of glory, truth, and the light of life. Faith in God often shines at its brightest and is most attractive in the reality of bitter trials. The suffering believer who clings to the Lord in times of trial is more likely to promote faith in others than, those who appear to have *successful* and *straightforward* lives.

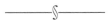

*Almighty God, we may not be aware that our interactions with non-believers may be the only reflection of Who You are. We pray Your light shines through us so others may choose to have our God be their God. Ruth's example of devotion to You is inspiring.*

*So the two of them continued on their journey. When they came to Bethlehem, the entire town was excited by their arrival. "Is it really Naomi?" the women asked. "Don't call me Naomi," she responded. "Instead, call me Mara, [which means "bitter"] for the Almighty has made life very bitter for me."*                                        Ruth 1:19-20 (NLT)

Pain, sorrow, grief, regret, poverty and loneliness had taken their toll. Ten years earlier Naomi had left Bethlehem with a husband and two sons, but she returned with only a Gentile girl. She was given one stranger for three loved ones. However, this was not nearly so tragic as it appeared on the surface, as subsequent events proved. Naomi committed the grievous error of placing the blame for all her trouble upon God. This has been symptomatic of the attitude of Adam from the very beginning. Adam inferred that the woman whom God had given him was responsible for the presence of sin. He thereby threw the blame back into the lap of God, suggesting that if God had not given her to him, the tragedy of the Fall would have been averted. God had not dealt bitterly with Naomi; she was reaping the fruit of the sin of disobedience. Naomi was but gleaning in the fields of a far country, away from the presence of God. God was not responsible for her misfortune, but He was responsible for the voice that had wooed her back home.

Our journey through life as Christians involves learning to trust the Lord's loving providence in life's changing scenes. We need to recognize that even the bitter experiences of life, that leave us feeling empty, are within His control and are designed for our good.

*Heavenly Father, forgive us for the times we have acted like Naomi and stepped outside of Your will for our life and found ourselves in deep distress and defeated. Rid us of bitterness because all of Your ways are pleasant.*

# God Doesn't Do Luck

*One day Ruth the Moabite said to Naomi, "Let me go out into the harvest fields to pick up the stalks of grain left behind by anyone who is kind enough to let me do it." Naomi replied, "All right, my daughter, go ahead." So Ruth went out to gather grain behind the harvesters. And as it happened, she found herself working in a field that belonged to Boaz, the relative of her father-in-law, Elimelech.* Ruth 2:2-3 (NLT)

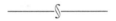

There is not a more endearing character presented in the Old Testament than Boaz, and there is not a more lovely woman in the Bible than Ruth. She compares favorably with her descendant Mary, the mother of Jesus. These two, Ruth and Boaz, stand out like bright lights on the dark background of that corrupt era. An industrious woman, Ruth hoped to find a friendly landowner who would allow her to follow behind the harvesters picking up—gleaning—the stalks which they might leave lying on the ground.

We might say, 'as luck would have it' she came to the field owned by Boaz. But the Lord does not do luck! His work is never haphazard. He plans; pre-arranges; and prepares. The field Ruth *stumbled upon* was the very field the Lord had planned. Events like this are often beyond our full comprehension. The Bible teaches that the Lord's sovereign plan incorporates the willing choices of men and women for which they are accountable. Ruth *chose* to go to that particular field, but she was doing what the Lord, in His power and will, had *decided beforehand* should happen.

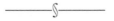

*God, nothing You do is by happenstance. You know in advance and plan every move we make. It is up to us to seek Your will and choose to obediently follow that will. When we do, Lord, Your blessings and outcomes are all for our good.*

*While she was there, Boaz arrived from Bethlehem and greeted the harvesters... Then Boaz asked his foreman, "Who is that young woman over there?" Boaz went over and said to Ruth, "Listen, my daughter. Stay right here with us when you gather grain; don't go to any other fields." Ruth fell at his feet and thanked him warmly. "What have I done to deserve such kindness?" she asked. "I am only a foreigner."*    Ruth 2:4,5,8,10 (NLT)

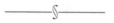

When Ruth set out that morning to glean in the fields, she was hoping someone who would show her grace. The channel of that grace was Boaz. No sooner had Boaz greeted his workers than his eye caught the presence of a stranger in the field, and a lovely stranger at that. We can get the impression that when he saw her, it was love at first sight. From that point on, Boaz focused his interest on Ruth and not on the harvest. Though an alien, Ruth was an eligible young woman whom the young men of the town would notice.

Boaz had already heard about Ruth, but now he set out to meet her personally. Boaz addressed Ruth in a most courteous manner. Since he was considerably older than the Ruth, he calls her *"my daughter."* Ruth could follow the women who worked for him from field to field during the harvest. Boaz had given strict orders to his male servants not to touch or in any way hinder the efforts of Ruth. He further invited Ruth to help herself from the water jars, which the servants might draw from some nearby well. But Boaz' kindness does not stop there.

*Heavenly Father, thank You for placing people in our lives that show incredible kindness. What an example Boaz has given for us to extend kindness to others, even if they are strangers. When heart-felt kindness is expressed the gratitude in return is genuine.*

# Kindness Rewarded

*"Yes, I know," Boaz replied. "But I also know about everything you have done for your mother-in-law since the death of your husband. I have heard how you left your father and mother and your own land to live here among complete strangers. May the Lord, the God of Israel, under whose wings you have come to take refuge, reward you fully for what you have done."*
Ruth 2:11-12 (NLT)

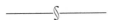

Boaz explains why he has shown Ruth such favor. What particularly impressed him were the reports he had heard about her treatment of Naomi after the death of Naomi's husband and sons. From this answer Boaz leads Ruth to believe that his generosity was simply his response to her acts of kindness toward her mother-in-law. He leaves her no hint that this was such an important issue to him because Naomi was his relative or that he is repaying her for her kindness to a member of his family.

First, Boaz has been kind to Ruth because he is fundamentally a good man, a man of noble character. Second, in Boaz's response we must recognize the providence of God. In v.2 Ruth had expressed the wish to Naomi that she might glean behind someone in whose eyes she might find favor. Although it was not expressed as a prayer, God had heard her wish. Boaz was kind to Ruth because God had prepared his heart for her! Boaz was confident that good things were in store for both Ruth and Naomi.

*Almighty God, You took the shattered lives of Naomi and Ruth, and turned everything around for their good. You do the same for us, as well. With You, we have hope and healing—what a blessing!*

*So Ruth told her mother-in-law about the man in whose field she had worked. She said, "The man I worked with today is named Boaz. May the Lord bless him!" Naomi told her daughter-in-law. "He is showing his kindness to us as well as to your dead husband.*

Ruth 2:19-20 (NLT)

———§———

How will Naomi respond to Ruth's experiences? The last time we saw Naomi, she was sharing her bitterness with the women of Bethlehem and blaming God for her sorrow and poverty. When Ruth had asked permission to go to the fields to glean, Naomi gave her daughter-in-law no word of encouragement, not even the promise of her prayers. But now we hear precious words from Naomi's lips— *"May the Lord bless him!"* She not only blessed Ruth's benefactor, but she is clearly stating from where those blessings come. Naomi had moved from bitterness to blessedness. When she heard that the man was Boaz, Naomi blessed the Lord. What a change has taken place in the heart of this grieving widow! This change came about because of the new hope she had in her heart, and the one who gave her that new hope was Boaz.

It is encouraging to see the changes that have taken place in Naomi because of what Ruth did. God used Ruth to turn Naomi's bitterness into gratitude; her unbelief into faith; and her despair into hope. One person, trusting the Lord and obeying His will, can change a situation from defeat to victory.

———§———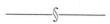

*Heavenly Father, the kindness of Boaz is a reflection of Your kindness, grace, mercy, and love with which You shower us. Like Naomi, if we look hard enough, we can see Your plans unfolding in our life and see how all things are working together for good for those of us who love You.*

# June 11             Hope in Redemption

*"That man is one of our closest relatives, one of our family redeemers."*
Ruth 2:2 0 (NLT)

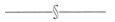

Naomi had hope because of who Boaz was—a near kinsman who was wealthy and influential. As we shall see, a near kinsman could rescue relatives from poverty and give them a new beginning. In the Old Testament social structure the kinsman-redeemer had three responsibilities: He had the right to recover forfeited property of a kinsman (Lev 25:25). Second, if one had fallen into slavery, the kinsmen-redeemer was to purchase his freedom (Lev 25:47- 49). And third, should a brother die leaving no male heir, the kinsmen-redeemer was to marry the widow to raise up offspring in the name of the dead relative (Deuteronomy 25:5-6).

It was not just the kindness and love of Boaz for Ruth that gave Naomi confidence, it was the principle of redemption that God had written in His Word that gave Naomi the assurance that Boaz would rescue them. As a close relative, Boaz could redeem the family property that Elimelech had mortgaged when he took his family to Moab. Naomi wasn't wealthy enough to redeem it, but Boaz could buy it back and keep it in the family. However, something else was involved: The wife of the deceased went with the property. Therefore, the kinsman redeemer had to marry her and bring up children bearing the name of the deceased. Those children would then inherit the property, and the family name and family possessions would continue to be theirs. This is known as "levirate marriage" (Deut. 25:5–10). The word *levir* is Latin for "a husband's brother."

*God, the exciting new hope the two widows was centered in a person, Boaz, just as our hope is centered in Jesus. Through faith in Christ, we have been redeemed into a living hope.*

# June 12 **Obedience Matters**

*One day Naomi said to Ruth, "My daughter, it's time that I found a permanent home for you, so that you will be provided for. Boaz is a close relative of ours, and he's been very kind by letting you gather grain with his young women. Tonight he will be winnowing barley at the threshing floor. Now do as I tell you—take a bath and put on perfume and dress in your nicest clothes. Then go to the threshing floor, but don't let Boaz see you until he has finished eating and drinking. Be sure to notice where he lies down; then go and uncover his feet and lie down there. He will tell you what to do."*     Ruth 3:1-4 (NLT)

There were other men who would gladly have married Ruth, but they could not have redeemed her. Only a kinsman could do that, and Boaz was that kinsman. Since Naomi knew that Boaz would be using the threshing floor that night and staying there to guard his grain, she instructed Ruth to prepare herself to meet him. There was nothing improper about this procedure, for it was the only way Ruth could offer herself to her kinsman redeemer. She had to put herself at the feet of the lord of the harvest, and he would do the rest. She was not only a hearer of the Word, but she was a doer. A willingness to obey the Lord is the secret of knowing what He wants us to do and being blessed when we do it. The will of God is not a cafeteria where we can pick and choose what we want. God expects us to accept *all* that He plans for us and to obey Him completely.

Suppose that on her way to the threshing floor, Ruth decided to take a different approach. Why lie at the feet of the man you want to marry? Why uncover his feet and then ask him to put a corner of his cloak over you? Certainly there ought to be a better way! Had she used another approach, Boaz would have been confused; and the entire enterprise would have failed.

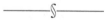

*Almighty God, we don't always understand Your plans and methods, but we know that all You expect from us is faithful obedience.*

*After Boaz had finished eating and drinking and was in good spirits, he lay down at the far end of the pile of grain and went to sleep. Then Ruth came quietly, uncovered his feet, and lay down. Around midnight Boaz suddenly woke up and turned over. He was surprised to find a woman lying at his feet! "Who are you?" he asked. "I am your servant Ruth, she replied. Spread the corner of your covering over me, for you are my family redeemer."*                                    Ruth 3:5-9 (NLT)

———§———

There is no suggestion that anything immoral or inappropriate happened between Boaz and Ruth. There is no hint of sexual impropriety. Boaz was an upright man and Ruth a woman of noble character. God's Word is clear that His good gift of sex is to be enjoyed only between a man and a woman who are married—after they are married. There is nothing here to suggest that Ruth and Boaz misused God's good gift. Besides, there's nothing sexy about smelly feet! Ruth was now asking for protection from a man God had provided, who was qualified to give her the protection she needed. In this, Boaz is a type of the Lord Jesus Christ. He prefigures the Christ Jesus, the Kinsman-Redeemer God has provided for all who will humbly ask Him to protect them.

Ruth's humble request therefore illustrates what is involved in both becoming and being a Christian. Becoming a Christian involves humbly asking the Lord Jesus Christ for protection as the Redeemer Who died on the cross. We all need His protection—His protection from the condemnation sin deserves. Self-protection is impossible. Only through His redeeming sacrifice on the cross is protection from condemnation available for all who take refuge in Him.

———§———

*God, we thank You for Your protection from sin and the evil ways of this world. You sent us the ultimate Redeemer, Who guaranteed our protection on the cross.*

*"But while it's true that I am one of your family redeemers, there is another man who is more closely related to you than I am. Stay here tonight, and in the morning I will talk to him. If he is willing to redeem you, very well. Let him marry you. But if he is not willing, then as surely as the Lord lives, I will redeem you myself! Now lie down here until morning."*

                                            Ruth 3:12-13 (NLT)

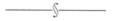

What seemed to Naomi to be a simple procedure has now turned out to be a bit more complicated, because there was another man in Bethlehem who was a closer relative—kinsman. Boaz didn't withhold this problem from Ruth, for he didn't want her to return home with false hopes in her heart. Joy and peace that are based on ignorance of the true facts are but delusions that lead to disappointments. The great concern of Boaz was the redemption of Ruth, even if another kinsman redeemer had to do it. Naomi could no longer say that her hands were empty. Now they were full because of the gift of grace and extra grain for Ruth and Naomi. Ruth's faith and obedience had brought about a complete transformation in their lives, and now they were living by grace from their *kinsman redeemer.*

It is through faith and patience that we inherit the promises. Since Naomi and Ruth believed that Boaz would accomplish what he said he would do, they waited patiently until they received the good news that Ruth would be a bride. Boaz was busy working for Ruth, and Naomi was confident that he wouldn't rest until he had settled the matter.

*Heavenly Father, it is encouraging to know that Jesus Christ is working unceasingly for us as He intercedes in heaven, and that He is working in us, seeking to conform us to His perfect will. He is our Lord of the Harvest.*

# June 15                    Cost of Redemption

*"If you want the land, then buy it here in the presence of these witnesses. But if you don't want it, let me know right away, because I am next in line to redeem it after you." Then Boaz told him, "Of course, your purchase of the land from Naomi also requires that you marry Ruth, the Moabite widow. That way she can have children who will carry on her husband's name and keep the land in the family." "Then I can't redeem it, the family redeemer replied, "because this might endanger my own estate. You redeem the land; I cannot do it."*                    Ruth 4:4-6 (NLT)

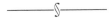

As widows, Naomi and Ruth needed a kinsman-redeemer who would provide an heir to inherit the land of Naomi's deceased husband, Elimelech. Boaz was ideal, but, as he told Ruth at the threshing-floor, there was a kinsman-redeemer nearer than him. Boaz had committed himself to see if the nearer kinsman was willing to act. Boaz waited at the city gate for the unnamed man to come along and got him to sit down before he raised the issue with him. Another *coincidence*?—hardly!

The un-named relative refused the offer because it was too much trouble—it would have meant a division of lands and inheritance to the detriment of the kinsman's own family and sons. Boaz, on the other hand, was different. He was prepared to accept that cost, illustrating the way the redeemers provided by God accepted the cost of redemption. There can be no redemption without the paying of a price. From our point of view, we might see salvation is free but from God's point of view, redemption is a very costly thing.

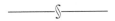

*Heavenly Father, pondering the truth about the cost of our redemption causes us to have feelings of gratitude, as well as bringing to light Your amazing grace! What was done on the cross is the ultimate act of redemption ever.*

*So Boaz took Ruth into his home, and she became his wife. When he slept with her, the Lord enabled her to become pregnant, and she gave birth to a son. Then the women of the town said to "Naomi, Praise the Lord, Who has now provided a redeemer for your family. May this child be famous in Israel. May he restore your youth and care for you in your old age. For he is the son of your daughter-in-law who loves you and has been better to you than seven sons!"*          Ruth 4:13-15 (NLT)

What wonderful changes came into Ruth's life because she trusted Boaz and let him work on her behalf! She went from loneliness to love; from toil to rest; from poverty to wealth; from worry to assurance; and from despair to hope. She was no longer *Ruth the Moabite*, for the past was gone and she was making a new beginning. She was now *Ruth the wife of Boaz*, a name she was proud to bear.

And for Naomi, she was over the moon. Even her friends couldn't contain their excitement as they began a spontaneous praise to God for how He had blessed her, and removed her empty bitterness, and filled it with grandson.

God had been gracious to Ruth back in Moab by giving her the faith to trust Him and be saved. His grace continued when she moved to Bethlehem, for He guided her to the field of Boaz where Boaz fell in love with her. God's grace continued at the town gate where the nearer kinsman rejected Ruth and Boaz redeemed her. After the marriage, God poured out His grace on Ruth and Boaz by giving her conception and then by giving her the safe delivery of a son, whom they named Obed, which means "servant".

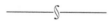

*Heavenly Father, Your Word is full of stories of people experiencing all facets of life. This story of Ruth, Naomi, and Boaz is one of hope, grace, faithfulness, promise, and extravagant love. We find all these things in You, and for that we are eternally grateful.*

*Naomi took the baby and cuddled him to her breast. And she cared for him as if he were her own. The neighbor women said, "Now at last Naomi has a son again!" And they named him Obed. He became the father of Jesse and the grandfather of David.*

Ruth 4:16-17 (NLT)

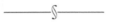

Naomi left Bethlehem *full* fulfillment in her family. She returned to Bethlehem *empty*—having lost both her husband and sons. With the birth of a grandson, however, she experienced anew the satisfaction and security afforded by male offspring. Throughout the book in all its artless simplicity there runs the note that God is supreme. He watches over people like Naomi, Ruth and Boaz and directs their paths. God never forgets His saving purposes. These events in Moab and Bethlehem played their part in leading up to the birth of David. We can also think of the genealogy at the beginning of the Gospel according to Matthew. He will reflect that God's hand is over all history. God works out His purpose—generation after generation. To David, God promised a royal lineage that would never end, and in David's descendant, the Messiah, our Lord, all the promises of the Bible come true.

The Book of Ruth opens with three funerals but closes with a wedding. There is a good deal of weeping recorded in the first chapter, but the last chapter records an overflowing of joy in the little town of Bethlehem. Not all of life's stories have this kind of happy ending; but this little book reminds us that, for the Christian, *God still writes the last chapter.*

*Heavenly Father, thank You for this beautiful story of love and redemption. We love and praise You and are blessed to be Your children. Thank You for Your grace and mercy.*

*"Which of these three do you think was a neighbor to the man who fell into the hands of robbers? The expert in the law replied, The one who had mercy on him. Jesus told him Go and do likewise."*

Luke 10:36-37 (NIV)

————§————

Most of us are probably familiar with Jesus' parable about the Good Samaritan. In Jesus' story, a man traveling from Jerusalem to Jericho was attacked; robbed; beaten nearly to death; and left along the side of the road. After two respected members of the religious establishment crossed to the other side of the road to avoid helping the beaten man in desperate need, a Samaritan—hated by the Jews of his day—went out of his way using his heart and hands to do what was right to assist the fallen traveler. This enemy of the Jews—the good Samaritan—cleaned the man's wounds; took him to an inn to care for him; and paid all of his expenses. The two religious men had no love—one man did. The Samaritan loved those who hated him. Jesus asked the lawyer, "which of these three was a neighbor to the victim?" The lawyer wanted to discuss "neighbor" in a general way, but Jesus forced him to consider a specific man in need.

It's easy for us to talk about abstract ideals and fail to solve concrete problems. We can *discuss* things like poverty and homelessness, and yet we may never personally do one thing to offer assistance to those in need. What the Samaritan did was help us better understand what it means to *show* mercy. God did say that we would always have the poor and needy in this world. That wasn't His original design, but in our fallen world, we have failed to be obedient to the two greatest commandments. So the question to us is not "who is my neighbor?" but rather, "whose neighbor am I?"

*Heavenly Father, help us to understand and apply Your truth that compassion isn't something we just talk about, it's something we do.*

# June 19 — Sin Separates Us from God

*"Those who live sinful lives are disobeying God. Sin is disobedience."*
1 John 3:4 (GW)

Sin is any personal lack of conformity to the laws of God, or His moral character. God has clearly outlined His standards and expectations in Scripture. Sadly in our nation today, we have been steadily redefining morality and have established "woke" ideologies; political correctness; entitlement; everything is racist; pro-abortion; inclusiveness; equity; and new pronouns for gender identity. These are all substitutes for the never-changing Biblical truths and principles. This has led to our diluting or dumbing down the impact of sin, which has caused many of us to rationalize our sinful acts with statements like, "I can do whatever I want as long as I don't hurt anyone" or "If it feels good, do it. What could it hurt?" or "Nobody will know, so no harm/no foul." These are *false* messages that never came from God! There are always consequences for our actions, and the idea that we can *do our own thing* because it isn't hurting anyone is a fallacy. Even if those around us are unaware of a sinful act we have done, God knows.

Sin is not confined to external conduct. Sometimes it is buried within our heart and very cleverly concealed from others—again, except from God. There are differences in the degrees of sin, as well as the effects and punishments that will come to those who are not redeemed. Some sins do more spiritual harm than others. Nevertheless, all sin separates us from God. As Christians, we have to steer away from our cultural or societal misbeliefs regarding our faith and instead rely solely on Biblical truths.

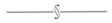

*Almighty God, as we strive to live righteous lives, while increasing our disdain of all our attitudes and actions that violate You. Help us realize our sins cause separation between You and us. We long to sin less and enhance our fellowship with You.*

*Jesus said, "I am the Way and the Truth and the Life. No one can go to the Father except by Me."*                       John 14:6 (NLV)

While it is true there is some common ground between many of the world's religions, particularly concerning basic values and morality, there are also significant differences. With this one outlandish assertion, *"I am the Way,"* Jesus boldly puts Christianity in a separate class all by itself. If the path to God is through Jesus, then Christianity cannot be reconciled with any other religion. This uniqueness of Christianity is rooted in the uniqueness of Jesus Himself. Some people believe that the sincerity of one's belief is what gives it power; or sincerity actually makes it true. Believing in the wrong thing doesn't make it right. While many have claimed deity, there are exceptional distinctions between Christ and them. How? (A.) His sinless life (B.) His substitutionary death (C.) His bodily resurrection (D.) and His offer of forgiveness by grace through faith. Christianity is not just another religion or philosophy. It is a reality—it is a relationship. Jesus didn't just claim that He was the One and only Son of God. He validated that claim with convincing, eye-witnessed evidence.

While other religious leaders can offer wise sayings; helpful advice; and insights, only Jesus Christ is qualified to offer Himself as payment for our sins, thereby guaranteeing eternal life with Him. Other major world religions teach that you must get yourself together; you must do something to earn God's grace. Christianity is radically different. God tells us that we will never *earn* salvation. So, it *does* matter in what or WHOM we place our sincere beliefs.

———§———

*Heavenly Father, You have provided the <u>only</u> Way to salvation and eternal life with You. We are truly blessed. Lord, guide us to be Your light to those who sincerely believe in the wrong thing.*

# June 21                 Take the Plunge

*Then Jesus came to them and said, "All power in heaven and on earth is given to Me. So go and make followers of all people in the world. Baptize them in the name of the Father and the Son and the Holy Spirit."*        Matthew 28:18-19 (NCV)

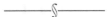

Baptism is one of the Lord's most treasured symbols or ceremonies. Jesus only left two of them with us in the church—*communion* and *baptism*. Whereas communion is a practice that is meant to be observed repeatedly throughout the life of a believer, baptism is generally a one-time occurrence. Baptism is not the act that *saves* us, but it is the act that *represents* that we are saved. Baptism by immersion illustrates, in dramatic style, the death; burial; and resurrection of Christ, while illustrating our death to sin and a new life in Him. Baptism is the *outward* expression of an *inner* change. It is an act of obedience *after* salvation has occurred. Jesus commanded baptism to be the first step of a new believer; an act of obedience and public testimony that honors Jesus as Lord of our life. Baptism separates the *browsers* from the *buyers*! In the Bible, only believers who had placed their faith in Christ were baptized. Therefore, infant baptism—Christening—is *not* a Biblical practice. An infant cannot place his or her faith in Christ and make a conscious decision to give their life to Christ.

Baptism is no trivial issue. It is a willing plunge into the public confession of faith: we claim God as our Father; and Jesus as our Savior; and proclaim that the Holy Spirit lives in us. In doing so, we submit ourselves to all three. After all, Jesus was baptized. Therefore, we must fulfill this divine and magnificent commandment.

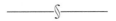

*God, for those of us who have been baptized by immersion, there is no greater experience— one that will remain as a prominent memory throughout our lives. May those who have accepted Christ as their Lord and Savior come to understand the magnitude of following Your command of baptism, and humbly submit in obedience to such.*

*"The Lord is my strength and shield. I trust Him, and He helps me."*
Psalm 28:7 (NCV)

————§————

Where does a toddler turn in times of anxiety? They turn to mommy or daddy, who are bigger than any problem they face. They run to them for protection, comfort, and for help. It is God's plan that as we mature, we would always turn to Him for help. Yet, somewhere along the way from the infant/toddler stage in our life, to where we are now, we developed a *Home Depot* approach to life—*"do it yourself!"* When this happens, we begin to rely less on God, and rely more on our own resources and abilities. This may go well for a season. But, too often there are consequences to this approach of self-reliance. We begin to over-estimate our own abilities to a point where we kind of *dethrone* God. We become prideful and arrogant, which keeps us from trusting in God to take care of us, as He desires to do. Humility is not a popular human trait in the modern world. It is not touted in the talk shows; or celebrated in valedictorian speeches; or commended in diversity seminars; or listed with the core values of a corporation. We may rely on God when tragedy strikes, but not in our everyday activities. We may rely on God when studying our Bibles, but not when it comes to applying His truths.

Reliance requires trust. When pride keeps us from trusting in God to take care of us, we feel a false sense of security based on our own imagined power and acumen to get through life's challenges. God willingly and lovingly helps us when we humbly submit ourselves to Him, trust in Him, and rely on Him for everything.

————§————

*Almighty God, forgive us for those times when we have drifted from all that You are and all You provide, and instead have forged through life in a self-sufficient, and self-reliant manner. God, You are the Creator of all things and are the Provider of all that we have. We are absolutely powerless without You.*

**June 23**                                                     **Good Fruit**

*"Yes, just as you can identify a tree by its fruit, so you can identify people by the actions."*                      Matthew 7:20 (NLT)

———§———

Being a Christian means allowing ourselves to be claimed by God, shaped and formed by Christ, and through His Holy Spirit, made in His image to become a brand-new person to live in the world differently than we have ever lived before. Throughout the Bible, God has a lot to say about "fruit" in the Christian's life. Leading a fruitful life means leading a life that's whole—spiritually, physically, mentally, and emotionally. A fruitful person is one who is implanted and is abiding in Christ—growing, increasing, abounding, flourishing, and exemplifying the characteristics of Christ—the fruits of His Spirit. Fruitfulness is a command of God; it's a sign of spiritual health; it's a source of deep satisfaction; it's a life of fulfillment and purpose; and it is an intimate and devoted partnership with God. God has set this world in motion, and He calls on every one of us to be in relationship with Him. He does this by filling us with His Holy Spirit that allows us to walk with Him, to talk with Him, to be guided, comforted, helped and encouraged by Him.

By receiving the gift of God's Holy Spirit, we are given the responsibility of recognizing and producing godly fruit in our lives. Not only is it important to recognize good fruit from bad fruit in others, it's just as important to cultivate the kind of fruit by which others would recognize Christ. What an amazing God we have, One Who is so near to us, and is so active in our lives!

———§———

*Heavenly Father, we realize that it is Your desire that we become more like Your Son. Help us to lean on Your Holy Spirit so that we can bear the best fruit to grow Your Kingdom. We pray that Your Spirit will fill us with discernment to recognize bad fruit, and to steer away from such. Help us to bear the best fruit to grow Your Kingdom.*

*"Look at My Servant, whom I have chosen. He is My Beloved, who pleases Me. I will put My Spirit upon Him, and he will proclaim justice to the nations."*

Matthew 12:18 (NLT)

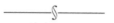

Matthew is describing how Jesus fulfilled what God told the prophet Isaiah in Isaiah 42:1-3. This describes God's original plan for Israel, who was not to remain separate from the other nations, but to be God's servant in taking the truth to the nations. The passage describes even more accurately the ministry of God's other Servant, Jesus the Messiah, who initiated the plan to take the truth throughout the world. Chosen by God, Jesus willingly cooperated with God's will. Though His ministry on earth dealt mainly with the Jews, the ultimate goal was to take it beyond to the Gentiles.

Jesus was not overly demonstrative by engaging in loud debates during His earthly ministry. Instead, He was more compassionate, gentle, and non violent—all the while fulfilling His responsibility as God's chosen Servant with Whom He was pleased.

Today in America, there are so many hot topics about which to ruffle our feathers. But, we need to use Jesus' example of calmness to communicate our point of view. Otherwise, we fall into the raucous mob-mentality of loud and often violent behaviors and words that have no positive impact on any message that is trying to be conveyed. Truth and justice should be shared with those with whom we agree, and especially with those who oppose those truths.

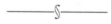

*Heavenly Father, thank You for Your Holy Spirit Who dwells in us to provide the calm, compassionate, and wise guidance we all need. May we rely on You when speaking truth about Who You are with others. God, we need justice to be proclaimed in our nation today.*

**June 25**                                        **God's Text Message**

*"Your word is a lamp before my feet and a light for my journey."*
Psalm 119:105 (CEV)

————§————

When was the last time any of us chose *not* to read a text message we had received on our mobile device? We display true devotion to reading text after text, regardless of how important, or not, the message is. Yet, many of us may opt not to read the most important message we could ever receive—the message from God. The Bible, God's text to us, is His love letter that tells us all about Who He is; what He has done for us; how much He loves us and wants the best for us; and informs us of our eternal future. The Bible is one of God's greatest miracles in that He gave His Word to mankind so that we may experience Him in a personal way and get to know Him better every time we open it up and read His message to us. The Bible is our *owner's manual* for this life, full of instruction and examples of how to have victory over sin; how to live a spiritually healthy life; how to gain wisdom, peace, and joy; and offers troubleshooting when things get a little broken.

When we choose to use any number of excuses we can call upon for not taking time each day to read God's unchanging truth, which is meant to be transformational, our lives get off course. Some of us might justify our choice to not read the Bible on a daily or regular basis based on our action of simply going to church once a week. As our bodies need food each day to sustain our physical health, our spiritual health will suffer if we only feed our souls on Sunday. We become *weak* Christians when we don't feed on His Word during the *week*.

————§————

*Almighty God, the Bible The Bible—God's text—is perfect, timeless, everlasting, unchanging, relevant to all. It is designed to bring understanding where there is ignorance; order where there is confusion' and light where there is spiritual and moral darkness. We thank You for this amazing lamp to light our path.*

*"Be diligent to present yourself approved to God as a worker who does not need to be ashamed, accurately handling the word of truth."*      2 Timothy 2:15 (NASB)

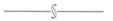

The Bible is God's revelation of Himself. The goal of interpreting God's Word is not to simply accumulate knowledge so that we can be the best at Bible trivia. The reason it is important to study and accurately interpret the Bible is so we can know God better; know what He expects from us; and know how we can live in a way that pleases Him. Christianity, like any other relationship, takes work. Studying the Bible is how we develop a deeper and more meaningful relationship with God. With the Bible, it is absolutely essential to know the context of a particular passage we are studying; to understand the context of the entire book in which the passage is found; and understand how that book fits into the context of Scripture as a whole. Or, to put it another way, our objective is to discover God's intended message.

No verse is ever an island. Interpretation has to be limited to the meaning that the original author—God—intended to convey. Popular Bible verses pop up everywhere, on T-shirts; on social media; on coffee mugs; on bumper stickers etc. However, verses without context can make it easy to miss the point. Misunderstanding verses in the Bible can lead to misapplying it in our lives, as well as misinforming others. When we pour into God's Word, we need to do more than simply read the words on the page. We must learn the context of those words. If we fail to ask questions, we might miss the point of the passage.

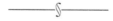

*Heavenly Father, Scripture tells us that Your instructions are perfect, Your commands are clear and give us insight for righteous living. What a blessing! Please impress upon our heart the value and importance of putting devoted effort into reading and studying the Bible daily to properly interpret Your intended message.*

        **Stop Making Comparisons**

*"Then I observed that most people are motivated to success because they envy their neighbors. But this, too, is meaningless—like chasing the wind."* Ecclesiastes 4:4 (NLT)

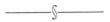

One of the greatest temptations facing the human race today is that of comparison. Making comparisons about virtually everything has become part of life from childhood to old age. We compare family background; physical appearance; intelligence; character; abilities; endowments; life achievements etc. It has systematically turned life in general to a kind of competition. Comparison will always make us ignore what we have and focus our attention on what we lack. It will push us to doubt God and ourselves, convincing us to seek solutions outside of God's provision. To be accepted or approved by people was not what God had in His mind when He created us. God intended for us to do His will and to be accepted and approved by Him. By making comparisons, we're implying that God made a mistake in making us as we are, and it allows others to define our worth.

The comparison game sprouts from jealousy, envy, and pride. It crushes our ability to authentically celebrate someone else's successes. When we keep our focus on Jesus, not the person to our left or to our right, it will be so fulfilling that we won't have the need or the desire to worry about how we measure up to others. When He cried out, *"It is finished,"* it was finished once and for all. Jesus broke the need for comparison in our lives.

*Heavenly Father, forgive us for those moments where we forget to Whom we belong. You're the One Whose opinion really matters. Help us to get back on track and run the race You have outlined for each of us, always looking to You, not man. Help us to stop playing the comparison game so that we can make our relationships with others more genuine.*

*Jesus answered: "You are completely wrong! You don't know what the Scriptures teach! And you don't know anything about the power of God."*     Matthew 22:29 (CEV)

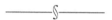

Ouch! What a stinging rebuke Jesus gave the Sadducees, whose question was based on the law of levirate marriage (Deut. 25:5–10). The Sadducees referred to this provision to demonstrate the absurdity of belief in the resurrection. Jesus produced evidence for the resurrection from the Pentateuch (Exod. 3:6), which the Sadducees recognized as their sole source for authoritative teaching. Yet, this calls for us to take a look in the mirror. How thoroughly do we examine Scripture to gain accurate interpretation in order to properly apply it to our lives, as the original Author intended? From cover to cover the Bible represents the whole counsel of God. His intent is not to confuse or stump us—His intent is that we would dig deep into His Word, for full understanding and obedient application in our lives. Looking for meaning in Scripture without understanding the true and appropriate context in which it was written is unwise and dangerous.

Perhaps the most neglected of spiritual disciplines is the serious study of God's Word. It is not enough to just read the words on the pages. We must understand the intended meaning; importance; and implications of what God has stated in His amazing gift to us—the Holy Bible. It is well worth our effort to do so.

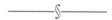

*Almighty God, You have given us this invaluable treasure by which our lives may be guided and measured. May each one of us do more than simply read the words on the pages of Your Holy Bible, and instead invest the time and effort to truly study Your Word. In doing so, we ask for discernment to glean and interpret Your intended message to us, so that we may properly apply it in our lives.*

# June 29                              Heart Surgery

*"For the word of God is living and active and sharper than any double-edged sword, piercing even to the point of dividing soul from spirit, and joints from marrow; it is able to judge the desires and thoughts of the heart."*                    Hebrews 4:12 (NET)

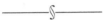

Communication with God is a two-way matter. We *speak* to Him through prayer; offering praise; confession; thanksgiving; petition concerning our needs and the needs of others; and seek His wisdom, strength, and guidance. Yet, how do we hear *from* God? While we marvel at the methods God used to speak to His chosen ones of old, our spirits long to engage in direct and meaningful communication in this present age. The very God of the universe speaks on every page into our minds and hearts. Full of life and power, the Word of God is able to probe the deepest recesses of the human heart and leave nothing hidden.

The inner life of a Christian is often a strange mixture of motivations both genuinely spiritual and completely human. It takes a supernaturally discerning agent such as the Word of God to sort these out and to expose what is of the flesh. When we read and study the Bible, God's Holy Spirit uses His Word like a scalpel to do heart surgery on us—carving us into the likeness of Christ. No other voice can reach us as deeply; lift us as high; or carry us as far as the voice of God we hear in the Bible. Therefore, we must choose a time, a place, and a plan to read, study—and hear—His Word daily.

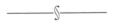

*Heavenly Father, how blessed we are that You are our God. We praise You for Your magnificence! God, Your Word is precious. Help us to love Your Word; to honor Your Word; to believe Your Word; to study Your Word; to obey Your Word; to defend Your Word; and to proclaim Your Word. Help us to make the commitments we each need to make in order to refresh our devotion to Your Word. In doing so, may our relationship with You grow deeper.*

*"Praise the Lord, O my soul. And all that is within me, praise His holy name. Prai.*
*the Lord, O my soul. And forget none of His acts of kindness. He forgives all my sin*
*He heals all my diseases. He saves my life from the grave. He crowns me with loving*
*kindness and pity. He fills my years with good things and I am made young again like*
*the eagle."*
Psalm 103:1-5 (NLV)

———§———

It's hard to find a more passionate doxology anywhere in Scripture than
David's heart cry in this Psalm. Springing from the depths of his soul, David
is stirred to pour out his pure praise about God in his self-directed "pep talk.
His prayer is absent any plea, complaint, or expression of need. Instead
with every fiber of his being, David is wonderstruck as he counts all ways in
which God has graciously blessed him and exclaims his adoration, gratitude
and praise for the Lord. We need to follow David's lead and continuall
count our blessings, because it is so easy to fall back on self-pity, complaint
and counting our woes. What greater blessing is there than the forgiveness
of our sins through the blood of Jesus? Without that blessing, there would
be no point to life—for without it, we would all be doomed to eterna
judgment and death.

God blesses us with healing from the spiritual disease of sin. Praise must
not just come from our lips. Praise must emanate from deep within our soul
recognizing all the great blessings God has given us. While God is absolutely
worth of our praise because He is Holy, majestic, and mighty, we have ever
greater reasons to praise Him. We praise Him for His never-ending grace
His love; His mercy; His kindness; His power; and for being our Heavenly
Father.

———§———

*Almighty God, we praise You for all that You have done in our lives. We praise You*
*for all that You are currently doing. And, we praise You for all the blessings that lie ahead*
*for each of us.*

# July 1         In Spite of Ourselves

*"The Lord is compassionate and merciful, slow to get angry and filled with unfailing love. He will not constantly accuse us, nor remain angry forever. He does not punish us for all our sins; he does not deal harshly with us, as we deserve."*     Psalm 103:8-10 (NLT)

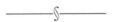

Do you ever wonder how and why God puts up with us? God knows each of us better than we even know ourselves. He made every molecule in our body and understands every complexity of our being. He knows how we are wired, and every intricate detail of our personality. He knows the temptations with which we struggle, and the unpredictability of our thoughts and feelings. He knows every good thing we have achieved, and every mistake we have made. He knows our deepest secrets, and unspoken desires. With God's amazing *personal omniscience* of us, no wonder we keep some distance between ourselves and God, because our *resume* is pretty pathetic! Yet, David knew God's heart and expressed that God is compassionate; merciful; patient; loving and forgiving. These characteristics of God Almighty are designed to lead us to repentance and into a personal relationship with Him.

We can often cover our *real* selves when dealing with our fellow man/woman. But, we can't hide our *true* self from God. When we totally absorb the truth in the deepest part of our heart and soul that God does love us; that He desires good things for us; and that He forgives our sins, then we can truly come to know His heart and finally understand how vital that is for our ability to fully trust Him. Then and only then will we seek God and praise Him with a heart that wants to *experience* God Himself, and not just what we might view as a required activity.

*Heavenly Father, how blessed we are that You love us and pour out Your grace and mercy <u>because</u> You know us! God, how grateful we are that You are so compassionate, in spite of sinfulness.*

## July 2                                          Ruler Over All

*"Lord, You are great and powerful. You have glory, victory, and honor. Everything in heaven and on earth belongs to You. The kingdom belongs to You, Lord; you are the Ruler over everything."*                                          1 Chronicles 29:11 (NCV)

———— § ————

God is sovereign over all of creation—He made it, and He directs it. God is sovereign over Heaven and earth, over disease, death, suffering, calamity, comfort; prosperity, joy, and peace. God is the Supreme Ruler of the universe and everything in it. He exercises His power as He wills; when He wills; and where He wills. Nothing will enter our life that God does not either decree or permit.

What difference does God's sovereignty make in our lives? It gives us courage to face our days. It helps us give thanks in adversity. And it humbles us in our planning, as well as our reflections of accomplishments with which we have been blessed. We will never attain a full understanding of the sovereignty of God, yet we can be grateful for it always.

Yet, we might have the question, "If God is sovereign and in control of my life, how can I have free will?" We are Christians *because* in His Sovereignty, God *chose us* to belong to Him! WOW! And, He did so before the earth was formed, so we can't take any credit for it. We did, however, have the responsibility of *accepting* His gift of salvation by *choosing to believe* in Jesus Christ and repent of our sins. It is only after this, that we are able to exercise our free will and choose the path He sets before us. God works through our choices. God's knowledge of what we are going to do does not mean that we can't choose something. Our free will is not restricted by God's foreknowledge.

———— § ————

*God, we praise You for how You work in our lives. Thank You for giving us free will to choose. Please guide us through those choices we make to ensure they align with Your will.*

# July 3                                          Beyond

*"I can testify that by their own free will they have given to the utmost of their ability, yes, even beyond their ability."*                       2 Corinthians 8:3 (ISV)

Just as our physical lives need routine check-ups to evaluate our health and help prevent disease, our spiritual lives must also be assessed and calibrated. That is when we can purge our unhealthy tendencies and replace them with the healthy habits that God desires, such as: faithful prayer; devoted service; humble confession; study of God's Word; joyful worship; and participation in Kingdom growth through our generosity. Grace is made visible when we live with an open-handed understanding of all we have, and all we are. Paul cites a great example of *visible grace* applied by the Macedonian churches, who buried any excuse that could have been employed, and willfully and joyfully demonstrated generosity *beyond* what was asked or expected.

Generosity does not have its origins in the human heart, but rather it is anchored in God's nature. Scripture reveals God's generosity in His acts of Creation; in entrusting His Creation to humanity; and in giving up His Own Son to redeem His Creation. Biblical generosity is the worshipful response—in acts of sacrificial giving beyond what is expected—from hearts that have been transformed by the amazing generosity of God. God gets the glory when His people are generous because it demonstrates how rich our God is! We must remember that the Macedonians were impoverished, yet their blessing and trust they had in Christ, was beyond their poverty.

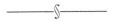

*Heavenly Father, help us to calibrate our hearts so that we may fully trust You and go beyond in our generosity. It is an absolute privilege to participate in advancing Your Kingdom.*

*"How blessed is the nation whose God is the Lord, the people whom he has chosen to be his special possession."*                                          Psalm 33:12 (NET)

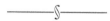

Despite the mistruths of CRT (Critical Race Theory), which is taught in many of our public schools, the Declaration of Independence was adopted on July 4th, 1776—and, thus America was born. Our Declaration of Independence states, *"... that all men are created equal, that they are endowed by their Creator with certain unalienable Rights, Life, Liberty and the pursuit of Happiness..."* But first, we need to acknowledge our dependence on God Who has so graciously granted these liberties to us. In spite of the fact that our nation has basically removed God from the public square, many of us remain faithful to Him.

As we celebrate our nation's independence, may we also acknowledge the flag, which is an emblem of our freedom. The proper folding of the flag involves twelve steps (folds) each representing something. The twelfth fold represents the Christian and glorifies God. The colors of our flag also stand for something—red for courage and the shed blood for our nation's independence; white for purity and freedom from corruption by another country; and blue for justice and perseverance. Is God still the God of our nation? Many things indicate that is not the case anymore. On this day of celebration, let's commit to turning that around.

*Heavenly Father, You promise to respond to us if we humble ourselves and return to You. Lord we a pray as individuals, and as a nation, that we whole-heartedly declare that You are Lord of our nation. We will not survive as an independent nation without You. Please give us the courage and wisdom to fight to bring You back.*

*"For the others have all contributed out of their abundance, but she out of her poverty has given everything she possessed, all that she had to live on."*      Mark 12:44 (NCB)

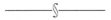

The commendation that Jesus gave about the widow's generosity was not prescriptive—He never suggests that every person should give everything away—but He singled her out to be *instructive* for us all. She was willing to sacrifice *all* that she had because of her complete trust that God would continue to provide her daily needs. Sacrifice means something different to everyone. For some, it may mean cutting back current spending to increase giving. Others might delay a major expenditure. Some people may find ways to increase their income in order to be more generous givers. And, for some, the idea of sacrifice is too frightening to make any adjustment. Yet, we must be careful that we do not confuse *sacrifice* with *amount*. While the amount of our offerings may differ, we are all able to make equal sacrifice.

As with the widow in this Scripture, the sacrifice—not the amount—is what meant the most to our Lord. This passage teaches that God considers the motive, attitude, and financial condition of the giver when determining the gift's value. He always measures the value of an offering by its worth to the person bringing it. The offerings from the wealthier religious leaders made lots of noise as they jingled into the offering receptacles, but the widow's sacrificial offering was heard in heaven. Here was a woman in need of *receiving* charity, yet she had a heart to *give*.

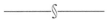

*God, we are eternally grateful for the greatest sacrificial gift ever—Your Son! It is a good reminder that the amount of our gifts and offerings may vary with our resources, but the attitude of our gifts and offerings should remain constant. Help us to see that giving which doesn't cost us anything, doesn't come from a generous heart.*

*"Everyone should give whatever they have decided in their heart. They shouldn't give with hesitation or because of pressure. God loves a cheerful giver."* 2 Corinthians 9:7 (CEB)

The heart is the command center of a person's life, where we collect and consider knowledge, where we make decisions and plans that determine the direction of our lives. The heart is where we determine to make and honor our commitments, and to keep our promises. The decisions and the commitments we make show our values; shape our character; and determine our destiny. This applies to our decisions and commitments to giving. Generosity is the response to the grace that we have through Jesus Christ. The spirit and practice of generosity is always an outward sign of an inward commitment to love. Giving is actually a relational commitment. No one is more tormented than the Christian who cannot trust God with his finances. On the flip side, no one is happier than the Christian who *totally* trusts God enough to give back to God what is already His. God wants our gifts to Him to be *our* idea, in an amount that in some way appropriately and faithfully reflects our unspeakable love and gratitude for Him.

Giving to the Lord is not an obligation; it's a privilege. God, Who knows and appraises our hearts, values only those gifts that come as a free expression of the deepest part of our souls. We have yet to see what God can do in, through, and for us when we are totally committed to Him. There are also other ways in which we can be generous. Certain organizations like *Tunnel to Towers, Samaritan's Purse,* and *St. Jude's Children's Hospital,* are amazing organizations that truly benefit others. God absolutely loves a cheerful giver because that is precisely what God is—a cheerful Giver!

*God, we praise You and thank You for unending love and mercy. You have blessed us with the opportunity to experience abundant joy, through our generosity, which reflects our heart condition toward You. May we continue to be open-hearted and open-handed.*

*"Glory belongs to God, whose power is at work in us. By this power he can do infinitely more than we can ask or imagine."*        Ephesians 3:20 (GW)

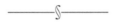

God's ability is beyond everything. His power has no limits and is not exhausted by anything He puts forth. It is truly infinite. What God is able to do through us and for us cannot be contained in a thought or explanation, and exceeds our ability to understand. If we think about it, God has never done anything to us that would cause us to hold back our complete and total trust in Him. With that said, why do we allow fear to thwart our efforts to commit to the plans and will for our life?

Christ dwells in the heart of every true believer, but not every heart is a comfortable home for Him when fear and doubt replace faith and trust. When we allow fear to take over, we can't do the things God calls us to do. What if God wants to show us something far greater than we've ever asked or imagined through this privileged opportunity to stretch our faith beyond where it's ever been? Are our eyes even looking up to see what He offers? The only way we can experience God's amazing abilities first-hand, is to fully trust Him. He is the One Who holds our future, though it may be invisible to us. At the end of the day there is one final question our fearful hearts may ask. Is God able? If we believe what He has communicated throughout the Bible, then the answer must be a resounding "Yes!"

*Heavenly Father, this spiritual journey with You has been awesome—and we're not done yet. We praise You for Your mighty power at work within us, and look forward to going infinitely beyond all that we can imagine or hope for because our faith has been stretched.*

*"One generation after another will celebrate Your great works; they will pass on the story of Your powerful acts to their children."*       Psalm 145:4 (VOICE)

God has only one plan for the preservation of His people from one generation to another. He has ordained that the story of His mighty works be passed from generation to generation, and thus shall the truth be preserved on the earth. God wants us to live trans-generational (not trans-gender) lives! God wants us to think beyond ourselves when we plan; carry out our commitments; serve; and pray. God is a generational God, the Bible is a generational book, and He has called us to be a generational people—but we must accept the challenge.

Legacies are passed through relationships—mainly parents to children, but also relationships with friends, co-workers, and neighbors. We are called to pass the baton of faith! Legacies are also passed through stories of what God has done. If passing the baton is important in a race, imagine how important it is in life. Whether it is a father trying to pass on to his son what it means to be a godly man, or a mother trying to pass on the lessons of womanhood to her daughter, we don't want to drop the baton! Unlike a race, we don't always get a chance to practice, do we? We all have the opportunity and duty to become *baton-passers* by living a life that exemplifies devotion to the Lord, and sharing our faith through godly relationships whereby we pass on the wondrous works of God, and remain committed to growing His Kingdom for generations to come.

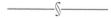

*Almighty God, we know that You have called upon each of us to love the truth, live the truth, guard the truth, and share the truth of Who You are. Help us to raise up and influence a generation of fully-devoted Christ followers, by passing the baton of faith.*

*"Everyone who hears these words of Mine and does them is like a wise man who built his house on rock. The rain fell, the flood came, and the winds beat against that house, but it did not collapse because it had been founded on rock."*    Matthew 7:24-25 (NET)

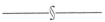

It's not enough to just read or hear the teachings of Jesus—such as His Sermon on the Mount—we must put them into practice and apply them in our everyday lives. Every person builds his or her life according to some design; belief; scheme; world-view; or philosophy. However, the difference lies in the foundation upon which we build. To build on anything other than the Rock—Christ Jesus—is to build our life on sinking sand, which is not a secure foundation. No one is exempt from the storms of life—believer or non-believer. The storms of life expose our foundation, and if it is not built on Christ and His Word, we find our very security, identity, and eternal future is threatened.

Many of the Proverbs in Scripture address wisdom and fools. Wisdom in Scripture is the ability to take divine truth and apply it to our life. The *fool* in Scripture is not necessary the person who lacks information. It is the person who does little or nothing with the information received. It takes more work to build on the Rock. It takes a greater investment of time and energy. On the flip side, it is easier and faster to build on the sand because one is tempted to take worldly shortcuts. While obedience to Jesus' words is not protection *from* the storms of life, it is protection *in* those storms. Building on the Rock is the best flood insurance there is. Let us all construct our life according to Christ's infallible building codes.

*Precious Jesus, You have clearly laid out the blueprint for us to build a rock-solid foundation for our life. You are our Rock, perfect in every way. May Your Holy Spirit guide and protect us through all of life's storms as we hear and apply Your truths in all seasons.*

*"Great is the Lord and worthy of the highest praise; no one can even begin to comprehend His greatness."*
           Psalm 145:3 (NCB)

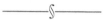

An inadequate view of God is the root of many sins. Wrong thoughts about God in Eden led to the *Fall*. Think of what would have happened in Eden if Adam and Eve had only turned from Satan's lies about God, and instead sought to know God better. Knowing that God's grace is wholeheartedly governed by His commitment to compassion; love; holiness; and justice in every circumstance is the very basis of our relationship with Him. This is especially important when we don't understand the *why* behind what is happening. In those times, our faith in the character of God enables us to trust that He is doing what is best in every circumstance. This is when we can begin to let go of our constant efforts of trying to be in control of our lives, and instead embrace the truth that the greatness and graciousness of God is all the control we need.

As we view our gracious loving and forgiving God, we realize that His love also demands that sin be punished. This is the very basis of God's grace. There is no way God can love what is good without hating what is evil. The very nature of God's grace forbids us to do what is wrong. It doesn't have anything to do with rules and regulations—it has everything to do with the character of Almighty God. His character is the very basis of life. Despite our limited ability to completely understand God's greatness, the more we come to know God and experience His attributes in our lives, the more we will come to adore who He is. And the more we adore Him, the more we will desire to imitate Him.

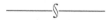

*Almighty God, we praise Your awesome greatness! There is no One greater than You. Lord, we give complete control of our lives to You. Thank You for Your power and grace so our weaknesses may to be used for Your glory.*

**Sharing His Goodness**

*"We have everything we need to live a life that pleases God. It was all given to us by God's own power, when we learned He had invited us to share in His wonderful goodness."*

2 Peter 1:3 (CEV)

The attributes of God are beyond our full understanding. His goodness doesn't stem from anything we have done or deserve. Every situation we experience in our life will be filtered through the loving and sovereign hands of God for His glory. God's glory is a revelation of His nature and character. It is through this, that we learn about His goodness. Before He created all things, He knew how everything would eventually turn out—particularly the long stream of sin that would flow out of Eden and corrupt mankind. Yet, in seeing it all and knowing it all in advance, God created man anyway. Why would He do that? Would *we* create a race knowing it would turn away from us; would rebel against us; would reject us; and would violently kill our son? The answer is an emphatic "No!"

While there are many mysteries concerning God, we can conclude that Creation—in spite of His full knowledge rebellion would occur—is clearly a mark of God's goodness! Although we were created last, we were not the *least*. He has designed it so when He calls us to Himself, that we have a hunger and desire to know Who He is. The goodness of God calls for a response from us. We must take time to recognize all His goodness and express our gratitude for it all. When we believe that God is good all the time, it frees us to take ever-increasing steps of faith, and enjoy a deeper relationship with our Lord. And, it might be helpful in these chaotic times to truly share His goodness.

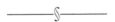

*Almighty God, what a privilege, honor and blessing it is to grow in our knowledge of Who You are. Your greatness and Your goodness are just some of Your amazing qualities that serve as reminders to us that You are all we need. We serve a powerful God.*

*"It is not good for the man to be alone, so I will create a companion for him, a perfect, suited partner."*

                                                    Genesis 2:18 (VOICE)

—————§—————

Unless we live in a cave where we are completely isolated from other people, every facet of our life touches a relationship in some way. Everything we do, or everywhere we go, we are in relationships with other people. We have relationships with friends; co-workers; neighbors; and family. And, regardless of how devoted and functional it may be, we all have a relationship with God. God created us for relationships—with Him first—and then with others. However, after Adam was placed in the Garden of Eden, God got the first declaration that something was missing. Adam was alone without a helper fit to aid him in fulfilling the Creator's mandate for humanity to multiply and exercise wise dominion over the earth. God solved this problem by creating a perfect companion for him—Eve. She was equal in importance, yet both would have completely different roles. She would be both a perfect mate and a perfect helper to Adam. Thus, when the two would come together, they would become one flesh. In love; in partnership; in decisions; and yes, even in flesh, the two would become one before God.

God wants marriages to be a strong and life-long union. He wants it to be a reflection of His relationship with His redeemed people. In Scripture, God has given us a blueprint of His design of marriage. In marriage, as God intends it, there are not two partners but three—Jesus is the third. God's design for marriage was for one man and one woman to give each other the God-crafted experience of loving and being loved. It is so sad that our nation has re-defined marriage. We can be sure that this breaks the heart of God.

—————§—————

*Heavenly Father, we thank You for the gift of our relationships with others. May You always be in the center of each one of them. We pray that our nation would turn from its evil ways and restore marriage to the way you designed it to be.*

*God blessed them and said to them, "Be fruitful and increase in number; fill the earth and subdue it. Rule over the fish in the sea and the birds in the sky and over every living creature that moves on the ground."* Genesis 1:28 (NIV)

————§————

Man and woman are equal in the sense that they bear God's image equally. When God made man, three Persons were involved: the Father, Son, and Holy Spirit. They created man in Their image—imparting Their nature to him —so that man, in a sense, had Their nature. Before the Fall, Adam, who was created first, was able to walk and talk with God in the way two close friends hang out and visit. During those talks, God made His will clear to Adam. Among the topics they discussed was work. Adam's work was pleasant and satisfying in a fertile garden where there were no weeds, no destructive insects, and no droughts. Then God gave Adam instructions to enjoy all the fruit of the garden, with one exception: the fruit of the tree of the knowledge of good and evil.

God gave Adam lessons about work; responsibility; leadership; and obedience even before He created a mate for him. Before sin entered the picture, God mandated a unique design for man: "headship." God brought man onto the scene first as leader. In God's order or pattern, the man—husband—is responsible to lead his wife and family in all aspects, including moral and spiritual matters. That pattern is God's expectation today, and work is still part of that equation. How sad that the work ethic taught to Adam, and expected for us to adopt, is quickly vanishing from today's generation(s). God never instructed Adam to just sit around waiting for freebies to roll in daily. God designed work for a purpose—a purpose America has ignored.

————§————

*Heavenly Father, our prayer is that we come to more clearly understand and embrace the roles of men and women, so that we might conduct our relationships in the manner in which You intended. God, we pray that the value and purpose of work will be restored to the fabric of our nation.*

*Then the Lord God said to the woman, "You will suffer terribly when you give birth. But you will still desire your husband, and he will rule over you." The Lord said to the man, "You listened to your wife and ate the fruit I told you not to eat. And so, the ground will be under a curse because of what you did. As long as you live, you will have to struggle to grow enough food."*      Genesis 3:16-17 (CEV)

————§————

The ideal parameters for marriage established by God were reversed by sin. Before the Fall, Adam and Eve lived in harmony with one another; in complete openness and vulnerability; trusting and loving each other. Each was satisfied with the responsibilities and roles God had given them. After the Fall, their marriage was tainted by self-centeredness; pride; anger; self-sufficiency; self-exaltation; condescension; desire to control; and hopelessness. Because Eve had sinned and changed her own human nature by listening to Satan, sin was going to make her job as a woman, wife, and mother much more difficult. Women now have an inward impulse—unless contained—to resist their husband's God-ordained headship, and try to control them.

Because Adam had failed in his leadership role and willingly sinned against God, work—which was God's original plan to be a blessing—would now become a life-long burden. God designed it that men would find a great deal of significance in their work. God's curse arranged things so that their work would never ultimately satisfy them. We find ourselves outside of the Garden. We find ourselves with no access to the tree of life. We find ourselves living under the shadow of death. Yet, the good news is that we can mitigate the curse through having Christ in the center of our lives—our relationships, our families, and our careers.

————§————

*Heavenly Father, we long for when You will restore the new Eden again, so we may live eternally with You, as You designed.*

*"Wives, submit to your husbands, as is fitting for those who belong to the Lord. Husbands, love your wives and never treat them harshly."* Colossians 3:18-19 (NLT)

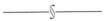

A good marriage is not based so much on *finding* the right person as it is on *being* the right person. Submission has nothing to do with equality, inferiority, or incompetence. Submission is not the exclusive responsibility of the woman. All Christians are called to submit to the authority of Christ. Submission has to do with accomplishing God's designed purpose. Jesus submitted to the Father in order to accomplish salvation. In marriage, submission means that a wife is to seek; to encourage; to welcome and look for ways she can strengthen her husband's leadership without resisting or undermining his leadership. Despite the fact that Adam and Eve were to be partners in exercising dominion over creation, God assigned the responsibility of headship in the family to Adam. We can liken that to the cockpit of an airplane where there are both a pilot and a co-pilot. Both fly the plane, but the pilot is assigned the leadership role.

Headship is never a license for any form of abuse. A husband is commanded to love his wife in a sacrificial and gentle manner, by putting the interests and feelings of his wife ahead of himself. When the husband allows his wife to be a true helpmate, she fulfills her innate role to support and assist him. God designed women to be helpers because men are not complete in and of themselves. God made woman the helper because man desperately needs someone to come alongside who will be different than him, in order to complete him, thereby fulfilling the Divine plan of God. A woman wants the security of knowing that she is loved and taken care of physically, emotionally, and of course, spiritually. And men fill that role.

*Heavenly Father, thank You for Your glorious plan for marriage. We pray all marriages would have Christ as the centerpiece.*

# July 16 Sanctity of Marriage

*"Husbands, love your wives the same as Christ loved the church and gave his life for it."*
Ephesians 5:25 (ERV)

———§———

When God designed marriage, He designed it for His glory, and our good. When a husband joyfully bears the primary God-given responsibility for Christ-like, servant leadership in the home, his wife can't help but feel the love and security she needs. Protection and provision are two most fundamental areas where a husband is called upon to fulfill his leadership responsibility. Protection and provision both have a physical and a spiritual meaning. There is physical provision (like food and shelter); spiritual *provision* (like the Word of God, spiritual guidance, instruction, encouragement); physical protection (as from intruders, natural disasters, or disease); and spiritual *protection* (like prayer and keeping certain influences out of the home). These are ways in which a husband's leadership is displayed.

In addition to his call for leadership, a husband is commanded to love his wife as Christ loved the church. A wife needs to see that their marriage is her husband's priority. *Falling* in love is somewhat easy and effortless; yet *remaining* and *growing* that love in a marriage is more challenging. But, by having Christ as the center of a marriage, love can be portrayed as a self-sacrificing, caring commitment that shows itself in seeking the highest good of the one loved. Women have a deep need to be valued, cherished and pursued—pursue her like you did when you were dating! Women want to be led to the Person of Jesus through the man God has placed in her life. A wife yearns for her husband to stimulate and nurture the spiritual growth of his whole family.

———§———

*Heavenly Father, it is through the strength and guidance of Your Holy Spirit that the sanctity of marriage, as You designed it, is upheld. Let us return to Your original design as the <u>only</u> form of marriage.*

*"God gives the gift of the single life to some, the gift of the married life to others."*

1 Corinthians 7:7 (MSG)

The wonderful gift of marriage is not the *only* design of God. He also designed that some people be single, because that, too, fits into God's will and purpose. In Paul's letter to the Corinthian church, he is offering himself as an example of the fulfillment of being single, by making it clear that singleness is not necessarily incompleteness. There are many reasons for singleness: Some are single because they are still young and haven't yet considered marriage; others have been single for a long time and are content with that situation; some may have the desire to be married, but have not found a partner; then there are some who have been married before, but are now single because of divorce or the death of a spouse.

Some have the *gift* of singleness, for which they are well suited. There are some blessings and opportunities that come with singleness, even if only for the short term. It allows for undivided service to Christ. As wonderful as marriage is, it will test your availability to be involved in serving or ministry because it will revolve around your marriage/family. That is not to say that single people are spiritually superior to those who are married. For single Christians, there is potentially more liberty and availability to serve. So, if you are single, then it is God's will and God's gift to you to be single—use His gift in a way that honors and glorifies Him. And if you are married, then it is God's will and God's gift to you to be married—you, too, are to use His gift in a way that honors and glorifies Him.

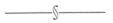

*Almighty God, our relationship with You is most important to us. Whether married or single, help us to fulfill You're will and Your purpose in every life. Your design for mankind is amazing. We pray we live our lives in ways that are pleasing to You.*

*They abandoned the Lord to serve Baal and the images of Ashtoreth. This made the Lord burn with anger against Israel, so He handed them over to raiders who stole their possessions. He turned them over to their enemies all around, and they were no longer able to resist them. Every time Israel went out to battle, the Lord fought against them, causing them to be defeated, just as He had warned. And the people were in great distress.*

Judges 2:13-15 (NLT)

———— § ————

It had been a generation since the Israelites had entered the Promised Land—a land that had been occupied by the Canaanites and their idolatrous religious system. The main deity in Canaan was Baal, god of rainfall and fertility, and Ashtoreth his spouse. These gods *weren't* living gods—simply carved idols. But the Israelites disobeyed God's command to wipe out the Canaanite religion completely. Instead, the Jews became so accustomed to the sinful ways of their pagan neighbors that those ways didn't seem sinful anymore. The Jews then became interested in how their neighbors worshiped, until finally Israel started to live like their enemies and imitate their ways.

For believers today, the first step away from the Lord is "friendship with the world", which then leads to our being spotted by the world. The next step is to *"love the world"* (1 John 2:15) and gradually become *"conformed to the world"* (Rom. 12:2). This can lead to being *"condemned with the world"* (1 Cor 11:32), the kind of judgment that came to Lot (Gen. 19) The sin in our lives that we fail to conquer will eventually conquer us. The people of Israel found themselves enslaved to one pagan nation after another as the Lord kept His word and punished His people. Will that happen to us? Will we keep going along with or allowing idolatrous and evil actions continue in our government, schools, and lives in general?

———— § ————

*God, we find our nation sinking deeper and deeper into a godless society full of idol worship, evil, and corruption. Help us turn back to you as individuals and as a nation. Forgive our sinfulness. We need Your intervention to restore us to You.*

*Then the Lord raised up judges to rescue the Israelites from their attackers. Yet Israel did not listen to the judges but prostituted themselves by worshiping other gods. How quickly they turned away from the path of their ancestors, who had walked in obedience to the Lord's commands.*          Judges 2:16-17 (NLT)

———§———

Whenever Israel turned away from the Lord to worship idols, He humbled them severely; and when in their misery they turned back to Him, He liberated them. But just as soon as they were free and their situation was comfortable again, Israel went right back into the same old sins. God delivered His people by raising up judges, who defeated the enemy and set Israel free. The Hebrew word translated "judge" means "to save, to rescue." The judges were deliverers who won great military victories with the help of the Lord—such as Gideon, Deborah, Samson etc. But the judges were also leaders who helped the people settle their disputes. Instead of trusting God to change their neighbors, the gods of their neighbors changed the Jews; and everything Moses warned them not to do, they did. The Jews broke down the wall of separation between themselves and their godless neighbors, and the results were tragic.

The cycle of disobedience, discipline, despair, and deliverance is seen today whenever God's people turn away from His Word and go their own way. God has great compassion for His people, but He is angry at their—and our— sins. The Book of Judges is the inspired record of Israel's failures and God's faithfulness. But if we study this book only as past history, we'll miss the message completely. *This book is about God's people today.* History does repeat itself!

———§———

*God, may we be awakened to fact that history does repeat itself, and we are seeing it for ourselves today. Removing You from so many aspects of our lives is proving this point. We need You desperately.*

*Deborah, the wife of Lappidoth, was a prophet who was judging Israel at that time…* *One day she sent for Barak son of Abinoam, who lived in Kedesh in the land of Naphtali. She said to him, "This is what the Lord, the God of Israel, commands you: Call out 10,000 warriors from the tribes of Naphtali and Zebulun at Mount Tabor. And I will call out Sisera, commander of Jabin's army, along with his chariots and warriors, to the Kishon River. There I will give you victory over him." Barak told her, "I will go, but only if you go with me." "Very well," she replied, "I will go with you. But you will receive no honor in this venture, for the Lord's victory over Sisera will be at the hands of a woman."*

Judges 4:6-9 (NLT)

————§————

God revealed to Deborah that Barak—no relation to the former U.S. President—was to assemble and lead the Israelite army and draw Sisera's troops into a trap near Mount Tabor; and there the Lord would defeat them. God would entice Sisera and his troops toward the Kishon River, where God would give Barak the victory. Barak's demand that the prophetess Deborah accompany him in the battle revealed his fear of the outcome and the weakness of his faith. The fact that Deborah agreed to accompany Barak suggests that his request wasn't out of God's will—although in granting it, God took the honor from the men and gave it to the women.

Along with the storm from the heavens and the flood from the swollen river, God sent confusion in the minds of the Sisera's troops. When you remember that the Canaanite god Baal was the god of storms, you can see how the sudden change of weather could have affected the superstitious Canaanites. Was the God of Israel stronger than Baal? If so, the wisest thing the soldiers could do was flee. And they did just that.

————§————

*Heavenly Father, we find peace in the fact that when we are battles with the enemy, that You are there to ensure our victory. We thank You for Your promise of victory and Your fulfillment such. We are currently in a battle with evil in our nation. We pray for Your victory in overcoming this.*

# Don't Fool Me

*Meanwhile, Sisera ran to the tent of Jael, the wife of Heber the Kenite, because Heber's family was on friendly terms with King Jabin of Hazor. Jael went out to meet Sisera and said to him, "Come into my tent, sir. Come in. Don't be afraid." So he went into her tent, and she covered him with a blanket.* Judges 4:17-18 (NLT)

Sisera fled in the direction of Hazor, where his army had been based. The battle had been so intense that he could not manage the journey without rest and refreshment. Since Sisera knew that Heber and his people were friendly toward Jabin, this settlement seemed a good place to stop and rest. When Heber's wife, Jael, came out to meet Sisera and invited him into her tent, the Canaanite captain was sure that he was at last safe. Jael gave him milk instead of water and then covered him with a blanket, and he was confident that he had found a dependable ally and could rest in peace. But Sisera made the mistake of telling Jael to lie if anyone asked whether he was there.

Being a wise woman, she concluded that Sisera was fleeing the battlefield, which meant that the Jews had won the battle and the Canaanite grip on the land was broken. If she protected Sisera, she'd be in trouble with the Jews, her own relatives. No doubt somebody was chasing Sisera, and whoever it was wouldn't be satisfied until the captain was dead. But Sisera had no reason to suspect danger. After all, Heber's clan was friendly to the Canaanites; Jael had shown him hospitality and kindness; and no pursuing Jewish soldier was likely to force his way into a woman's tent. What Sisera didn't know was that God had promised that a woman would take his life.

*Heavenly Father, You know who our enemies are. When we rely on Your guidance and trust You explicitly, You orchestrate everything for Your desired outcome and victory is achieved. What a blessing!*

*But when Sisera fell asleep from exhaustion, Jael quietly crept up to him with a hammer and tent peg in her hand. Then she drove the tent peg through his temple and into the ground, and so he died.*     Judges 4:21 (NLT)

For a captain to flee from a battle was embarrassing. For him to be killed while fleeing was humiliating. But to be killed by a *woman* was the most disgraceful thing of all. So what should we make of Jael; was she a heartless murdering woman who became God's tool for justice? There is no doubting the fact that she was not a woman to be scorned! But faced with the choice of giving refuge to a man who murdered, raped and pillaged God's people or bringing his life to a swift end, she chose an option that, in the long run, would be less violent. When faced with a choice, Jael sided with God's people and in doing so she was used by God to bring about their deliverance.

Perhaps we find passages like this difficult because we try to *sanitize* the Bible and smooth over the parts, with which we are not comfortable. Of course, the events we have been thinking about do not call on Christian women to arm themselves with tent pegs! There is a significant shift of emphasis from the Old Testament to the New, because the Old focuses on a physical kingdom and the New on a spiritual one. But even in the NT there are still issues we might rather gloss over. We like to think of God's love and compassion—but not about His judgment. We might enjoy talking to people about heaven—but not be so comfortable speaking about hell. These are not issues that our politically correct culture finds palatable, but they are addressed in the Bible and we must be faithful to what it says. And as for political correctness—God's not interested in that!

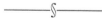

*Heavenly Father, Your ways and thoughts are not always the same as ours, but that is why You are God, and we aren't. Thank You for the lesson on holding accountable, those who are disobedient, or turn away from You. May we not make the same mistakes.*

*Again the Israelites did evil in the Lord's sight, so the Lord handed them over to the Philistines, who oppressed them for forty years.*        Judges 13:1 (NLT)

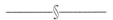

The Lord had given the Israelites into the hands of the Philistines. They were the fiercest enemy they had faced yet, and this particular conflict stretches right back to the days of Joshua and projects forward to the reign of David, when they were finally defeated. The Philistines were among the "sea people" who, in the twelfth century B.C., migrated from an area of Greece to the coastal plain of Canaan. The Jews weren't able to occupy that territory during their conquest of the land, as they had been commanded to by God in Joshua's time.

The years of affliction under the Philistines, like the previous oppressions by other nations, were God's doing. It introduces the longest period of oppression that God sent to His people—forty years of Philistine domination. The Hebrew tribes had grown cold in their faith and loyalty to God, turning to corrupt and idolatrous Canaanite customs. It's worth noting that there is no evidence given in the text that Israel cried out to God for deliverance at any time during the forty years of Philistine domination. The Philistines disarmed the Jews and therefore had little fear of a rebellion.

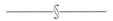

*Heavenly Father, this doesn't sound far off from how our nation has been operating. People today march and rally to promote the killing of innocent babies, and claim it's a woman's right to choose. We allow our cities to be burned and damaged because <u>some</u> lives matter more than others. We put up with a continual flow of lies coming from our government officials. Then there's a number of us who stand up for life, peace, and truth—and rely on You to ensure those will again rule the day. So, we are crying out to You. We need You to save our nation.*

*"You will become pregnant and give birth to a son, and his hair must never be cut. Fo*
*he will be dedicated to God as a Nazirite from birth. He will begin to rescue Israel from*
*the Philistines."*

                                                      Judges 13:5 (NLT

————§————

When God wants to do something really great in His world, He doesn'
send an army but an angel. The angel often visits a couple and promises t
send them a baby. His great plan of salvation got underway when He called
Abraham and Sarah and gave them Isaac. When He wanted to deliver Israe
from Egyptian bondage, God sent baby Moses to Amram and Jochebed; and
when in later years Israel desperately needed revival, God gave baby Samue
to Hannah. When the fullness of time arrived, God gave Baby Jesus to Mary
and that baby grew up to die on the cross for the sins of the world. The
baby in this verse is Samson. Like John the Baptist, Samson would be :
Nazirite from his mother's womb. The word *Nazirite* comes from a Hebrew
word that means "to separate, to consecrate." Nazirites were persons who
for a stated period of time, consecrated themselves to the Lord in a specia
way.

Babies are fragile, but God uses the weak things of the world to confounc
the mighty. Babies must have time to grow up, but God is patient and is
never late in accomplishing His will. Each baby God sends is a gift from
God—a new beginning—and carries with it tremendous potential. What a
tragedy that we live in a society that sees the unborn baby as a menace instead
of a miracle; an intruder instead of an inheritance. We need to stand up for
these innocent lives before they are ripped from women's wombs. Our
nation holds demonstrations and riots for black lives to matter, yet hold
demonstrations to murder babies. Don't their lives matter? Yes, they do!

————§————

*Heavenly Father, life is precious. How it must break Your heart when the innocent life*
*of baby in the womb is intentionally ended. Help us to end this sinful and abhorrent*
*practice. All Human lives matter! We are all made in Your image!*

# July 25                                    Reckless with Power

*Then Samson prayed to the Lord, "Sovereign Lord, remember me again. O God, please strengthen me just one more time. With one blow let me pay back the Philistines for the loss of my two eyes." Then Samson put his hands on the two center pillars that held up the temple. Pushing against them with both hands, he prayed, "Let me die with the Philistines." And the temple crashed down on the Philistine rulers and all the people. So he killed more people when he died than he had during his entire lifetime.*

Judges 16:28-30 (NLT)

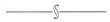

How do you assess the life and ministry of a man like Samson? It is an interesting story well worth reading. His decline began when he disagreed with his parents about marrying a Philistine girl. Then he disdained his Nazirite vow and defiled himself. He disregarded the warnings of God; disobeyed the Word of God; lived dangerously through his weakness with women; and was defeated by the enemies of God. He probably thought that he had the privilege of indulging in sin since he wore the badge of a Nazirite and won so many victories for the Lord, but he was wrong. He was physically strong, but spiritually weak.

Spiritual and moral carelessness begins with an attitude that says, 'it could never happen to me'. It will lead us to toy with temptation, which will result in sin. Blessings from God and success in our work for Him do not make us immune from temptation and spiritual danger. Samson is one of three men in Scripture who are especially identified with the darkness. King Saul lived for the world; Samson yielded to the flesh; and Judas gave himself to the devil—and all three ended up taking their own lives.

*Heavenly Father, Your Word provides us with valuable life-lessons. Give us the discipline and desire to pour into the treasures that lie in the pages of the Bible, and may we glean the wisdom therein.*

*Then Christ will make his home in your hearts as you trust in him. Your roots will grow down into God's love and keep you strong. And may you have the power to understand, as all God's people should, how wide, how long, how high, and how deep his love is.*

Ephesians 3:17-18 (NLT)

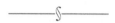

When we trust Jesus, He dwells in our hearts. This is personal; this is relational. Our faith is based on His love. Faith is the requirement—the attitude—that receives Jesus into our hearts. His presence means not only strength, but wisdom; inspiration; and above all love. True knowledge and understanding of God is unattainable without love. The breadth of His love is incomprehensible, yet we can still experience it to the best of our ability. God's love has many dimensions that work to weave into the fabric of our life. To experience genuine love, we need to get out of our heads and into our hearts. God wants us to be planted deeply in His love like a solidly rooted tree that grows to be massive and strong. Even a child may start to gain *knowledge* of a parent's love, but true *expressions* of that love— affirmations, affection, verbal encouragement—is what provides the fullest understanding of love. God's love comes from eternity past, and stretches on into the eternal ages to come. It is a love that is everlasting, and available to *all* people.

If we ever doubt the immeasurable vastness of God's love, just remember the most extravagant expression of love—*"For God so loved the world that he gave his one and only Son, that whoever believes in him shall not perish but have eternal life."* (John 3:16)

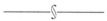

*Heavenly Father, regardless of all that happens in our broken society and world, we can find peace and comfort in knowing You love us more than we can fathom. Help us to rest in that truth and may it provide us with the strength and wisdom to share that love with others and stand up against those who are against You.*

# Do You Love Me?

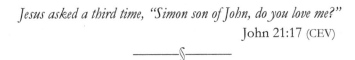

*Jesus asked a third time, "Simon son of John, do you love me?"*
John 21:17 (CEV)

————§————

Peter arrived on shore, dripping wet, yet filled with excitement to see the risen Lord. At the same time, he was feeling a deep shame for his sins just days earlier. As they sat around the fire on the beach, there might have been an awkward silence. Peter's thoughts might have flashed back to the glow of another fire. There, he denied the Lord.

Grace is certainly on display here following Peter's three-fold denial of Jesus during the sham trial of Him prior to His ultimate crucifixion. God has commanded us to love Him with all of our being—heart, soul, mind, and strength. How often, like Peter, have we failed to keep this command? How often have we denied Jesus?

Jesus didn't bring up the three times Peter had denied Him. Instead, Jesus lovingly confronts Peter—not shaming, but reconciliation—to have him face his failures. Jesus wasn't asking for Peter's promise to never deny Him again. He was asking for Peter's heart.

Once we completely surrender to our Lord and Savior and love Him with all that are—warts and all—we can face our failures head-on and willingly accept the task ahead that Jesus provides. Our significant failures can lead to significant service in the Kingdom of God.

————§————

*Almighty God, the love, compassion, and kindness You extended to Peter, You extend to us. The offer of forgiveness You extended to Peter, You extend to us. The commission of Kingdom work You extended to Peter, You extend to us. Thank You for Your grace and Your promise of eternal life with You. Lord, we <u>do</u> love You!*

*As He approached Jerusalem and saw the city, he wept over it and said, "If you, even you, had only known on this day what would bring you peace—but now it is hidden from your eyes."*
Luke 19:41-42 (NIV)

—————§—————

Jesus was sending a message to Israel on that first Palm Sunday—a message that decision time had come. For three years of Jesus' ministry the people had seen or heard about His acts of healing the sick; freeing the oppressed; feeding the hungry; and even raising the dead. As thousands of people crowded into Jerusalem for the Passover, Jesus made His way past the crowds to a place overlooking the Holy City, and he stopped and His tears burst forth. His heart sank as He considered the people's celebration and the realization that they had missed it. They *didn't get it.* They didn't understand. The people mistook Jesus for someone else.

During His *parade* into Jerusalem, they shouted "Hosanna—Save us!" Yet, Jesus did not make a triumphal entry into Jerusalem that day to be a *Santa Clause*—to give everyone what they wanted or thought they wanted. Jesus came to Jerusalem for one thing—to die! In five short days, the adoring crowd would change their cheers of "Hosanna" into jeers of "Crucify Him" because Jesus wasn't what they *wanted* Him to be. As Jesus overlooked Jerusalem, He wept because He was able to look beyond their superficial celebration and see into their hearts. They did not understand the power of His message. They did not understand the gravity of their condition. We, too, should be brought to tears when He is being rejected today.

—————§—————

*Heavenly Father, we thank You for the gift of life in Christ. We pray that those who have yet to receive this gift of eternal salvation will now do so. We pray Your work will be done in every heart so ultimately there will be no more weeping.*

*They came to Jerusalem, and Jesus entered into the temple, and began to throw out those who sold and those who bought in the temple, and overthrew the money changers' tables, and the seats of those who sold the doves.*                                Mark 11:15 (WEB)

————§————

The Lord came to His Own house; and found it in total disarray. He took all the necessary steps to set things right. The Temple had ceased to be about the Lord. It had become a house that was man-centered, not God-centered. This angered Jesus! The anger of Jesus was the righteous anger of a King Who saw a system, which deprived His people the right to worship, and took financial advantage of those who were there solely for the purpose of praying and worshipping God. After all, Jesus had come into the world to be the Savior of all men—Jew and Gentile. The racket of selling and changing money, and the noise of animals made it impossible for the Gentiles to have a place of reverence for prayer and worship. Business had pushed worship right out the door, and God's purpose in the temple was being destroyed by greed.

Some may wonder if Jesus' anger was sinful. We are not commanded to never be angry, but instead to deal with it properly. Jesus' anger had the proper motivation; focus; control; and duration. It is important to note that Jesus' actions of clearing the Temple did not result in physical harm to anyone. The only thing that Jesus hurt was the pride and pocketbook of those corrupters. The only blood that was shed was His Own—four days later on the cross.

These days the White House and the People's House (both Congress and Senate) have become dens of corruption and greed. And, besides a morning benediction—until they stop that from happening—God has basically been thrown out of those places too.

————§————

*Heavenly Father, we pray that You might impress upon our hearts Your greatness and glory. Let the thought of Your complete sovereignty over all things cause us both to revere and worship You with greater faith, undivided devotion, and joyous awe.*

*"For many are called, but few are chosen."* Matthew 22:14 (NLT)

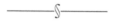

This verse closed the third in Jesus' trilogy of judgment parables given in response to the Jewish religious leaders who maliciously challenged His authority just days before His crucifixion and resurrection. This parable about the great wedding feast was both an invitation and a warning. The parable represents God's dealing with the nation of Israel. They were His invited guests, but they rejected the invitation, as they rejected the Messiah. Those invited refused to come, some because they were too busy with their own worldly pursuits, and some because they were positively hostile toward the King.

God has now extended that invitation to all. No one is excluded from the gospel invitation. God's generous call to Jews and Gentiles alike must be matched by our wholehearted response. Admission to the Kingdom of God is on God's terms, not ours. It is by God's grace—not by our goodness—that entry is granted. Just as modern restaurants post the sign, *"No Shoes, No Service,"* God's heavenly banquet says, *"No Surrender; No Celebration."* And the man who wanted to be at the party on his own terms was equally judged. And, that judgment was (and is) tragic! It is eternal darkness and separation from the glory of God's Kingdom. To reject the invitation of God to share in the Kingdom is folly—it is to choose death. To accept this amazing invitation full of God's love, grace and mercy, is to delight in the ultimate celebration for all eternity.

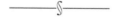

*Almighty God, we whole-heartedly accept Your invitation to the greatest wedding there will ever be. We thank You for Your grace and mercy and thank You for calling us into an eternal intimate union with Jesus.*

# July 31                          A Beautiful Thing

*While he was in Bethany, reclining at the table in the home of Simon the Leper, a woman came with an alabaster jar of very expensive perfume, made of pure nard. She broke the jar and poured the perfume on his head. Some of those present were saying indignantly to one another, "Why this waste of perfume? It could have been sold for more than a year's wages and the money given to the poor." And they rebuked her harshly. "Leave her alone," said Jesus. "Why are you bothering her? She has done a beautiful thing to Me."*

Mark 14:3-6 (NIV)

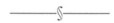

During Jesus' final week, He experienced the hatred of the priests; the love and worship of the woman (Mary); then the hateful treachery of Judas. Mary's extravagant act of devotion stands in stark contrast to the religious leaders' indignation and Judas' act of betrayal, and represents a beautiful picture of a woman who understands the superlative worth of Christ. He is worth the embarrassment; judgment; or scorn we might receive from friends, family, and outsiders. He is worth the awkwardness that oftentimes accompanies genuine expressions of worship. And He is certainly worth more than all of our worldly possessions.

Mary's act of extravagant worship was fairly public, but it was not for the others to see—it was all for Jesus. This woman pours out her love on the Savior by sacrificing the most precious thing she owns. The whole house is filled with this sweet, sweet fragrance—that is until Judas and the other disciples cause a *stink*. This truly was a *beautiful thing*. Yet, Mary thought it was a privilege and a joy.

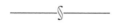

*Heavenly Father, we thank You for Your Word that so beautifully displays Mary's act of selfless, sacrificial, and extravagant worship of Jesus. It reflects her grasp of the majesty and greatness of our Lord and Savior. May our worship always be uninhibited and extravagant in all ways.*

# August 1                                    Greatest Expression of Love

*"But God shows His great love for us in this way: Christ died for us while we were still sinners. So through Christ we will surely be saved from God's anger, because we have been made right with God by the blood of Christ's death."*                    Romans 5:8-9 (NCV)

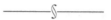

Has this ever truly sunk in with us? Have we ever really allowed time to stop and marvel at the magnitude of this sacrifice in our place? In the death of this One Man, all the sins of the human race are fully paid for—past, present and future. As a result, those of us who believe in Jesus find that our sins are forgiven forever. This is the heart of the Gospel: God's holiness demands that sin be punished. God's grace provides the sacrifice. What God demands, He supplies. Thus, salvation is a work of God from first to last. It is *conceived* by God, *provided* by God, and *applied* by God. The great truth is that the cross is a place of God's wrath. The cross is the place where Jesus—in a voluntary act of love unequaled in the history of the universe— bore the sins of all of us unworthy sinners, causing God to momentarily turn His back on His Own Son.

The cross reveals the great heart of God, a heart overflowing with love. On the cross, our Savior endured unthinkable pain and soul-wrenching agony hanging by the nails in His hands for hours on a rough wooden cross—all for our sake. When Jesus' mission was accomplished and He breathed His last, the Father preached a sermon without words when He tore the curtain from the top to the bottom. It was God's way of saying; "You are welcome in My family for eternity. Let nothing keep you away." So, how do we respond to what Jesus accomplished on the cross?

*Almighty God, every day is a time to go inward to rest in heavy silence as we feel wholehearted gratitude for Your abiding love. You fully expressed that love through sacrificing Your One and only Son for our sinfulness, so that we will not experience spiritual death and separation from You.*

# August 2                                    Lukewarm Christian

*"I know you well—you are neither hot nor cold; I wish you were one or the other! But since you are merely lukewarm, I will spit you out of my mouth!" You say, 'I am rich, with everything I want; I don't need a thing!' And you don't realize that spiritually you are wretched and miserable and poor and blind and naked."* Revelation 3:15-17 (TLB)

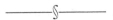

The water situation in Laodicea was reflected in the church. By the time the piped-in water reached their city, it no longer possessed the therapeutic properties of the hot water out of the springs in Hierapolis; nor did it provide the refreshing quality of the cold waters from Colossae. In Laodicea, the condition of the water was tepid and undesirable, which reflected their spiritual condition. One of the perils of the Christian life is that of becoming lukewarm or spiritually anemic. The idea of being neither hot nor cold means that they were not affecting their environment in any way. They were making no difference in their community.

Their church was not wicked or evil—it was simply meaningless. The so-called believers of Laodicea were so well off they thought they needed help from neither man nor God. They had become indifferent and apathetic, and were unmoved by the cross of Jesus; the Word of God; and the condition of the lost people around them. These folks were not burning with hot passion for Jesus. If we are more concerned about *offending* someone for simply sharing the wonderful things about our Savior, we need to think again. That's just as bad as being *meaningless,* or *lukewarm.*

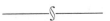

*Heavenly Father, our prayer is that we would all examine ourselves as individuals, as well as a church body, to ensure that we are not spiritually anemic and lukewarm. The last thing we wish to do is sicken or disgust You in anyway. God, help us calibrate our spiritual temperature so that our faith and our deeds will become pleasing to You, and beneficial to Your Kingdom. May we all go overboard in our words and actions as we share with others Your greatness.*

*"In the morning, O Lord, You will hear my voice. In the morning I will lay my prayer before You and will look up."*
　　　　　　　　　　　　　　　　　　　　　　　　　Psalm 5:3 (NLV)

————§————

Prayer is mankind's most vital link with Almighty God. It is our human-divine connection, allowing us the privilege of spending time in heart-felt communication with God. Prayer is not for God's good, but for ours. He doesn't need our prayers—but we need to pray! Sadly, however, our prayer life is severely lacking. A lack of prayer means we are still trying to run the show. It's a sign that we've decided we can handle things on our own. The primary failure of prayer is our failure to pray! Although God longs to come to our aid, He waits until we ask Him specifically and boldly in prayer. Sometimes He wants us to come to the end of our own pitiful resources and surrender in prayer—before He intervenes. Or, we may have been praying yet our prayers lack power because we pray in our own strength rather than in the strength of the Holy Spirit within us. We forget that God has all the resources at His disposal so that He is able to answer our prayers in His way; in His time; and in accordance with His will.

Fervent prayers get God's attention because they come from a heart that believes God's power is unlimited. What matters is the posture of our heart. Let's wrap our minds around the amazing truth that God, Creator of the universe, takes the time to listen each and every time we are willing to meet with Him in prayer—all because of His endless love for us. God has invited every one of us into His presence, and we can never overstay our welcome. He delights to hear from us through prayer. He delights in our trust. Let's pray big, bold, and specific prayers!

————§————

*Heavenly Father, thank You that Your provision is far greater than our need. We ask forgiveness for our doubting Your omnipotence when we present prayers that are too small. Stir us to faithfully present You with big, bold, and passionate prayers.*

# August 4                                       Rest in Him

*Then Jesus said, "Let's go off by ourselves to a quiet place and rest awhile." He said this because there were so many people coming and going that Jesus and his apostles didn't even have time to eat.*                 Mark 6:31 (NLT)

The disciples had just returned from what was apparently an intensive mission. Their activities had created much interest. So many people were coming and going that the disciples had no time even to eat. Since the disciples were obviously tired from their missionary activities and from the demands of the crowds, Jesus decided to seek rest for them.

We live in a culture where rest is often viewed negatively. We work hard; play hard; and fill our lives with endless activities. We put rest at the end of our *to-do list.* Even if we are filling our time doing God's work, we become vulnerable to worldly influences, as well as reactions to those influences, when we deprive ourselves of the necessary rest—designed by God for us to have.

It's not a surprise that we are living in turbulent times, and no one is more pleased about that than Satan. We are certainly in a battle with this invisible enemy. And because of that, we need to prepare for battle each day. A vital part of that preparation must include rest—for our bodies and for our souls. In addition to sleeping or an occasional nap, rest involves quiet time with the One Who can restore us and give us strength. We need to be mindful if we start running on empty. When this happens, we need to fill our tanks with God's Word, His love, and His peace. Just as Jesus did with His disciples, we need to seek the necessary rest and refreshment from our wearisome activities we experience each day—rest in Him.

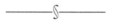

*Father God, thank You for the wonderful way in which You designed us. We can always find rest in Your presence from our toils, as well as refuge from our fears and worries. Guide us to refocus our time and energy on You each day. We can find rest in You to renew our spirit and give us strength when we are weary, overwhelmed, anxious, or fearful.*

# August 5                               Direct Access

*"Through Him we have obtained access to this grace in which we stand, and we rejoice in our hope of sharing the glory of God."*           Romans 5:3 (RSV)

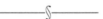

To understand this let's go back to the book of Genesis and read the story of the transgression of Adam and Eve, and how God drove them out of the Garden of Eden. Man was no longer to have immediate access into the Presence of God because God can't be around sin. Since then, whenever He interacted with anyone, He did so on a restricted basis. After God made a covenant with Moses at Mount Sinai, He promised to be in the midst of his people in the Tabernacle. Even then, however, it was only the High Priest who could enter God's immediate presence. Only once a year on— the Day of Atonement—the High Priest had to go through complex rites of purification and cleansing before he dared enter the Holy of Holies. People could draw near to God, but no one was allowed direct access into His presence, except the High Priest under the circumstances just described.

A massive curtain of several folds and layers, which was far more difficult to destroy than a huge wooden door, kept people out of the Holy of Holies. This veil was a reminder to the people that God was inaccessible. The veil hung in the Temple in Jerusalem until the hour of the death of Christ. At the moment Christ died on the cross, the veil of separation was torn in two—as if a giant hand had reached down from heaven and ripped it like tissue paper from top to bottom. Why? Because the barrier between God and man was removed. The sin of man was now atoned for, and those who are justified are now able to come into the presence of God—not by merit but by God's grace and mercy. We now have direct access to God.

*Almighty God, despite what is going on in our world, we are so blessed that we live in an age when we do have direct access to you 24/7. We no longer have to go through a human high priest to communicate on our behalf. Your Holy Spirit resides in us and now we can share in Your glory.*

# August 6                                Teach Me

*"Teach me Your way, O Lord; I will walk in Your truth; Unite my heart to fear Your name."*                      Psalm 86:11 (NKJV)

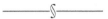

From the beginning, God gave men and women freedom of choice. From God's perspective, there are only two options to choose from—one that is righteous and in accordance with God's will, and the other that leads to sin and evil. In this Psalm, David is expressing his desire to walk in the path that God would prefer he take. We should pray the same for us. Most of us instinctively pray for quick deliverance or answer to our requests. We must remember, God is not a genie in a bottle—He is our Creator. But David prays that he will learn God's ways so that he will walk in obedience to God's truth. He prays that his loyalty will not be dispersed or split up, but rather be united or single-minded. His desire is to be wholly devoted to God—and only God.

This is how to experience the most amazing relationship ever. It is essential to let the ways of God become the controlling force in our lives. Knowing His ways for every situation we encounter is a life-long pursuit. It involves a willingness to *learn*, then a desire to *follow* His ways. Our relationship with God doesn't get much closer than when we truly commit ourselves to seek His truth through Scripture; listen to the guidance of His Holy Spirit; and choose to walk in the path He has designed for each of us to follow.

*Lord, You are truly the only Source of all that is righteous. We ask for a more disciplined heart in order genuinely grow in the grace and knowledge of You. Let Your Word guide our steps each day. Let our ears be tuned into Your voice and drown out the voices of this world. Unite our hearts with Yours, to worship You above all else.*

# August 7                                          Escape Corruption

*"And because of His glory and excellence, He has given us great and precious promises. These are the promises that enable you to share His divine nature and escape the world's corruption caused by human desires."*

2 Peter 1:4 (NLT)

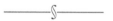

Participating in the divine nature simply means that as believers—through the power of the Spirit—we begin to change positively and demonstrate more and more of the character of God in our lives. At the same time, we demonstrate less and less of the character of the society. As a result, we escape the internal decay or rottenness that accompanies so much of the evil desires of the world. Peter wrote a great deal about false prophets or teachers in churches, yet some of what he wrote in his letters can also be applied to our influencers in our schools and governments—local, state, federal. We can't avoid the negative impact evil and corruption has on our life, but we don't have to take it lying down either. We can fight back because we have God on our side.

Suffering and pain will accompany the battles of this life, yet God has promised us that victory is certain. None of us who have endured attacks by the enemy emerges without some measure of pain. The battle will shake us, shock us, and often leave ugly scars. But what happens when the dust settles? We are blessed with the benefits that come with God's heavenly version of the *Purple Heart.* We find comfort in God's promise that He will perfect us; He will confirm us; He will strengthen us; and He will establish us.

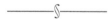

*Heavenly Father, Your promises are true and unfailing. They give us hope in this broken and corrupt world. It seems to be getting worse each day. Please give us strength and courage to combat this corruption. We trust that You will ultimately rid this world of all evil and that we will have eternal peace with You.*

# August 8                                         Build an Ark

*The earth was corrupt before God and filled with violence. God looked on the earth and saw it was corrupt, for all flesh had corrupted their way on the earth. So God said to Noah, "The end of all flesh is come before Me, for the earth is filled with violence because of them. Now I will destroy them with the earth. Make an Ark of cypress wood for yourself."*  Genesis 6:11-14 (MEV)

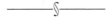

In the Gospels of Luke and Matthew, Christ teaches that the days before the rapture and the Tribulation will be like the days of Noah. We are living in the *days of Noah* today. We see such parallels as the multiplication of people in the population explosion; moral corruption of every kind; unspeakable violence; lack of conscience; and true believers being in a minority. The characteristics of those awful and tragic days in Noah's time, strange as they may seem to our *enlightened* culture today, are starting to be repeated, and will explode in the last days of this present age. It is urgently important—from the standpoint of both understanding past history and seeking guidance for the future—that we understand the events, which took place in the days of Noah.

God's sorrow at man, and the grief in His heart, are striking. This does not mean that creation was out of control, nor does it mean that God hoped for something better but was unable to achieve it. God knew all along that this was how things would turn out, but the Bible tells us loud and clear that as God sees His plan for the ages unfold, it affects Him. God is not unfeeling in the face of human sin and rebellion. His heart is broken over men and women who choose to live without Him; rebelling against His laws; and ignoring His kindness.

*Heavenly Father, we need You. History is repeating itself and we are in midst of it. We are willing to fight with You as our Commander.*

# August 9                                    Spared

*"I will bring a flood of waters on the earth to destroy all flesh, wherever there is the breath of life under heaven, and everything that is on the earth will die. But I will establish My covenant with you; you must go into the Ark—you, and your sons, and your wife, and your sons' wives with you. Bring every living thing of all flesh, two of every kind, into the Ark to keep them alive with you."* Genesis 6:17-19 (MEV)

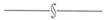

The Bible says *"Noah was a righteous man"* not because he was perfect or had a preceding righteousness, but because he believed God. Noah was no doubt a sinner—being human—but he had believed God's promises and sought—by God's grace—to obey His word and follow His will. Though Satan had managed to corrupt the whole world, the one man whom he wanted most of all to destroy, was under the invulnerable protecting shield of the grace of God.

In Genesis 6:10, we are introduced to Noah's three sons by name— Shem, Ham, and Japheth. They had all been born within the last century before the Flood, and they had lived in the midst of this corrupt society all their lives. The marvel is that they themselves somehow escaped the corruption. Had it not been for the example and teachings of their godly parents and grandparents, no doubt they also would have been inundated in the wickedness. One factor, which possibly helped, was that Noah probably kept them busy for many years in building the Ark and making preparations for the Flood. Besides Noah's family, God saved two of each kind of animal for His re-start of the world. His Creation was not a mistake, but God knew before Creation that this *do-over* would be necessary.

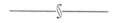

*God, it breaks our heart to know that we have broken Yours. We know there are no half-measures in dealing with sin. At the same time, we know that there are no half-measures in effecting salvation. Thank You, Lord, for Your grace and mercy.*

# August 10        He Simply Obeyed

*Noah did this; he did all that God commanded him.*
Genesis 6:22 (MEV)

According to God's instructions, the Ark was to be designed for capacity and floating stability rather than for speed or navigability. Building the ark required careful planning and engineering and a century of sweat, as well as obedience to God's command. We are not told exactly when God's instructions to Noah were given, though it was probably soon after His prophetic warning that man would have only 120 more years before judgment would come (Genesis 6:3). The work probably was going on throughout most of the century immediately preceding the Flood.

At the time Noah began building his Ark, it must have seemed ludicrous to the people in his community. They had never seen any kind of flood—or even rain for that matter (Genesis 2:5)—and Noah's preaching and construction work no doubt gave them much occasion for ridicule. Nevertheless, Noah had been warned by God of things not yet seen and, believing God's Word, he proceeded steadfastly to complete the task. Specifically, God said that only eight people would be on board: Noah, his wife, his three sons, and their wives. God foreknew that none from that generation would be converted through Noah's preaching and so all would perish in the waters of the Flood. Of course, there were some believers during the construction phase—e.g., Lamech, Methuselah—but the would die before the coming of the flood. The tasks God had given Noah to do were monumental, extremely difficult and discouraging, and yet Noah never questioned or complained. He simply obeyed!

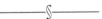

*Heavenly Father, this is a wonderful example of trust, faith, and obedience. We don't know what lies ahead in our future on earth, yet all we can do is to obediently put our trust and faith in You alone.*

*In the six hundredth year of Noah's life, in the second month, on the seventeenth day of the month, the same day, all the fountains of the great deep burst open and the floodgates of the heavens were opened. The rain fell upon the earth for forty days and forty nights.*

Genesis 7:11-12 (MEV)

———§———

Having entered the Ark six days earlier, Noah, the animals, and his family had to wait in the Ark seven days for the rain to come. They had never seen rain up to this time. This was a real test of faith—to wait a week after more than 100 years of preparation. They all entered with Noah evidently being last. Then a remarkable thing took place. Once inside, verse 16 states *"The Lord shut him in."* How God did this is not recorded, but somehow the door to the Ark was shut and sealed, without the help of any human hands. This provided a final assurance to the occupants that they were in the will of God and under His protection.

The old world was forever dead to them from that moment on. They had drowned in their sin. Noah and his family were given a new life and they were to live in a new world. The Ark of safety endured the battering of the Flood, which destroyed the world of the ungodly. In its history, the earth has suffered much under the effects of the *Original Sin in the Garden.* Heat; cold; fires; floods; droughts; earthquakes; volcanic eruptions; and all kinds of physical upheavals have disturbed its crust and the inhabitants dwelling on its surface. But immeasurably greater in magnitude and extent than all other catastrophes combined was the great Flood. In our modern age of scientific skepticism, the enormity of this great event of the past has been all but forgotten. It would be prudent to remember it as God remembered Noah.

———§———

*Almighty God, although we are not experiencing a catastrophic event like the Great Flood, we are drowning in the evil and corruption of our nation and world. God, You are our Ark where we find protection.*

# August 12             He Never Forgets

*God remembered Noah and every living thing and all the livestock that were with him in the Ark. So God made a wind to pass over the earth, and the water receded.*

                                          Genesis 8:1-2 (MEV)

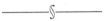

When we're going through a storm, it's easy to feel forsaken. Feeling forsaken is a normal human emotion that most of us have experienced, whether we admit it or not. Even Jesus cried out from the cross, *"My God, My God, why have You forsaken Me?"* (Matt. 27:46) The word "remember" in verse 1 doesn't mean to call something to mind that may have been forgotten. God can't forget anything because He knows the end from the beginning. Rather, it means to fulfill a promise and act on behalf of somebody.

Noah, his family, and the animals had been together in the Ark for over a year, which is a lot of *togetherness*. Did they ever get impatient with each other or with the animals? We can only imagine. There's no record that God spoke to them after He had shut them into the ark, so perhaps somebody in the family experienced an occasional fleeting fear that maybe God didn't care for them anymore. God not only remembered Noah and his family, but He also remembered the animals that were with them in the Ark. God spared these creatures so they could live on the renewed earth and reproduce after their kind. It was His desire that His creatures enjoy the earth and contribute to the happiness of the people He had created in His own image. We can depend on Him no matter what our circumstances or no matter how we feel.

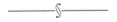

*Almighty God, we can be sure that You never forget or forsake us, not only because of Your promises, but also because of Your character. You are love, faithful, constant, perfect, and holy. May we be as devoted to You as You are to us.*

*Then God spoke to Noah, saying, "Go out of the Ark, you and your wife, and your son and your sons' wives with you. Bring out with you every living thing of all flesh that is with you, birds and animals, and every creeping thing that creeps on the earth, so that they may breed abundantly on the earth and be fruitful and multiply on the earth."*

Genesis 8:15-17 (MEV)

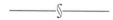

Where did the floodwaters go? Never underestimate the power of moving water! It's possible that the Flood greatly altered the contours of the land and created new areas for the water to fill, both on the surface of the earth and underground. Since there were eruptions from beneath the earth, whole continents and mountain ranges could have risen and fallen, creating huge areas into which the water could spill. The winds that God sent over the earth helped to evaporate the water and also move it to the places God had provided. A God powerful enough to cover the earth with water is also wise enough to know how to dispose of it when its work is done.

After he stepped out of the ark and stood on the renewed earth, Noah was so filled with gratitude that his first act was to lead his family in worship. He built an altar and offered some of the clean animals as sacrifices to the Lord. Noah was a balanced believer—he walked with God in loving communion; he worked for the Lord in building the Ark; he waited on the Lord for instructions concerning his leaving; and once he was standing on the earth, he worshiped the Lord. The true worship of the Lord had been restored on the earth. God blessed mankind with a fresh start.

*Heavenly Father, we ask that we, too, can be "balanced" believers. May we treasure our quiet moments with You; work for Your Kingdom; wait for Your instructions; and worship You always.*

       # Rainbow Promises

*"When I look and see the rainbow in the clouds, I will remember the agreement that continues forever. I will remember the agreement between Me and every living thing on the earth."*      Genesis 9:16 (ERV)

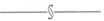

In this covenant, God promised unconditionally that He would never send another flood to destroy *all* life on the earth. He simply stated the fact that there would be no more universal floods. From that day on, Noah and his family could enjoy life and not worry every time the rain began to fall. God's covenant with Noah and the animal creation was sealed with the sign of the rainbow. Whenever people saw the rainbow, they would remember God's promise that no future storm would ever become a worldwide flood that would destroy humanity.

But the rainbow isn't only for us to see, for the Lord said, *"When I look and see the rainbow"* (Gen. 9:16). Certainly, God doesn't forget His covenants with His people, but this is just another way of assuring us that we don't need to be afraid. When we look at the rainbow, we know that our Father is also looking at the rainbow; and therefore it becomes a bridge that brings us together. The personal lesson for us is simply this: In the storms of life, always look for the rainbow of God's covenant promise. We may see the rainbow before the storm; we may see it in the midst of the storm; or like Noah, we may have to wait until after the storm. But we will always see the rainbow of God's promise if we look by faith.

*Heavenly Father, whenever we see a rainbow, we are in awe of its beauty. But more importantly, we are aware of Your promise. God, how blessed we are that despite our sinfulness, You still love and protect us from eternal separation from You. May we be as faithful as Noah and feel the security of Your Ark in our daily lives, until You return.*

*"The law of Moses could not make anything perfect. But now a better hope has been given to us, and with this hope we can come near to God."*     Hebrews 7:19 (NCV)

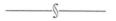

Mosaic law was written to point out the fact that we are sinful, and was intended to hopefully curb or restrain our commission of sin. Yet compliance or enforcement of moral or ceremonial law alone does not lead to salvation. The Old Covenant kept us apart from God, whereas the New Covenant—our faith in Christ—gives us a clear picture of God's grace and mercy, and allows us to freely have an intimate and eternal relationship with Him. Jesus has fulfilled the purpose for which the law was given.

The Mosaic Law was not totally useless; but just inadequate at building a meaningful relationship with God. Although the law performed a valuable function, its essential *inadequacy* was that it could not give life and spiritual energy to those who kept it—let alone to those who failed to do so. Its purpose was to offer a standard by which man could measure his own moral status. The new law offers us an unrestricted direct access to God—anytime and anywhere. That is huge! We no longer have to go through a human to speak to God on our behalf. God desires that we seek Him without barriers or interference. It is nice that we are living under the New Covenant.

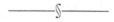

*Heavenly Father, we're so grateful that we are the time of the New Covenant. God, we pray that as You draw us nearer to You, that we will learn more of Your ways and apply them in our lives; that we will delight in humility; judge less harshly; forgive more easily; listen more intently; speak more softly; and love more deeply. God, thank You for the unlimited access to You through Your Holy Spirit.*

# August 16                                          Shout to the Lord

*"Shout to the Lord, all the earth; break out in praise and sing for joy!"*
Psalm 98:4 (NLT)

We must rejoice *shout to the Lord* whenever we draw near to Him for He is not only our Savior, but He is our King. Through whatever means possible, we are to rejoice and praise Him through singing, shouting, dancing, clapping, playing a musical instrument etc. Believe it or not, when done in a crowd, it becomes infectious—in a good way. May all this joy be directed to God. Think of the magnitude and volume of the praise Jesus received when He made His triumphant entry into Jerusalem. Sadly, this joyful display of worship turned dark as in just a few days, their singing of *"Hosanna! Blessed is the one who comes in the name of the Lord!* would quickly turn shouts of *"Crucify Him!"*

In light of the wonders of grace and righteousness displayed in God's salvation, all of creation is invited to unite in singing praises to Him. Praise is our expression of delight in God Himself; our response to God revealing Himself to us; our acknowledgment of His character and His acts; and our expression of the love we feel as we consider how great He is. It matters not, the way in which we worship God. He welcomes it all as a joyful noise—it is music to His ears. Perhaps our loud rejoicing can drown out the ugly chants of hate and evil pouring from the mouths of those who hate God and hate America.

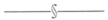

*Heavenly Father, it is an absolute honor to praise Your Name and worship You with exuberant shouts and songs of joy. Our salvation cannot remain quiet, and for that we cannot contain joy and jubilation of that fact. It is a delight to break out in praise for You. And during these times, we need to do it more emphatically.*

*"Where is another God like You, Who pardons the sins of the survivors among his people? You cannot stay angry with your people, for you love to be merciful."* Micah 7:18 (TLB)

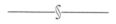

Once again through His mercy and grace, God has forgiven the repentant remnant of Jews who survived God's judgement of allowing enemy nations to invade Israel. As God kept his promise to Abraham, in the age of Moses and Joshua, by bringing Israel up out of the bondage of Egypt and into their inheritance of Canaan, He keeps His promise in Micah's time by delivering them from the hand of the Assyrians.

No God compares to the Lord in pardoning sin. Those who live by God's forgiveness must imitate it. If God had our human attitude regarding forgiveness, we would not have the blessed assurance of eternal life with our Creator. Forgiveness is a decision made in our hearts to refuse to live in the past. It is not an optional part of the Christian life. Our willingness to forgive is in direct proportion to our remembrance of how we have been forgiven. God has given us the perfect template of how to graciously forgive ourselves, and others. We *hold on* to the memory of abuse, betrayal, and all other wrongdoings we have experienced from others, yet God *forgives and forgets*. What a different world we would live in if more people would follow God's command and formula to forgive.

*Almighty God, thank You for Your infinite grace and mercy. Help us to break the cycle of bitterness that binds us to the wounds of yesterday. When we become hard on the inside to protect ourselves from further pain, help us to hear the gentle call of Your Holy Spirit to soften our hearts. Help us to be more like You, Jesus, by forgiving freely, graciously and completely.*

*"My dear brothers and sisters, always be willing to listen and slow to speak. Do not become angry easily, because anger will not help you live the right kind of life God wants."*

James 1:19-20 (NCV)

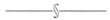

This letter by James is designed to correct a variety of disorders that existed among all of us. We are often rigid in our own opinions and less willing to hear what others have to offer—especially when those opinions greatly differ from ours. That has created a huge mess in our nation today. The shear unwillingness and adamant refusal to discuss, debate, or casually converse about the goings-on in our world is shameful and has led to a serious divide. Sadly, when discussions do arise, they often end up in angry reactions or outcomes. This pattern has grown monumentally in the past decade, that only God can rectify our current condition.

Anger is part of the makeup of our human nature. We feel that anger is caused by an event outside of ourselves, when actually it is not the event, but our interpretation and reaction to the event that makes us angry. The *experience* of anger is different from the *expression* of anger. James wants us to possess a teachable spirit, to which the willingness to listen is the key ingredient. Is there such a thing as anger without sin? We find the answer by looking at the emotions of Jesus. His anger was a righteous anger. His anger was not about self but about injustices against others and against God. Can we say that about our own anger?

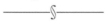

*Precious Jesus, You took on the anger of this world as You hung all alone on a cross. Yet, You felt no anger when You were tortured and crucified. Instead, You offered a prayer of forgiveness "Father, they know not what they do." God, we ask for strength to fully use the ears You have given us to listen to others, and to help us control our tongues when we speak.*

# August 19              Faith, Hope, Love

*"Three things will last forever—faith, hope, and love—and the greatest of these is love."*
1 Corinthians 13:13 (NLT)

The Apostle Paul wanted to address a serious concern with the church in Corinth—pride and arrogance. If untreated, this toxin would only lead to unbridled evil. We can see a similar situation today in our government—at all levels. The arrogance, greed, and thirst for power have brought our nation into a critical condition. Yet, there is hope—and that hope is found in Jesus!

From cover to cover, the Bible is God's love story to us. Faith, hope, and love are the most enduring of all human virtues, but even among these, love is the greatest because: Love is the root of faith and hope. While faith and hope are largely personal, love is focused on others. *Faith* is our trust in and commitment to God. *Hope* is linked with God, yet we cannot live without hope. *Love* is the very essence of God Himself. Without love, there would be no redemption and no eternal hope. Our love—though completely unlike Christ's in its measure—may be like His in its expression. Let's all get caught up in how God loves us and watch our lives respond by becoming more like Him. Let us all commit to keeping the love for one another alive, and heal our nation.

*Father God, You are love! It is Your very nature! You fill us with that love so that we might honor You as we love others with Your love. Mercy, grace, love, forgiveness, cleansing, and life eternal—all this and more You give to sinners like us. Thank You! God, enable us to bring to life the faith and hope we have in Christ by extending love to one another. Give us strength to endure all that may try to get in our way of that love.*

# August 20          Stay Alert

*"Stay alert! Watch out for your great enemy, the devil. He prowls around like a roaring lion, looking for someone to devour. Stand firm against him, and be strong in your faith."*

1 Peter 5:8-9 (NLT)

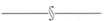

C. S. Lewis once suggested that there are two mistakes Christians make in talking about Satan—we either joke about him, or we ignore him. Biblically, Satan or the devil is described as the prince of this world. His residence is on this earth, and he moves from place to place. Because this earth is the devil's territory, believers are constantly under attack. Additionally, the Bible speaks of the devil as a personal spiritual being in active rebellion against God. He leads many demons like himself. Peter envisions the devil as a cunning and evil personal being who has the ability to attack Christians and to disrupt the life and unity of the church. We must never allow ourselves to underestimate the adversary's ability to outwit, deceive, and attack us.

Satan's aim is to destroy the faith we have in our Lord and Savior, Jesus Christ. Through his tempting; false teachings; and lies, he wants us to abandon our faith in God, and our relationship with Him. These days Satan is on rampage and infecting people with his evil. He knows his time on earth is limited, so he is holding nothing back. We can see his influence throughout our nation and world. We must always be clear-headed, vigilant, and control our affection to worldly things. Equipping ourselves with the Word of God will help us to discern truth from lies. Our ability to stand firm against Satan's deceptive attacks comes from the power of the Holy Spirit, not our own. We must stay alert!

*Lord, thank You for being our Comforter, Counselor, and Protector through Your ever-present Holy Spirit. There is no stronger foundation than Your Truth, upon which our faith is built. God, help us to remain steadfast in our faith and give us the ability to discern truth from lies. Use us to be a light to others, who have been deceived also by the prince of darkness.*

# August 21                    Momentary Troubles

*"For our light and momentary troubles are achieving for us an eternal glory that far outweighs them all. So we fix our eyes not on what is seen, but on what is unseen, since what is seen is temporary, but what is unseen is eternal."* 2 Corinthians 4:17-18 (NIV)

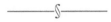

Being a Christ follower does not make us immune to troubles, set-backs, or challenges in this life. The intent of this verse is *not* to deny we have problems; to down-play the seriousness of our difficulties; or to inspire us to take *pleasure* in our suffering. Instead, the purpose is to shift our focus from our problems to our eternal future—where there will be the absence of troubles of any kind. The Apostle Paul is asking us to put on our eternal glasses and look to our eternal future to carry us through our troubles and give us hope.

What lies ahead for our eternal souls far outweighs any problems or suffering we may be experiencing in the present. This was Paul's attitude, which allowed him to refer to the physical suffering he had endured as "light." The faith we have in our eternal future with God provides us with a bit of understanding when we ask "why?" regarding our circumstances. The good news we never have to endure our problems and challenges alone, for God has promised to be with us. There is no affliction that we have to face alone, for He has promised to provide us with the sufficient strength we need to endure it and supply us with the hope of eternity. The present world, including the physical body of a Christian, is subject to decay or corruption. The world, which is to come, including the glorious resurrection body of believers, is eternal and incorruptible.

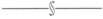

*God, this is our comfort when we are going through difficult times in our lives. We ask for the strength, courage, and vision to equip us to look beyond our pain, elective or not. You are our paramount focus of what is on the other side of our suffering, and our faith lies in knowing that in the end, we will be with You for eternity.*

# August 22                                      No Excuse

*"For ever since the world was created, people have seen the earth and sky. Through everything God made, they can clearly see his invisible qualities—His eternal power and divine nature. So they have no excuse for not knowing God."*     Romans 1:20 (NLT)

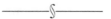

What do we imagine God to look like? Is He like the witty cigar-smoking character that George Burns played? Is he the long-bearded bigger-than-life being with a scowl on his face? Is the god of our imagination simply that—imaginary? Our One True God has revealed Himself throughout the Bible, and He doesn't quite fit the previous descriptions.

Seeing the beauty and complexity of creation carries with it the responsibility of acknowledging there is a Creator. The Apostle Paul is indicating in this verse that to witness God in nature is so clear and so constant that ignoring it is indefensible.

All we need to do is look around to see the works of the Workman to know that there is only One, Sovereign God. Yet, stopping there will not allow us the privilege of sharing eternity with our Creator. Through various means, God has invited us to discover more than His creation; He invites us to discover His truth, His Word, and His infinite love for us. When He knocks, we must answer and seek Him with fresh eyes, ears, and hearts so we can discover His awesomeness, and share it with others. If we do not believe in God, it is because we are suppressing the truth about God—denying God's own revelation of who He is. And for that, we have no excuse.

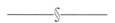

*Almighty God, thank You for Your glorious Creation. More importantly, God thank You for knocking on the door of our hearts because You wanted to give us the gift of Your life, and gift of Your love. God, use us to help remove the blinders of those who elect not to see and accept Your love and grace.*

## August 23                                      Faith Defeats Doubt

*John the Baptist, who was in prison, heard about all the things the Messiah was doing.*
*So he sent his disciples to ask Jesus, "Are you the Messiah we've been expecting, or should*
*we keep looking for someone else?"*                      Matthew 11:2-3 (NLT)

———§———

The definition of doubt is 'uncertainty' or 'questionable.' Matthew informs us about John's doubts, which lead him to send his followers to question Jesus. John's doubts may have been prompted by Jesus' works that may not have fit his preconceptions of what the Messiah would be like. Or perhaps in his discouraging and lonely time in prison, his uncertainty temporarily grew a bit, wondering why Jesus would allow His forerunner to languish in prison. Or, maybe John sent his disciples to Christ for *their* satisfaction—to counter their doubt about Who Jesus truly was. Remember, Satan introduced doubt into the world when he caused Eve to question if God *really* said that she and Adam should not eat from the tree of knowledge of good and evil.

Doubt is not the opposite of faith, but the opportunity of faith—the growing pains of an eager, seeking spirit. Doubt asks questions—unbelief refuses to hear answers. The Bible is full of people who doubted. They weren't heroes for simply having doubts; they were heroes for confronting and conquering them with God's help. We can have confidence, even in the things we cannot see, because God has proven Himself righteous, faithful, and true. If we doubt God's ability to respond to our prayer requests, what would be the point of asking in the first place? In order for us to have faith in God, we must study to know what He has said. Once we have an understanding of what God has done in the past; what He has promised us for the present; and what we can expect from Him in the future; we are able to act in faith instead of doubt.

———§———

*Heavenly Father, we thank You for allowing us to come to You when we experience doubt.*
*Genuine wisdom can only be found in You, so teach us to turn to You for wisdom, truth,*
*and understanding so that our doubt can be erased, and our faith can grow even deeper.*

*"God has also given us a desire to know the future. God certainly does everything at just the right time. But we can never completely understand what he is doing."*

Ecclesiastes 3:11 (ICB)

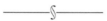

It's hard to fully understand the present, let alone the future. Life is a mystery. We can't explain why bad things happen to good people, while the crooked and corrupt go unpunished. We are inundated each day how people in power are doing things that are so destructive to our nation. So many people get caught for criminal acts, but aren't held accountable. On the flip-side, other people who don't possess radical or woke views on life and justice—are punished for lesser acts. It is hard to understand how far God will allow this corruption and destruction of our nation to continue. We need to trust that God will keep His promises to administer His judgement and wrath against wickedness.

Instinctively, we ponder our future and sometimes think we control it. Yet, God has ordained and designed the human experience. Every aspect of His administration of affairs is flawless and beautiful in its own time. All the events of life are marked by harmony of purpose, which God has determined. Since we can't unravel the mysteries of God, we should instead concentrate on seeking and accepting God's will for our lives. Since we can't grasp the good that may come out of difficult circumstances, we should instead place greater trust in God's providence, and respond obediently when He calls us into action. We just have to wait on His direction.

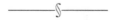

*Lord, even when Your will seems too difficult, we pray for trusting hearts when we are experiencing situations we simply don't understand. We will never comprehend Your extraordinary ways, yet help us to not look too far ahead and thus miss the joy of our day-to day living for, and serving such a loving God as You.*

# August 25                   Quality Recipe

*"And beside this, giving all diligence, add to your faith virtue; and to virtue knowledge; and to knowledge temperance; and to temperance patience; and to patience godliness; and to godliness brotherly kindness; and to brotherly kindness charity."* 2 Peter 1:5-7 (KJV)

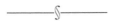

These verses remind us that God has given us all that is necessary for the divine life. And, because He has, we must be diligent in cultivating it. There must be a desire, determination, and discipline on our part. We must supplement our faith by exercising specific characteristics in order to live more Christ-like lives. The first is virtue, or the courage to stand up for what is right. This courage is to be supplemented with the knowledge of spiritual truth through studying the Bible. Next, under the operation of the Holy Spirit, we can demonstrate discipline and self-control when it comes to greed, excess, or temptations of this world. While temperance has to do with the *pleasures* of life, patience relates primarily to the *pressures* or *problems* of life. Godliness describes a person who is right in his/her relationship with God, as well as his/her fellow man. Finally, we can show kindness and love by giving our time, our talents, and our treasures for others.

This recipe begins with faith and ends with kindness. Once prepared, it is the foundation of exhibiting Christ-likeness in our lives, and love in our hearts.

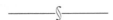

*Almighty God, thank You for being the steadfast, ever-present Source of all that we need. We confess that so often we fail to honor You by not utilizing all the gifts and resources You have supplied for us to live lives that please You and serve others. God, we pray for Your guidance to get our priorities right by putting You above all else. We pray for a deeper faith that comes to life through our exercising temperance, patience, kindness and generosity despite whatever challenges we may face. Give us a hunger and thirst for Your Word. We trust in You and love You.*

## August 26                                     Seek Wisdom

*"If you need wisdom, ask our generous God, and he will give it to you. He will not rebuke you for asking. But when you ask Him, be sure that your faith is in God alone."*

James 1:5-6 (NLT)

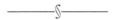

Should we only seek wisdom when we are faced with important decisions to make, or when we find ourselves in challenging situations? The truth is that we should be on a daily quest for wisdom—God's wisdom. We need to have teachable and willing spirits to recognize our lack of and need for wisdom—before decisions are made.

We make decisions every day; some are more difficult than others. Wisdom is required because we don't always choose what is in alignment with God's will. Wisdom is a gift from God and is the practical application of His teachings to everyday situations. It is not automatic, and therefore must be sought. Yet, we must approach God in faith and believe that He loves and cares for us and that nothing is impossible with Him. If we doubt His goodness and power, we will have no stability in times of trouble. We can fearlessly approach God, and He will be overjoyed to hear us. He will pour out wisdom when we ask Him in faith. God is unreserved and unwavering in His intent to give us His gift of wisdom to those of us who ask.

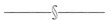

*Father God, You are always watching over us and ready to give us much needed wisdom whenever it is needed. God, forgive us when we fail to seek Your counsel and receive Your divine wisdom when we are faced with important decisions. Lord, we faithfully come to You now through prayer and through studying Your Word. We ask for wisdom to make decisions in our lives that will be beneficial, righteous, and in harmony with Your will. God, we are so grateful that You enjoy hearing from us when we offer prayers to You.*

*"We have not stopped praying for you since the first day we heard about you. In fact, we always pray that God will show you everything He wants you to do and that you may have all the wisdom and understanding His Spirit gives. Then you will live a life that honors the Lord, and you will always please Him by doing good deeds. You will come to know God even better."*                     Colossians 1:9-10 (CEV)

Despite not having yet visited the church in Colosse, the Apostle Paul was praying for them from a Roman prison. He wanted to impress upon them to resist the false teachings they had received that were causing confusion. This intercessory prayer was for the Colossians to gain true spiritual wisdom.

The true purpose of spiritual wisdom and understanding is to enable Christians to live our lives in a way that fully pleases and honors God. How do we acquire spiritual wisdom and understanding of His will for our lives? We do so by investing our time through prayer and continual study of God's Word. God doesn't reveal His will just to satisfy our curiosity. Rather, He does it so we might live fruitful lives. Although a person is not saved *by* good works, he most certainly is saved *for* good works. Knowing God is itself an activity. Obedience and service are a form of devotion. The return on this wise investment of our time is priceless and eternal. Spiritual wisdom reveals itself in a transformed character.

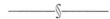

*God, forgive us when we veer off our spiritual path. God, stir in our hearts to have the desire to diligently invest our time in You, Your Word, and Your will. Forgive our foolish thinking that our guidance could come from anywhere but You. God, help us to exercise discipline in spending more time in Your Word, and growing in our relationship with You. We want grow in our wisdom of You, and have all of our decisions be ones that honor and please You.*

# August 28                                      The Biggest Test

*Sometime later God tested Abraham. He said to him, "Abraham!" "Here I am," he replied. Then God said, "Take your son, your only son, whom you love—Isaac—and go to the region of Moriah. Sacrifice him there as a burnt offering on a mountain I will show you."*                                      Genesis 22:1-2 (NIV)

What? Are you kidding? Sacrifice my own child? Yes, this is the test that God gave to Abraham—who had been faithful to God. The test was very real; he was to give his son Isaac back to God. Not every difficult experience in life is necessarily a personal test from God. Of course, any experience *could* become a test or a temptation, depending on how we deal with it. Sometimes our own disobedience causes the pain or disappointment. Sometimes our hurts are simply a part of normal human life. As we grow older, friends and loved ones relocate or even die; physical challenges come into play; life changes around us; and we must make painful adjustments.

We must learn to distinguish between *trials* and *temptations*. Temptations come from our desires within us; while trials come from the Lord who has a special purpose to fulfill. Temptations are used by the devil to bring out the worst in us; but trials are used by the Holy Spirit to bring out the best in us. Temptations seem logical while trials seem very unreasonable—as in the trial that God put before Abraham. Abraham, however, did not know that it was only a test. God commanded Abraham to take Isaac to Moriah and sacrifice him—his beloved son—as a burnt offering. Abraham trusted God and obediently followed His order.

*Heavenly Father, the test You gave to Abraham is one that many of us would find impossible to fulfill. God, help us trust that You would not ask us to do anything that would cause great harm. May our faith be as strong as Abraham's.*

*So Abraham placed the wood for the burnt offering on Isaac's shoulders, while he hims(
carried the fire and the knife. As the two of them walked on together, Isaac turned
Abraham and said, "Father?" "Yes, my son?" Abraham replied. "We have the f(
and the wood," the boy said, "but where is the sheep for the burnt offering?" "God w(
provide a sheep for the burnt offering, my son," Abraham answered. And they bo(
walked on together.*

Genesis 22:6-8 (NL1

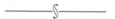

Can we even imagine the wrenching in Abraham's heart? The son fc
whom he had waited for one hundred years was about to be taken away—
would he still follow God? Our faith is not really tested until God asks u
to bear what seems unbearable; do what seems unreasonable; and expec
what seems impossible. Abraham heard God's command and immediatel
obeyed it by faith. He knew that God's will never contradicts God's promis
so he held on to the promise *"for Isaac is the son through whom your descendan(
will be counted"* (Gen. 21:12). Abraham believed that somehow, in some way
God would spare Isaac's life through this ordeal.

Do we have that kind of faith in God? When the going gets tough, do w
have a mind that defaults—not to brainstorming our own solutions, but t(
brainstorming the miraculous ways God might work the situation out fo
our good and His glory? To reverence God as sovereign, we must trus
Him implicitly and obey Him without question. If we do, then we will hav(
enough light at the end of the tunnel to keep going—and to do what Go(
says! God will provide!

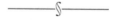

*Heavenly Father, we marvel at the strength of Abraham's faith, not to mention Isaac's
who believed that You would provide the sacrifice. God, it is refreshing to see children hav(
the faith of their parents.*

*When they arrived at the place where God had told him to go, Abraham built an altar and arranged the wood on it. Then he tied his son, Isaac, and laid him on the altar on top of the wood. And Abraham picked up the knife to kill his son as a sacrifice. At that moment the angel of the Lord called to him from heaven, "Abraham! Abraham!" "Yes," Abraham replied. "Here I am!" "Don't lay a hand on the boy!" the angel said. "Do not hurt him in any way, for now I know that you truly fear God. You have not withheld from Me even your son, your only son." Then Abraham looked up and saw a ram caught by its horns in a thicket. So he took the ram and sacrificed it as a burnt offering in place of his son.* Genesis 22:9-13 (NLT)

———§———

Just as Abraham, hands trembling and forehead dripping with sweat, draws his killing knife, the Lord comes through, as promised. Abraham had passed the test! He had laid aside his doubts and fears and done what God said. Did God know ahead of time what Abraham would do? Yes. The Bible teaches that God always knows the end from the beginning. Abraham's faith and obedience set the bar quite high. Through his willingness and obedience, Abraham did indeed love and trust God to the fullest. Our best evidence of fearing God is our faith to serve and honor Him with that which is dearest to us. This is a portrayal of an obedient servant worshiping God in faith and at great cost, and in the end receiving God's provision.

And because of Jesus' sacrifice, we won't be tested in this manner. There was no substitute for Jesus. Jesus was acting as the substitute for *us all.* There was no ram in the thicket for Him because He Himself was *our* ram in the thicket. God gave Isaac to Abraham, and Abraham gave Isaac back to God. What two men did on a lonely altar would one day bring blessing to the whole world!

———§———

*Almighty God, Abraham did not withhold his son, and You did not spare Yours. Isaac felt neither knife or fire and was with his loving father. Jesus was tortured beyond belief and forsaken by You because of our sin. God, what a reminder of Your greatness.*

*"I became a servant of the church when God gave me the work of telling you His entire message. In the past God hid this mystery, but now he has revealed it to His people. God wanted His people throughout the world to know the glorious riches of this mystery—which is Christ living in you, giving you the hope of glory."*          Colossians 1:25-27 (GW)

The Apostle Paul calls the message he was to preach about the Gospel a "mystery." This terminology is not in reference to a "who done it" novel but instead means "secret." Since the beginning of mankind, God has given hints and prophecies about this mystery, yet it was still just that—a mystery.

So what exactly is this secret. Jesus Christ is the Secret! Secondly, the secret now revealed is that this Secret is available to everyone. Hidden for generations is now disclosed to all—including the Gentiles. For generation after generation God has communicated to us through His Word. God's Word tells that, *"In the beginning there was the Word. The Word was with God, and the Word was fully God... Now the Word became flesh and took up residence among us."* (John 1:1, 14) The secret is that the Word—Jesus Christ—lives in the hearts of those who have put their faith in Him.

Before Christ came to earth in the flesh, there was a great deal of animosity between the Jews and the Gentiles. Jesus came and broke the wall between them so that both Jews and Gentiles could experience the saving grace of Christ. The mystery revealed and the indwelling of Christ in believers' hearts is what made that miracle possible. We need a miracle of unity in Christ today to save our nation.

*Heavenly Father, we are blessed that You sent Your Son to have Your Word come to life. Forgive us when we act in a stingy fashion about You, because we must share Who You are with others instead of keeping You to ourselves. Thank You that we are beneficiaries of Your revealed mystery.*

# September 1                                     Fear Not

*After these things the word of the Lord came unto Abram in a vision, saying, "Fear not, Abram: I am thy shield, and thy exceeding great reward."*      Genesis 15:1 (KJV)

———§———

Throughout the Bible we are reminded by God to "fear not." In fact, in the King James Version, *fear not* is stated three-hundred sixty-five times— perhaps a good reminder for every day of the year. (I guess the only day we can be afraid is February 29th of a Leap Year.) There are two types of fear in the Bible: One type is fear or reverence of the Lord; being in awe of all that He is. The second type is the fear of being harmed or damaged in some manner. To overcome any type of fear requires that we put our total trust in God—our Shield; our Protector.

When the Bible says to us, "Fear not" or "Do not fear," we are to interpret that to mean we should not *succumb* to that fear, and we shouldn't let panic set into our hearts and minds. Instead, we are to lean on our faith. We are in a spiritual battle with Satan—the father of lies—who would love nothing more than for us to be in constant fear. Look at what the COVID crisis did to America. Mis-truths and fear tactics were utilized by those in charge to force unreasonable and unnecessary mandates that proved to be as harmful as the virus. Fear is a tool of the devil. We are *not* to fear the evil and corrupt plans and actions of wicked leaders, who unfortunately are running all levels of our government. Trust God because He is our Shield and is in total control, so fear not.

———§———

*Heavenly Father, we are so grateful for Your protection, and all the ways You calm our fears. Let Your Holy Spirit tug on our hearts to remind us that You are in control and all that You ask is that we put our total trust in You.*

# September 2                 Just Believe

*While Jesus was still speaking, some people came from the house of the synagogue leader. They said, "Your daughter is dead. There is no need to bother the teacher anymore." But Jesus paid no attention to what they said. He told the synagogue leader, "Don't be afraid; just believe."*        Mark 5:35-36 (NCV)

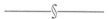

Jesus had experienced some challenging times in the synagogue. And Jairus, the synagogue leader was not really a fan of Jesus. So, it wasn't his fondness of Jesus that made him go to Him—it was his desperate need, and his fear that his daughter would die. In the meantime, Jesus performed another miracle for a woman with a bleeding disorder who had placed her faith in Him for healing. That act somewhat boosted Jairus' hope.

But Jesus challenged Jairus to believe big!—to believe in a resurrection instead of a healing. Though his faith wobbled through this, Jairus somehow broke through the fear and believed. When his friends approached to inform him that his daughter had died, Jesus told him to ignore their report. Jesus asked him to do, in spite of all the worldly-wisdom of the hired mourners who filled the house, to believe the impossible. Jesus went to Jairus' house and was mocked by the crowd for claiming that the little girl was simply asleep, not dead. The unbelief of the mourners shut them out of seeing the miracle. Jesus entered the house and went to where the little girl was lying. He tenderly told the dead girl to "arise." Faith can *always* trump fear!

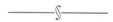

*Jesus, with Your calming voice You speak to our fears. You have cast out demons; healed the lame; given sight to the blind; calmed the raging sea; and restored life to the dead. We pray that whenever we are in doubt, in trouble, and especially when we are in fear, that we would trust and lean on You without fear, and just believe.*

# September 3                  Eternal Rock

*"You will keep in perfect peace all who trust in You, all whose thoughts are fixed on You! Trust in the Lord always, for the Lord God is the eternal Rock."*     Isaiah 26:3-4 (NLT)

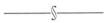

Faith is not a flash in the pan, but a life-long commitment because of the One in Whom it rests. Those who know Him to be a God of infinite wisdom will trust Him further than they can see Him. Those who know Him to be a God of almighty power will trust Him when troubles come. Those who know Him to be a God of infinite grace and goodness will trust Him even when we don't deserve such love. The more we trust God, the deeper and more intimate our relationship with Him grows. The better God is known, the more He is trusted.

It is so advantageous for us when we depend on God for guidance, protection, peace, and love. When we place our trust in the things of the world, the results are temporary and of little value. God is our eternal Rock, and when we build our life's foundation on that Rock, it will withstand any storm. We are called to a life-long trust that is based on God's rock-like faithfulness and His promise of eternal life with Him. God has promised peace for us who abide in Him. Let's make sure we don't let go of that promise.

*Heavenly Father, how blessed we are that You are a loving and trustworthy God. Often we forget that You invite us to lean on You in all our circumstances. In Scripture You have told us countless times to place our trust in You alone. God, when we do, we are blessed with a perfect peace we can't experience from any other source. God, help us to realize that our relationship with You can flourish to unimaginable levels if we would surrender and trust You like never before. It just doesn't get any better than that.*

# September 4            Faith Through Trials

*"God is keeping careful watch over us and the future. The Day is coming when you have it all—life healed and whole. I know how great this makes you feel, even though y₀ have to put up with every kind of aggravation in the meantime."*    1 Peter 1:5-6 (MSG)

In this life we face many trials or "walls" that with God's help, we can g₀ over, under, around, or through. Because of God's greatest sacrifice and th₀ resurrection of Christ, we are born again into a living hope filled with a₀ eager and confident expectation of the life to come. Because of His gift ₀ eternal salvation, we can experience a glorious joy through daily fellowshi₀ with Jesus Christ, even when we face the temporary walls in this life. Go₀ matches these temporary trials to our strength and growth needs.

There are a number of truths about trials. They are humbling and take ou₀ attention from self to God. They are difficult and painful. They are divers₀ and happen at different times, for different durations. They point us to th₀ genuineness of our faith. Though we don't rejoice over the trial itself, w₀ can rejoice over the result brought about by our God. We do not rejoic₀ because suffering is great. We do not rejoice because we're out of touc₀ with reality. We rejoice because we have a living hope; a permanen₀ inheritance; a divine protection; a developing faith in an unseen Savior; an₀ a guaranteed deliverance. Our eternal life begins now!

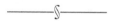

*Precious Jesus, may we revive our appreciation of the fact that Your death and resurrectio₀ means forgiveness, freedom, and the ability to walk with You through this fallen worl₀ into the eternal world that lies ahead. When we hit our walls, may we experience You₀ peace amidst the chaos and aggravations in our lives because of Your ever-present love₀ Your endless resources, and the assurance of an everlasting life with You.*

# September 5                    Angels Watching

*"God's purpose in all this was to use the church to display his wisdom in its rich variety to all the unseen rulers and authorities in the heavenly places. This was His eternal plan, which He carried out through Christ Jesus our Lord. Because of Christ and our faith in Him, we can now come boldly and confidently into God's presence."*

Ephesians 3:10-12 (NLT)

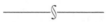

There have been cosmic dramas taking place from the beginning and into our present day. God is the Author and Director of this drama, and the church is the cast of actors. So who is the audience?—angels. Peter writes in his epistle, *"Even angels long to look into these things"* (1 Pet. 1:12) The mysteries of God have not yet been revealed to the angels, so they are watching HIS-tory unfold. And through all of this it is being presented to us, and because of Jesus, we too, get a front-row seat.

There is no limit to God's power; He is in control of everything! When we fully comprehend that fact, then we can boldly come to Him in prayer. This is an unspeakable privilege and liberty we have to enter His presence, all because of what Christ has done. We're not fooling God when our prayers withhold what is truly in our hearts—such as what we really need, or what we fear. Whether we actually bow our knees when we pray is not the important thing; that we bow our *hearts* and boldly surrender ourselves to faithfully ask Him for what we need is what's vital. God's answer to our prayer is always what He knows is best for us.

*Heavenly Father, we will never know all the mysteries of You this side of Heaven, yet we are blessed to be part of Your drama. Besides the angels watching this play out, may we invite those who have yet to surrender to You, get a peek at Who You are.*

# September 6                                    Seek, Not Stress

*"Seek first God's kingdom and what God wants. Then all your other needs will be met as well. So don't worry about tomorrow, because tomorrow will have its own worries. Each day has enough trouble of its own."* Matthew 6:33-34 (NCV)

We are to be in a constant pursuit of God's Kingdom. In other words, we are to seek the things of God as a priority over the things of the world. Our salvation is inherent in the kingdom of God and it is of greater value than all the world's riches. Everything in nature works together, because nature trusts God. Our Heavenly Father cares for us much more than all else He created, so why wouldn't we trust Him to care for our critical needs. When we seek first the Kingdom of God, we seek to feed our hearts with spiritual food; we seek to have spiritual garments of kindness, humility, patience, and love; and we seek to quench our thirst with the living water that Christ provides. Our allegiance is to Him first, and from this righteousness abounds.

Worry pulls us apart. The anxious heart receives all kinds of blows through anticipatory anxiety that will never happen. If we truly trust that we will have an eternal life of glory, grace, and unimaginable joy in the presence of God, how can we not trust that He will provide our needs now? God never promised freedom *from* trouble. But He did promise He would be with us during troubled times. These days we are experiencing pretty troubling times in our nation. But we don't need to worry because God is in this with us.

*Heavenly Father, we thank You for Your past blessings, the assurance of blessings to come, and for Your eternal promises. You are always faithful, even when we lack faith. God, going forward, our focus is on how we can further Your Kingdom. We trust that You will take care of our critical needs in this life because of the promise of eternal life with You. God, we ask to be used mightily by You to bless others, as an extension of Your arm. What a privilege it is to serve Your Kingdom.*

# September 7        Think About These Things

*"In conclusion, my friends, fill your minds with those things that are good and that deserve praise: things that are true, noble, right, pure, lovely, and honorable."*
Philippians 4:8 (GNT)

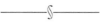

Our mind is the greatest treasure we have in terms of those gifts of human life. To protect it, our thoughts must be in concert with the Spirit of God. As our physical body needs exercise, so does our mind. Paul has given us six words that should guide our thought-life. As we think about such things, they will shape our attitudes and direct our words and actions. No word is spoken or action taken which did not first originate as a thought. And our thoughts are conditioned by repetition. As Paul identifies the objects of our thinking, we discover that they are grounded in God's revelation of Himself. The command is that our thought-life is to have a very regular orbit around things that are true, noble, right, pure, lovely, and honorable. So we must ask ourselves: "Am I filled with God's gift of peace and joy?" If the answer is "no," then perhaps it is because our thought-life may be out of orbit.

The things we allow our mind to dwell on will be revealed by the way we live. God does not force upon us the things about which we think. He has given us the ability to choose how we think, and ultimately how we behave. The truths of God give us direction for a Christ-like life, and an avenue for obedience, which results in a walk of peace with Him, and unspeakable joy.

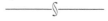

*Heavenly Father, Your written Word gives us an endless well of clear and refreshing water of truth. Forgive us when we lose sight of You and give our minds over to the world, instead of the Creator of the universe. Lord, strengthen us as we choose to give our thoughts and minds to you. Help us to take each thought captive and dwell upon those things that bring you glory and honor. God, we do have choices in this life—and we choose the joy that comes from You.*

*"The rain and snow come down from the heavens and stay on the ground to water th* *earth. They cause the grain to grow, producing seed for the farmer and bread for the hungr* *It is the same with My word. I send it out, and it always produces fruit. It will accomplis* *all I want it to, and it will prosper everywhere I send it."*     Isaiah 55:10-11 (NLT)

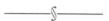

Rain is a heavenly gift that creates transformation by turning deadness int life, and producing nourishment. The Word of God, found in the Hol Scriptures, is His chosen instrument to achieve His purposes. God's Wor is seed. Just as the rain and snow are never wasted but accomplish Hi purposes, so His Word never fails. The Bible reveals His thoughts and ways sets His targets; voices His promises; and is powerful to achieve what i expresses. Just as rain enlivens and strengthens withering vegetation, God' Word produces life in our sinful hearts, enabling us to be fruitful in Hi Kingdom.

Now we know that God's promises not only last, they are life-sustaining Hope in the Gospel keeps us alive—it's our rain. Like rain to the crops God's Word it is a slow and silent work that transforms us in due time. Th promise of God to save sinners never fails. We never know when we shar just a little of God's Word, how it will flourish in someone's heart.

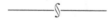

*God, we are so grateful for Your amazing grace, mercy, and love. You have uniquel* *designed for each of us to enjoy prosperous and successful lives. Yet, we cannot achieve that* *on our own. God, alone we cannot live the way You want us to live. We need the truth* *of Your Word and the guidance of Your powerful Spirit. God, we are so blessed to have* *the gift of Your Holy Scriptures to give us the daily nourishment our hearts require.*

# September 9                                    Active Faith

*"What good is it, dear brothers and sisters, if you say you have faith but don't show it by your actions? Can that kind of faith save anyone?"*                    James 2:14 (NLT)

Faith is not some kind of vague feeling that we concoct; faith is confidence that God's Word is true, and the conviction that acting on that Word will bring His blessing. Is it a prerequisite that we must do good works in order to be saved? No. Faith is the foundation. The kind of faith God wants us to have should naturally manifest itself into doing good for others. Our faith shouldn't just be an *intellectual* faith—knowing Scripture, but never applying it in real life. *Active* faith, on the other hand, is just that—active. People with active faith do not merely hold to ancient doctrines; they practice those doctrines in their everyday life.

As sinners, we are saved by God's loving grace. Yet, genuine saving faith leads to works. Our commitment is to surrender to God and have His Holy Spirit transform us to conduct ourselves in a Christ-like manner. God's love in our heart motivates us to obey Him and serve others. As our faith deepens, the evidence of that faith should flow out of us as good works that bless others and honor God. Do we merely *voice* that we have faith in our Lord and Savior? Or, are our hearts stirred by His truth to the point that we exercise genuine faith through our actions?

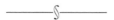

*Almighty God, how privileged we are to be recipients of Your loving mercy and saving grace. Forgive us for the times we just say we are followers of Christ, yet do nothing to demonstrate it. Ignite in us a fire that produces a passion to represent You to the world through our actions. God, we pray that our relationship with You deepens and that we will walk in ways that please You. We pray that we will bear the fruit of the works You have planned for us long ago. May our faith yield actions that honor and glorify You.*

*The Lord spoke His Word to Jonah, son of Amittai. He said, "Leave at once for the important city, Nineveh. Announce to the people that I can no longer overlook the wicked things they have done."* Jonah 1:1-2 (GW)

————§————

This was a tall order God gave Jonah, which we will get into more detail in the coming days. For now, we need to face some glaring similarities the wicked city of Nineveh had with the current state of the cities in our nation today. It didn't just happen overnight; it has been brewing for some time—and now it is coming to boil. The evil, corruption, violence and hate that is penetrating the fabric of America needs to be revealed and dealt with—immediately. We have an election coming in a couple of months, which is one of the tools we can use to combat this wickedness. Like God sent Jonah, He is sending us.

We can no longer deny what is taking place: carjacking; looting; defecation in our streets; pushing people down stairs or onto subway tracks; burning pro-life clinics; arrests and imprisonment of many innocent people who attended January 6th rally; adding ridiculous pronouns to our language; the lies, hypocrisy and withheld evidence regarding January 6th; the lies and hidden truths about the deadly side-effects of the *untested* COVID vaccines; the retribution for speaking up about the vaccine and ludicrous and harmful mandates, and the overall mis-handling of COVID itself; the lies about the open border which has created havoc on our cities with rampant human trafficking and thousands of Fentanyl overdoses; allowing transgender men to frequent women's locker and restrooms; public schools indoctrinating our children without parental knowledge; ending our energy independence; and reckless government spending resulting in an economic recession. This list is endless. We need God more than ever to remove Nineveh from our nation.

————§————

*God, we need You now to help us combat the destruction of our nation. You have been removed from our nation, but we are fighting to bring You back. Help us, God.*

## September 11                              Runaway Prophet

*Jonah immediately tried to run away from the Lord by going to Tarshish. He went to Joppa and found a ship going to Tarshish. He paid for the trip and went on board. He wanted to go to Tarshish to get away from the Lord."*                          Jonah 1:3 (GW)

———§———

Old Testament prophets ministered primarily within the borders of the nation of God's people, Israel. Yet, this time, God commissioned the prophet Jonah to deliver His message to Nineveh, a city located outside of Jonah's nation. Those living in this capital city of Assyria were pagan enemies of Israel; a civilization of murdering terrorists; and violent annihilators of everyone who stood in their path. Because of his utter disdain and hatred of the Ninevites, Jonah didn't want to deal in any way with them, especially with the *possibility* that they might receive mercy from God. Jonah didn't argue with God about the mission; he simply ran from it. Then he boarded a cargo ship to get as far away as possible from God. He was hoping that distance away from God's power would prevent God making him have to preach to an enemy of Israel—Assyria. What Jonah failed to understand is that whenever God calls us or commands us to do something, He enables us to do it.

What Jonah didn't realize was that he was being chased. Despite a head start, the prospect of escaping the God Who cared both for the soul of Jonah, as well as the souls of the Ninevites, was hopelessly doomed. It wasn't just bad luck on Jonah's part that his ship ran into a storm at sea. God orchestrated this disastrous event as part of His plan to get Jonah back on track. God's purposes were essentially restorative, rather than punitive.

———§———

*Heavenly Father, there are times in our life when we run away from You. We thank You that You are always in pursuit of us; to restore us and bring us back to Your presence. God, help us to be obedient to Your instruction and direction for our lives, and to trust You with our whole heart that You will be with us when we are called to "Nineveh" so that we don't run in the opposite direction to "Tarshish."*

# September 12                        Man Overboard

*The storm was getting worse. So they asked Jonah, "What should we do with you to calm the sea?" He told them, "Throw me overboard. Then the sea will become calm. I know that I'm responsible for this violent storm."*                      Jonah 1:11-12 (GW)

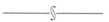

In the full teeth of the storm, Jonah could no longer ignore and run away from the truth that God, Who sent the storm, was also the only One Who can calm the storm. Through this storm, the rest of the crew on the ship were facing death, from which their gods could not save them. They suspected this supernatural storm had something to do with the runaway they brought on board. To end his turmoil, Jonah proposed that they throw him overboard to lighten the load on the ship. In their desperation, the crew's single remaining hope was the death of Jonah—a solution that came from the Lord via His prophet. If he dies, they live.

When we are in a storm, we must consider what should be done to the sin that raised the storm in the first place. It must be realized; confessed; and repented. Before throwing Jonah overboard, they prayed to Jonah's God that they would not be held responsible for Jonah's death. So, for a moment, at least, they acknowledged the One true God. Praise God for that storm. It was a sign that God was not yet through with Jonah. Our God is too merciful and too loving to let His children drift off into open rebellion without trying to save them. As Jonah was thrown overboard and the sea was closing over him, God commissioned a great fish.

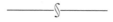

*Heavenly Father, as Jonah offered himself to be cast into the raging and stormy sea, we can't help reflect on the fact that Jesus did the same, and completed the ultimate sacrifice on the cross to save not only a boat full of people—but every single one of us. Praise Jesus!*

# September 13          Sanctuary in a Fish Belly

*From inside the fish Jonah prayed to the Lord his God. Jonah prayed: "I called to the Lord in my distress, and He answered me. From the depths of my watery grave I cried for help, and You heard my cry…" Then the Lord spoke to the fish, and it spit Jonah out onto the shore.*       Jonah 2:1-2; 10 (GW)

———§———

Out of Jonah's suffocating and unimaginable circumstance comes this amazing prayer. The man who recoiled at the thought of God extending mercy to Assyria, now knows that God better extend mercy to him or there's no future. We might wonder, where Jonah's prayer life had been hiding. He could have prayed *before* booking passage to Tarshish, or before his *nap* during the storm. He had plenty of chances, yet he waited until he was on death's doorstep.

The Lord used the sea as His hand of correction, and provided a great fish as a sanctuary for Jonah. The three days and nights Jonah spent in the belly of the fish was the time he needed to empty his sinful heart. Inside the fish, Jonah recognized his utter dependence on God. Inside the fish, God stripped the wayward prophet of his pride; his rebelliousness; and his self-righteousness. God removed these idols or spiritual distractions. In his distress, he allowed the Word of God—the Psalm he was quoting—to permeate his thoughts. This reminds us of the value of preserving God's Word in our hearts. God's Word softened Jonah's rebellious heart, and guided him to understand and acknowledge God's thoughts about him. When Jonah was ready to obey God, the fish was ready to release him.

———§———

*God, forgive us for our self-directed living that causes us to drift, and sometimes sprint away from You. Despite the depth of our sin, the truth is that Your grace and mercy is infinitely deeper.*

## September 14                    Second Chance

*Then the Lord spoke to Jonah again: "Go to that great city, Nineveh," He said, "and warn them of their doom, as I told you to before!" So Jonah obeyed and went to Nineveh. Now Nineveh was a very large city with many villages around it—so large that it would take three days to walk through it.*                    Jonah 3:1-3 (TLB)

————§————

The events of the third chapter of Jonah describe one of the greatest evangelistic campaigns to ever be recorded in the Bible. It shows what God can do with a frail human instrument. Jonah was given a second opportunity to obediently do the will of God—by preaching His message to an evil nation. Though Jonah had rebelled and completely blew it the first time God called him to this task, God still gave him a second chance, which demonstrates God's marvelous grace and forgiveness.

Like us, Jonah did not deserve a second opportunity, but thankfully we serve a God that is full of tender mercy. The first time God gave His orders, Jonah rose up to *flee*. But this time he rose up to *preach* God's warning. There was no delay; no procrastination; no waiting for a more convenient time; no running away. Jonah immediately obeyed. There are so many ways in which the Lord could have spoken to Jonah. He could have reminded him of the disasters surrounding the first commissioning. The Lord could have warned him that He was only going to give one last chance to prove himself—or He could have gently told him to *go*. The job of ridding the wickedness of Nineveh was just as urgent as God's first request of Jonah. The only change was in the heart of Jonah. The job of ridding the wickedness in our nation is also urgent!

————§————

*Heavenly Father, You are certainly a God of second-chances. We are so blessed that when we fail to follow Your will and direction for our lives, that You never give up on us. Thank You for Your amazing grace and mercy.*

# September 15                    They Repented

*"But the very first day when Jonah entered the city and began to preach, the people repented."*

Jonah 3:4 (TLB)

————§————

As soon as the people of Nineveh heard Jonah's bold and uncompromising message of warning and devastating judgment, the entire city—everyone without exception—turned to God in faith and gave evidence of genuine repentance of their sins. Jonah's successful preaching campaign had nothing to do with Jonah's ability, or the Assyrian's worthiness. God had a purpose beyond human understanding. If we take John 3:16 seriously, then we must conclude that before God showered Nineveh with grace, He reached to them with love. Perhaps we can look at God's choice to save the Assyrians differently. Maybe this represented God's plan to produce added good in the world by saving the worst people in the world. No doubt their murderous ways stopped—at least for a short time. In the end, the revival at Nineveh is nothing short of a sovereign work of forgiveness that produced change.

Repentance is more than saying "I'm sorry." It means following through on that conviction and turning around. It means changing our mind and transforming our heart so that we are no longer at odds with God, but instead are in perfect sync with Him. Change, repentance, and new life comes from God, not us. It was God, not Jonah, Whom the Ninevites believed. God is the hero of this story. He is a holy and just God Who would have every right—with no warning at all—to destroy all the Ninevites; all the pagan sailors in the boat; Jonah himself; and for that matter, all of us. This is about a God Who deserves all glory and worship. This story is about our holy God Who is patient with sinners; pursues the rebellious; and gives grace to the undeserving. He is a God of second chances!

————§————

*Father God, Your grace—Your transforming love and acceptance—is the most precious gift. You still love us in spite of ourselves. Our nation is rebellious and we ask for Your pursuit of us. We need Your divine intervention now.*

*Jonah was very upset about this, and he became angry. So he prayed to the Lord, "Lor isn't this what I said would happen when I was still in my own country? That's why tried to run to Tarshish in the first place. I knew that you are a merciful an compassionate God, patient, and always ready to forgive and to reconsider Your threats destruction. So now, Lord, take my life. I'd rather be dead than alive." The Lord aske "What right do you have to be angry?"*      Jonah 4:1-4 (GW)

———§———

Each chapter in the Book of Jonah has a story to tell—chapter one, *rebellic* chapter two, *repentance*; chapter three, *revival*; chapter, *resentment*. Eve though Jonah obeyed his second commission given to him by God, h wasn't happy about the outcome. Jonah didn't want the Ninevites to repen he wanted them to perish. Jonah was unconcerned about the people c Nineveh, and not really concerned about the will of God. He wanted h: way, and when he didn't get it, he complained to God—although it's calle a *prayer*. While Jonah's heart was full of judgmental and bitter selfishnes: he was oblivious to the heart of God.

The Book of Jonah is different from the other prophetic books in the Bibl in this way: With Isaiah, Jeremiah, and Daniel, we see stories of men wh obeyed God explicitly. They heard God's call and delivered the messag they were summoned to deliver. Not so with Jonah. He initially ran fron the request to be on mission with God. Then finally Jonah obeyed, but ther was still work to be done in his heart. His obedience was not coming fron a changed heart. Jonah was compliant, but he wasn't committed. Wha Jonah completely overlooked was the fact that he himself was a product o the same mercy of God that was bestowed on the Ninevites. If it had no been for these divine qualities and gifts of God, Jonah would still be in th belly of a fish.

———§———

*God, pride and prejudice are characteristics that You detest. God forgive us when w display these sinful attitudes. Please rid all of us, including our leaders, of these things Yo hate.*

*The Lord replied, "This plant grew up overnight and died overnight. You didn't plant it or make it grow. Yet, you feel sorry for this plant. Shouldn't I feel sorry for this important city, Nineveh? It has more than 120,000 people in it as well as many animals. These people couldn't tell their right hand from their left."* Jonah 4:10-11 (GW)

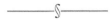

After telling God he'd rather die than see mercy shown to Nineveh, he went outside the city to pout. God caused a plant to grow to provide Jonah with much-needed shade. The next day, God sent a worm to devour the plant, and a strong wind to carry the withered plant away, exposing him to the hot sun. Now Jonah *really* wanted to die! God's reply to Jonah pointed out the absurdity of his thinking. Jonah was more upset about the loss of the plant, than the potential loss of thousands of human souls. Did Jonah produce the plant that provided shade and protection? No, it was God. Jonah needed to get over himself!

Jonah's anger stemmed from prejudicial bitterness. He did not want to see bad people—his enemies—receive God's grace. He did not desire the salvation of others. The story of Jonah should challenge us to swallow our pride; quench our anger; and put God's perspective ahead of our own. Loving people who love us is natural. Loving our enemy requires grace. It requires the Gospel. Loving our enemies is so difficult when they are causing so much destruction to our nation, through lies, violence, and corruption. We need an intervention from God. The story of Jonah ends with a question. We can only hope that Jonah learned the lesson God was giving to him—that God's will in this world is all that really matters, and He can extend His grace and mercy as He chooses. We need to learn the same lesson—with God's help.

*God we pray that we can put aside all the things that cloud our vision of Your will, as well as our hurts, desires, and our wills so that we might be better able to do Your will in the world. Transform our hearts to be more like Yours.*

## September 18                              God's Possession

*"Once you were not God's people, but now you are. Once you were not shown mercy, but now you have been shown mercy."*                              1 Peter 2:10 (GW)

How we identify ourselves determines how we approach life. At times we may have asked ourselves, "Who am I?" Am I what I do? Am I what I achieve? If so, we will always have to do more, and achieve more to find our value. "Am I defined by the things I have done right, or the things I have done wrong?" "What about what others think about me? If we claim our identity in what others say, we will always try to please people instead of pleasing God. This results in an *identity crisis*. If we are not seeking to find our identity in Christ alone, then we are seeking it in something else. We can either let the world tell us who we are, or let God tell us who we are. If we listen to who God says we are and embrace His identity in us, we'll find the freedom to live out all He has planned for us.

He has clearly and repeatedly told us who we are in numerous Scripture verses. We are God's possession—created to be enjoyed by Him. Nobody on this earth will accept us the way God accepts us. In Genesis 1, a beautiful and majestic God makes us in His image. No other creature was made in the image of God—only us. The value of something is measured by the price one is prepared to pay. Yet, the most amazing thing is that God was willing to pay the price of His Son to give us the prize of Himself. Now, if that doesn't make us feel extremely valuable, nothing will.

*Heavenly Father, saying 'thank You' does not begin to scratch the surface of the gratitude and awe we have for Your decision to choose us as Your very own possession, long before we were ever born. Thank You for sending Jesus Christ to die for us, so that we can be forgiven and have the privilege of living the life You have planned for us.*

# September 19 — Loyalty and Kindness

*"Never tire of loyalty and kindness. Hold these virtues tightly. Write them deep within your heart."*
                                                                    Proverbs 3:3 (TLB)

———§———

The word loyalty brings to mind a powerful sense of belonging and solidarity. With it comes the idea of whole-hearted fidelity coupled with unwavering devotion and duty. We are also commanded to not copy and become loyal with the ways of the world, because it will cripple our spiritual growth. Unfortunately, our hearts often times become divided. And, when the heart is divided, we don't correctly choose on who's team to play—God's team or Satan's. Living with a divided heart eventually messes up our mind.

Discipleship is more than a promised loyalty. Discipleship demands a practiced loyalty—an operating, functioning kind of loyalty that holds up under every kind of pressure. In a world of selfishness and self-centeredness, we need to rediscover loyalty to our families, friends, communities, and church. But above all, we need to be loyal to our God and Savior. *"The Lord keeps close watch over the whole world, to give strength to those whose hearts are loyal to Him."* (2 Chronicles 16:9) Let us hold tightly to the virtue of loyalty by making God the center of our lives.

Let us always remember and treasure in our hearts the love, grace and mercy of God. And when we truly accept their value, we can in turn apply them in our daily lives to others. What would our world be like if we had more of this?

———§———

*Almighty God, as we take a personal inventory, we can no longer deny that we have often failed in our loyalty to You, our family, our friends, our community, and our church. God we ask that You would purify and seal our hearts so that our loyalty and kindness would no longer be divided between Your will and ways, and the things of this world. We pray our loyalty will be expressed in our words and our actions.*

# September 20                                     Purity

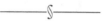

On this side of heaven our hearts seek after many things. People may pretend that they are seeking God with all their heart and with all their strength, but often the tell-tale signs betray their true motives. Purity of heart deals with motives and hidden purposes. Something that is pure is unmixed with any other matter. It is unified; all of one substance; and without contamination. At its core, purity is having a heart for the Lord that isn't watered down or polluted by lesser things. Purity of heart means that our thoughts, our desires, our attitudes, and our speech are focused on God's will instead of our own. Purity is about God because God is holy, and separated from sin.

Because of God's amazing grace, when we are saved we are deemed pure because of our position in Christ—our names are written in the Lamb's Book of Life and declared His. Too often, we fall out of step with God and our hearts become impure. Yet, that does not change our *position* before Christ, but it does affect our fellowship with Him because we allow the impure things in our lives to become a wedge between the pure and righteous nature of Jesus. So, if we want a clean and pure heart, we need to ask for one. Purity is worth it because the pure in heart see God. To do this, we must guard our heart above all else. (Prov. 4:23) Guarding our heart is critical to experiencing all that God desires for our life.

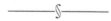

*God, You shine Your light upon us as we live in the darkness of our sin and our denial. Lord, we humbly come before You seeking to have our hearts cleansed and made pure so that our relationship and communion with You will be all that we need to sustain us through each day.*

# September 21                    Who Will Take a Stand?

*"Who will rise up for me against the wicked? Who will take a stand for me against evildoers?*
                                                            Psalm 94:16 (NLT)

———§———

The author of this Psalm had the same concerns we do today. He had a love and reverence for God. He wanted righteousness to thrive, and evil and wickedness to cease.    Every day we read or hear news reports about escalating crime; economic inflation; our failing education system; rampant drug addiction and homelessness; a porous border threatening the health and safety of our citizens; big pharma and big tech lying to Americans; an energy crisis caused by a useless executive order; corruption at every level of government; and a society that has turned their back on God. We ask, how long will this continue?

Well, it will continue as long as we—all of us—*allow* it to continue. We have fallen into a trap of putting up with the evil and wickedness of a few. Their voices have been louder than ours; their actions have been more demonstrative; and their fear-tactics have shut us down. The truth is, that all of this evil is being done by far fewer people than we realize. Yet, we are afraid to speak up—to take a stand against them. Is the fear of being "cancelled" the root of our reluctance? We can all recall the countless times when one of these extremists made an outlandish claim like, "It's all about your white-privilege;" or "It's racist to keep criminals in jail;" or "Blacks in America suffer from voter suppression." Here is one way to stand up—ask them to give you an example and/or explain how they can justify their claim. We have allowed their loud, never-ending, and baseless claims to dominate the news and influence our thinking.    This has shut us down to fight back…why? Don't we know that we have God on our side? He hates sin and evil just as much as we do. Perhaps He is waiting for us to rise up and take a stand against evildoers.

———§———

*God, we ask for Your guidance and courage to take a stand against the evil and wickedness in our nation today. Help us to be victorious in returning You to the heart of our nation.*

*"They went, and while still on their way, became clean. One of them, when he realiz that he was healed, turned around and came back, shouting his gratitude, glorifying G He kneeled at Jesus' feet, so grateful. He couldn't thank him enough—and he was Samaritan."*

                                                                    Luke 17:15 (MSG

———§———

Gratitude is an essential virtue—a fountain from which all other blessing flow. Ingratitude, on the other hand, is the leprosy of the soul. It eats awa on the inside; destroys our happiness; cripples our joy; withers ou compassion; paralyzes our praise; and renders us numb to all the blessing of God. In a series of questions, Jesus expressed disappointment in the nir men who didn't return after being healed by Jesus. All ten of the lepers wer cleansed and had an equal motive for gratitude. Therefore, it might b expected that all ten of them would give thanks and praise to God. Bu apparently the nine were so absorbed in their new happiness that they coul not spare a thought of its source. The one exception was this foreigner, Samarian who did not even belong to God's chosen people, the Jew However, before we judge the nine too harshly, we need to examine or ow gratitude quotient.

How often do we take our blessings for granted and fail to give thanks t the Lord (and others). Too often, we are content to enjoy the gift or blessing but we forget the Giver. Being thankful is not a natural part of our sinfu human nature, which has led us to be big on requests and small on thanks Sadly, this has evolved into mentality of entitlement for some. The truth is that the only thing any of us are entitled to is damnation and hell. Ye because of the love, grace and mercy from our Heavenly Father, we hav been given the gift of eternal life and salvation for which thanks should b given each and every day.

———§———

*God, we pray that You would rid us of the senseless mentality of entitlement an unwarranted pride, and replace it with humble and grateful hearts. We are eternall grateful for our salvation.*

# September 23                                    Courage

*"This is my command—be strong and courageous! Do not be afraid or discouraged. For the Lord your God is with you wherever you go."*                    Joshua 1:9 (NLT)

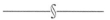

Every new thing can be scary; every unknown step is risky. However, every time we are afraid of the future, we should bring to mind other steps we have taken in this life with Jesus and ask ourselves if He has ever abandoned us or left us without help. Courage has a memory of God, and it is this memory of God that moves us courageously into the future. Joshua knew a thing or two about encountering adversity. Without question, forty years of wandering in the wilderness had qualified him to understand hardship and challenges—physical, relational, spiritual, mental, and emotional. As a successor to Moses, and having the received the benefits of his mentorship, Joshua knew that God not only understood the dangers that would test his courage, but also the provided him with the strength to courageously overcome them.

Courage is not to be confused with pride. Pride is thinking that we do great things because we are great. Courage is doing great things because God is great. The basic motivation for courageous living is the promise that God is with us and will not abandon us regardless of situation, or task at hand. The teachings and commands from God never left Joshua's heart, and because he clearly knew God's will, he was virtually assured of success. God has made a costly investment in each one of us, and He wants to see that we fully trust Him as we faithfully and courageously cross our *Jordan River* with the knowledge that God will be with us every step of the way.

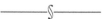

*Lord, our prayer is not only to have confidence in Your presence, but to also have confidence in Your purpose. God, use us to humbly, obediently, and courageously follow Your plan for our life. God we pray that Your Holy Spirit would bless us with the courage to stand firm for the temptations and challenges that come our way.*

*"Do nothing out of selfish ambition or vain conceit. Rather, in humility value others above yourselves, not looking to your own interests but each of you to the interests of the others."*

Philippians 2:3 (NIV)

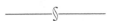

Selfishness, pride, and conceit come naturally to us. On the other hand, God's standard of humility does not. Humility is not our favorite virtue, but it is certainly among God's favorites. We cannot come to God without it. We cannot love Him supremely without it. We cannot love and serve others without it. And, we cannot have the same attitude as Christ and be all He wants us to be without it. Humility is evident when we demonstrate a complete understanding of our position before God—the One to Whom we belong. When this happens, our attitude, our words, and our deeds will take on a posture of lowering ourselves for the purpose of living with a servant's heart.

The premier example we should follow is that of Jesus. On a cold night in a manger, God shed His glory and put on human skin. He did not come to make Himself big. He came with great humility to bend His knees—for His family; for His disciples; for His people; and for us today. He bent His knee every time He showed compassion; every time He healed the sick; touched the untouchable; and fed the hungry. He got down on His hands and knees and washed the dirty feet of His disciples the night before He obediently hung on the cross. When Jesus modeled a humble rendering of His full love, He did it in service. Are we willing to empty ourselves and humbly serve others?

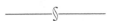

*God we are eternally grateful that You sent Your Son to clearly show us what humility looks like. We ask that You would help us rid ourselves of pride and selfishness and replace it with humility so that we will obediently pour ourselves into others through service. God, help us dispose our self-centeredness as we seek and appreciate the value of others, by keeping our ears open and our "I's" closed,*

# September 25                    Nobody to Somebody

*"Now I am sending you to the king of Egypt so that you can lead My people out of his country." But Moses said to God, "I am nobody. How can I go to the king and bring the Israelites out of Egypt?"*                    Exodus 3:10-11 (GNT)

———§———

When the Hebrew-born Moses lived his first forty years as the adopted son of the ruler of Egypt, he was a great prince—wealthy; highly educated; powerful; and respected. Yet, God did not call Moses at the height of his notability. Instead, God called Moses after he became a murderer; a fugitive; and a poor shepherd who did not even own the sheep he tended. This once prominent man spent the next forty years of his life eking out his existence living with his wife, his father-in-law and raising his two boys on the backside of the desert. After his life-shattering failure and all those years of obscurity that followed, Moses certainly must have felt like a *nobody*. He couldn't imagine God choosing a rejected utensil such as him, and finding any use in him.

Often times, failure produces in us a servant's attitude. And, what does a servant do? He/she does the next task that is given. On one ordinary day in the desert, Moses stopped to look at a particular bush, and nothing was ever normal and ordinary for him again. The now eighty-year-old, resisted and questioned God when He finally did call Moses into service. The best part is that God promised to be with Moses every step of the way. Despite Moses' checkered past, God used him to save the Israelite people. Our past doesn't limit God. Our poor decisions; awful events; or hurtful encounters do not deter God. He can recycle our past and use us in remarkable ways for His Kingdom.

———§———

*Heavenly Father, how grateful we are that the confessed sins of our past have no bearing on how You want to use us in the present and future. God, may this truth that Your grace is greater than our past be at the forefront of our mind and heart.*

*"Celebrate and worship His holy name with all your heart. Trust the Lord and his mighty power. Remember his miracles and all His wonders and His fair decisions."*
Psalm 105:3-5 (CEV)

In addition to the sound doctrine, prophecy, wisdom, and instruction found in the Book of Psalms, we also glean expressions of delight in God through our remembering Who He is, and celebrating in all He's done and continues to do for us. When God marched the Israelites out of Egypt and moved them toward the Promised Land, He began to instruct them in the particulars that would identify and preserve them as His people, and emphasized the importance of remembering Who had done these wondrous things so that future generations would benefit from those truths. Sadly, during their long journey, they experienced numerous incidents when they failed to remember. It was sad not merely for their circumstances, but for their wandering hearts—which turned to idols.

And yet, we can each attest to the times in our lives when we have failed to recall God's goodness and turned underserved attention to idols. Faith is the confidence in the goodness of God, which builds our trust in Him when we remember His faithfulness in the past. Let's pause and recall: God's faithful attention to our deepest needs; His provision in our desperate hours; His salvation through His crucified and resurrected Son; His mercy and forgiveness in spite of our sin; His peace when the circumstances around us are swirling; His hope for wondrous and everlasting life in His presence; and His abundant blessings—which are far beyond what we deserve.

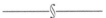

*Heavenly Father, thank You for Your wonders and miracles recorded in the Bible, as well the countless blessings bestowed on each of us, which help to encourage us to trust You with the future. God, help us to be mindful that You are always walking with us. We praise You and thank You for Your goodness and mighty power. We love You and celebrate all that You are and all that You do.*

# September 27          Offering A Child

*And she made a vow, saying, "Lord Almighty, if You will only look on your servant's misery and remember me, and not forget Your servant but give her a son, then I will give him to the Lord for all the days of his life, and no razor will ever be used on his head."*

1 Samuel 1:11 (NIV)

———§———

A woman named Hannah was in a polygamous marriage, and she was barren. Many times she prayed to the Lord that she would be blessed with a son. But God delayed in answering her prayers, and for good reason. God was looking for a man to lead Israel during these desperate days of transition—from having judges to having kings. He needed a man that He could speak to, and that would speak to the people for Him. Additionally, God was waiting, bringing Hannah around to where her heart was completely towards God; the things of God; and that which God wanted. This is what God was desiring; this is what God was looking for, and so when God brought her around to this place of that commitment to God, then the Lord answered her prayer. She gave birth to a boy and named him Samuel, which means "appointed by God."

When he was weaned, she *offered* him to the High Priest, Eli, who raised him into one of Israel's greatest prophets. Now Eli had sons who were also priests, as they were from the tribe of Levi. Yet Eli's sons were worthless men. Eli had never shown good parenting skills and did not properly discipline his sons. That, coupled with the wickedness of his sons, resulted in God taking action—ending their lives. Yet Samuel, who was growing up under Eli's tutelage, chose a godly path. Hannah's sacrificial offering was used mightily by God.

———§———

*Heavenly Father, the Bible gives us numerous examples of those who devoted their lives to You, and those who failed to do so. Sometimes, it comes down to parenting, and other times, it is the work of the enemy. God, when we lean into You for all our guidance in this life, we will not stray from the path You have set forth.*

# September 28          Give Them What They Wan

*"But be sure to fear the Lord and serve Him faithfully with all your heart; consider wh* *great things He has done for you. Yet if you persist in doing evil, both you and yo* *king will perish."*
                                                                    1 Samuel 12:24-25 (NIV

———§———

Samuel grew up and became one of Israel's finest prophets. At this tim Israel was a nation let by judges—counselors and lawmakers. Yet, Israel wa actually a theocracy, governed by God. The Israelites started rejecting th theocratic form of government and they were demanding now a monarch They were saying, "We want a king like the other nations." The Lord tol Samuel to explain the good, bad, and ugly things that having kings woul bring. Knowing what would happen, God told Samuel something lik "Okay, give them what they want." Eventually, Samuel made it public th Saul is the first king of Israel.

At this point, Saul was humble and not anxious to be in the spotlight. H started out with much promise. He was chosen and anointed by God. H was filled with the Holy Spirit. He had the support of a godly man lik Samuel. He had been given gifts appropriate to royalty. He had th enthusiastic support and goodwill of most all the nation. He had valiant me around him, men whose hearts God had touched to support him. And, h had the wisdom to not regard every doubter, or every critic, as an enemy But despite all these great advantages, Saul would still blow it. Would h walk in the advantages God had given him so far, or would he go his ow way? The rest of the book of 1 Samuel gives the answer to that question We too have seen elected officials who start off on a good foot—only to g against the will of God.

———§———

*Heavenly Father, this is a reminder that those times when we think we know what is bes* *for us, ultimately are proven otherwise. Help us to stay with the plans that You hav* *made for us. We pray that our elected representatives will stay on the righteous path, a* *well.*

*"You have done a foolish thing," Samuel said. "You have not kept the command the Lord your God gave you; if you had, He would have established your kingdom over Israel for all time. But now your kingdom will not endure; the Lord has sought out a man after His own heart and appointed him ruler of His people, because you have not kept the Lord's command."*        1 Samuel 13:13-14 (NIV)

————§————

Saul had a son named Jonathan who was a remarkable military leader. He led a victorious attack on the Philistines, but Saul took credit for it. This was a bad sign in the heart and character of Saul. His own sense of insecurity would not allow any of his associates (even his own son) to receive credit. But the Philistines would not be completely defeated and staged a counterattack, by surrounding the Israeli forces. The Israelites became fearful and hid out in thick brush and caves. Samuel had told Saul to wait seven days for him at Gilgal, where Samuel would preside over the sacrifices, and Israel would be spiritually prepared for battle. When Samuel didn't arrive on time, Saul got impatient and took it upon himself to offer the sacrifices—Saul was a king, not a priest and was not authorized to do that.

As a result of his disobedience, God told Saul that his descendants would not reign after him. Though he was a king, he would not establish the monarchy in Israel. We might have expected that Saul would be "impeached" as king right then and there. But Saul would actually reign another twenty years. He would still be on the throne as a king, but it would never be the same, because the end of his kingdom was certain. Though God had rejected Saul, He had not rejected Israel. Because God loved Israel, He would raise up a new king, a man after His own heart.

————§————

*Heavenly Father, this is a sad story of a once prominent leader who, through pride, failed in his leadership role. Guard the hearts of our nation's leaders that they don't fall into the same trap. And for those who have already fallen, we pray they would confess and repent.*

*So he asked Jesse, "Are these all the sons you have?" "There is still the youngest," Jesse answered. "He is tending the sheep." … Then the Lord said, "Rise and anoint him; this is the one." So Samuel took the horn of oil and anointed him in the presence of his brothers, and from that day on the Spirit of the Lord came powerfully upon David.*

1 Samuel 16:11;12-13 (NIV)

Jesse was the grandson of Ruth. Jesse presented all of his seven sons to Samuel, but the Lord rejected all of them as the one He would anoint to be the next king. Since Samuel knew God's word was true, he knew there must be another son of Jesse who had not been presented. This shows the low regard David had among his own family. First, his father doesn't even mention him by name. Second, he wasn't even invited to the sacrificial feast that they were having. Third, he would not have been brought in unless Samuel insisted on it. So God chose this humble, ordinary, spiritual young shepherd boy to become the future king of Israel. At that time in David's life, his primary responsibility was protector of his sheep.

When we think of a man after God's own heart, many of us think that this is a title reserved for a few *super-spiritual* folks. We want these kinds of people around us, but we never think we can be one of them. We aren't spiritual enough. But look at David—a warrior who killed hundreds of men with his own hands; a fugitive; a traitor; a man who had seasons of backsliding; an adulterer; and a murderer. Yet he could be called *a man after God's own heart.* If David can have our sins, then we can have his heart. We can love God and pursue Him with the kind of focus and heart David had.

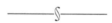

*Heavenly Father, this is more evidence of what a forgiving and passionate God You are. We are blessed to be chosen by You.*

# October 1                                    Play Me A Tune

*Now the Spirit of the Lord had departed from Saul, and an evil spirit from the Lord tormented him. Saul's attendants said to him, "See, an evil spirit from God is tormenting you. Let our lord command his servants here to search for someone who can play the lyre. He will play when the evil spirit from God comes on you, and you will feel better." So Saul said to his attendants, "Find someone who plays well and bring him to me."*

1 Samuel 16:14-17 (NIV)

The same equipping Spirit which came upon David, left Saul. He no longer had the resources to effectively administer after the kingdom. This was the effect of his rejecting God. His own mental and spiritual health was deteriorating. David, on the other hand, communicated with God through his music and poetry, which I'm sure pleased God. He had a heart for God.

After Samuel had privately anointed David to be the next king, David returned to his regular job tending his sheep. Saul's attendants told him there was a young man who played the harp, which might soothe Saul's mental anxiety; so David was summoned to serve Saul. It worked—David's music calmed Saul's disturbed mind. At the same time, the Philistine army was setting the stage for a battle with Israel. The Philistines had one *big* advantage—Goliath! This giant of a man was over nine feet tall, and wore a helmet and body armor weighing one hundred twenty-five pounds. For forty days Goliath would taunt the Israelites by shouting, *"Choose one man to come down here and fight me! If he kills me, then we will be your slaves. But if I kill him, you will be our slaves!"* (1 Sam. 17:8-9). God had left Saul—had He also left the rest of the Israelites? Just because many in our nation have left God, we can only pray that God won't leave the rest of us who haven't.

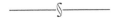

*God, may we never reject You; the penalty is too enormous. We can see how our faith and trust in You is pleasing to You, and we are blessed, as a result. Help us to face the giants in our lives. Give us the wisdom and strength to bring You back into all matters of life.*

# October 2                                    It Doesn't Fit

*"Don't worry about this Philistine," David told Saul. "I'll go fight him!" "Don't be ridiculous!" Saul replied. "There's no way you can fight this Philistine and possibly win! You're only a boy, and he's been a man of war since his youth..." "The LORD who rescued me from the claws of the lion and the bear will rescue me from this Philistine!"*

1 Samuel 17:32-33, 37 (NLT)

David's father, Jesse, told David to go the military camp where his older brothers were and give them some food. David learned about Goliath's challenge and Saul's reward for whoever would step up to that challenge. His brothers were not amused with David's apparent willingness to be the one to challenge the giant. So, David went to Saul. Despite Saul's initial response of "are you kidding?" David explained that he had fought off lions and bears as a shepherd, and he could do the same with Goliath.

Our experiences ought to be improved the more we trust in God and pursue the duty the Lord has set forth for us. Afterall, He has delivered us, and will continue to do so. Saul agreed to let David put his life on the line. He even offered David his armor and sword—neither fit because David's method of warfare differed from the norm—so he declined Saul's offer. Saul's armor didn't work because his armor did not *physically fit* David. And, it didn't work because his armor did not *spiritually fit* David. Armor, military technology, or human wisdom would not win this battle. The Lord God of Israel would win this battle! We have a battle of divisiveness and corruption brewing in our nation today. We need the Lord to be on the front lines with us to achieve victory.

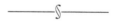

*God, we need to be rescued from the jaws of "wokeness" and radical ideas and practices. It seems like a giant task, but we trust that You will help us to be victorious and restore Your rightful place in our nation.*

# October 3             God Delivers

*"Come over here, and I'll give your flesh to the birds and wild animals!" Goliath yelled. David replied to the Philistine, "You come to me with sword, spear, and javelin, but I come to you in the name of the Lord of Heaven's Armies—the God of the armies of Israel, whom you have defied. Today the Lord will conquer you, and I will kill you and cut off your head."*      1 Samuel 17:44-46 (NLT)

————§————

We can imagine Goliath's loud voice reverberating against the tall hills surrounding the Valley of Elah. It must have struck fear into the heart of every Israelite soldier, and probably even some of the Philistine soldiers! Then David answered with his teen-age voice. The Philistines probably laughed when they heard David practically screaming in his cracking voice, and the Israelites were probably mortified. Then to top it off, David adds he would cut off Goliath's head...nice, emphatic touch! It was like David said something to the effect, "Those are some pretty fancy weapons you've got there, mister. But I've got something far better than your weapons."

David was a representative of the Lord and was a sent man—on a mission from God. David was careful to say that the *Lord* would deliver Goliath into David's hand. David was bold, but he was bold in God, not himself. David's attitude was completely different than the other men of Israel, including King Saul. David was concerned with God's cause before everything. Before his own personal safety; before his own personal glory; before his only personal honor; he had a passionate concern for God's cause. He cared about the things God cared about. He saw the problem in spiritual terms, not in material or fleshly terms. It would be so nice if more people in our government would care more about spiritual things, than worldly things. What a difference that would make.

————§————

*God, may we be like David and be concerned about the things that concern You. Thank You for delivering us from our giants, and we trust You will do so in the future.*

# October 4                              True Friends

*After David had finished talking with Saul, Jonathan became one in spirit with David and he loved him as himself. From that day Saul kept David with him and did not let him return to his father's house. And Jonathan made a covenant with David because h loved him as himself.*                              1 Samuel 18:1-3 (NLT)

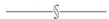

For some insight on who David really was, we only need to read the Psalm He had a deep hunger for God and a strong commitment to what was right In many of his Psalms, he was basically saying, "Wherever You are, Lord that's where I want to be—just as close as I can get. That's the chief desir of my life." David would make a great friend, wouldn't he? When Davi finished the *"ding dong, the giant's gone"* conversation with Saul, his fame and renown in Israel was assured. He had performed a remarkably heroic deed and was initially well-received by the leadership of Israel.

Earlier, we were introduced to Jonathan, the son of Saul. He was th remarkably brave man of faith who once initiated a two-man war against th Philistines. God delivered the Philistines into the hand of Jonathan and hi armor bearer that day. Jonathan and David just immediately hit it off. Ther was an immediate bond that was formed between them. They both wer bold; they both were men of great trust in God; and they both were men o action. Most of all, they both were men who had a real relationship with God. Jonathan, by all human expectation, would be the next king. However because of his father's disobedience, the Lord—through the prophe Samuel—had anointed David to be the next king. Yet they made a covenan of friendship that would prove stronger than jealousy; stronger than resentment; and stronger than ambition. Jonathan was in David's corne and could see the hand of the Lord upon David.

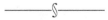

*God, we thank You for the true friends You have placed in our lives. You are the bon that binds authentic and righteous friendships.*

*"Do you hear this? They have said that David killed tens of thousands and that I only killed thousands. What else is left for him but my kingdom?" From that moment on, Saul was suspicious of David.*         1 Samuel 18:8-9 (VOICE)

———§———

It would be some twenty years until David took the throne of Israel and replaced Saul. David became very successful in Saul's army and very popular among the people—to the point of them singing songs about David's fetes. This didn't sit well with Saul. Saul's heart grew hard with hate and envy. For the next twenty years, David would be a fugitive on the run from Saul's desire to kill David. Through it all, dodging spears from Saul; hiding out in caves; and even hiding out among the enemy—the Philistines—David's heart remained the same. His time in the caves gave him an opportunity to have quality time with God. When David had no idea how God would get him to the next place, he simply trusted and obeyed. Isn't that what God wants from all of us?

At first, David didn't see through Saul to get a picture of his true character. But it soon became apparent that Saul had turned his back on God. Because Saul was making himself the enemy of the Lord, he was also the enemy of David. It didn't *have* to be like this, but Saul's heart was set on this destructive course—where David's heart was set on God. But as David kept a humble heart before the Lord, God protected him. We often think that being a humble servant and being in control contradict each other. We wrongly think that if you are a humble servant, then you must be at the mercy of events. But the example of Jesus, Who was completely in control, yet always submitting that control to God the Father, was always a humble servant, and a caring shepherd.

———§———

*God, we see clearly how jealousy, anger, and life apart from You is a losing battle. May we take on humility and submit control of our lives to You. We thank You for Your grace and Your patience with us.*

# October 6 Tragic End

*Saul groaned to his armor bearer, "Take your sword and kill me before these pagan Philistines come to run me through and taunt and torture me." But his armor bearer was afraid and would not do it. So Saul took his own sword and fell on it. When his armor bearer realized that Saul was dead, he fell on his own sword and died beside the king. So Saul, his three sons, his armor bearer, and his troops all died together that same day.*

1 Samuel 31:4-6 (NLT)

———§———

The Philistines had attacked deep into Israeli territory and Saul's army assembled and prepared for battle at Mount Gilboa. Because of his deep rebellion against the Lord, Saul was not ready for battle. This once promising king utterly threw his away his life, ending up so desperate and spiritually bankrupt that he sought counsel from a witch, instead of taking his fears to the Lord. Tragically, Saul's sons were affected in the judgment of God against their father Saul. The brave and worthy Jonathan died as we might expect him to—loyally fighting for his God, his country, and his father the king unto the very end.

In the same battle, Saul's armor bearer could not bring himself to kill the man and king he served. So Saul took matters into his own hands and fell on his own sword. Seeing this, the armor bearer followed suit by falling on his sword, and they died together. Their death was tragic, yet important in God's plan. In taking the logical heirs to Saul's throne, God cleared the way for David to become the next king of Israel. We know that if Jonathan had survived, he would have gladly yielded the throne to David. But the same could not be said of Saul's other sons, so God was merciful to the nation and to David in taking Saul's sons in battle. God provided strength, mercy, courage and protection for David throughout those twenty years—and beyond.

———§———

*God, David always found strength in You. When he was completely broken he asked You for strength. May we do the same. When we are broken and empty, please fill us with Your strength, mercy and grace.*

# October 7               Smooth Sailing?

*In the spring, at the time when kings go off to war, David sent Joab out with the king's men and the whole Israelite army. One evening David got up from his bed and walked around on the roof of the palace. From the roof he saw a woman bathing. The woman was very beautiful, and David sent someone to find out about her. The man said, "She is Bathsheba, the daughter of Eliam and the wife of Uriah the Hittite."*

2 Samuel 11:2-4 (NIV)

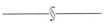

When this incident took place, David had ruled Israel for twenty years. He had moved from victory to victory, with success and God's favor at every turn. No doubt about it, King David was on a roll, and paradoxically...that's a time when we really need to be on our guard. When we're walking through a time of crisis, we naturally look to the Lord for help and guidance. But when life sails along smoothly on a calm sea, with no clouds on the horizon, we tend to become careless. We lower our guard...and the devil pounces.

Remember when Jesus faced that period of intense temptation when he went one-on-one with the devil in the wilderness? When did that happen? Right after His baptism. David had already set the scene for his defeat by actions he had done in direct disobedience to God. This reminds us that the sins we commit today may not have their full impact on us until much later. David didn't fall suddenly—as with everyone, it was a process. David had already defied God's laws, David took concubines after he became king. God had specific laws for kings, such as: *"He must not take many wives, or his heart will be led astray."* (Deuteronomy 17:17) This is exactly what was happening to David—his heart was slowly but surely turning away from God.

*God, when our lives are sailing along nicely, we tend to leave You behind. That never works. We need You always, not just when times are tough. Your laws serve a vital purpose. Help us to be obedient.*

# October 8          Adultery and Murder

*"When Uriah's wife heard that her husband was dead, she mourned for him. After the time of mourning was over, David had her brought to his house, and she became his wife and bore him a son. But the thing David had done displeased the Lord."*

2 Samuel 11:26-27 (NIV)

———§———

Not long after this one-night-stand with Bathsheba, she sent him a note that said, *"David, I'm pregnant!"* David should have paid attention to this second red-flag warning. When it dawned on him that he had actually impregnated another man's wife, he should have repented before God and come clean. But instead, David did what most people try to do when they're caught in sin—we try to cover it up. But there is something about sin that just doesn't want to stay covered. Instead of heeding God's red flags, David dreamed up the most wicked scheme of all. At this point, David's sin had gone beyond lust, adultery, and deception. Now he was planning a murder. He ordered that Uriah be sent in the front line of the fighting, where death was almost certain. Brave Uriah died in battle that day, and after a brief period of mourning, Bathsheba married King David and came to live in the palace, and gave birth to a son.

It certainly looked as though everything was working out, and that David and Bathsheba had successfully covered up a potential scandal. But David forgot to take God into account. God was certainly not pleased with what had taken place. Why are we tempted to cover up our sins, rather than confess them? The whole concept of hiding our sin is deceptive. Our sin is never hidden before God and only hidden with difficulty from our conscience. Our hidden sin hinders our fellowship with God and others and is a barrier to spiritual life and power. What a burden we carry until we lift it off ourselves through confession and repentance. Remember, God forgives and forgets.

———§———

*God, we can't hide from You the sins we commit. Thank You for restorative grace You have provided through our confession and repentance. It is the same protective grace You give that can keep us from falling in the first place.*

# October 9                      Reap What We Sow

*Then David said to Nathan, "I have sinned against the Lord." Nathan replied, "The Lord has taken away your sin. You are not going to die. But because by doing this you have made the enemies of the Lord show utter contempt, the son born to you will die."*

2 Samuel 12:11-14 (NIV)

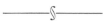

So one day in David's life the best thing that could possibly have happened, happened. David got busted. The prophet Nathan came to pay the king a visit. Nathan then gives David a sober reminder of the effects of his sin. The damage to our witness; our integrity; our reputation; to our family and friends; and to the work of Christ in our world can't even be calculated. The prophet went on to tell David that the sword would never leave his house. And that's exactly what happened. David faced the repercussions for his sins for years to come. The child born from this encounter between David and Bathsheba died. Then as the years passed, David's own children repeated this very behavior.

One of David's sons treated his half-sister as David treated Bathsheba, taking advantage of her. Then Absalam, another of David's sons, treated his brother as David treated Uriah and became a murderer, eventually leading to a rebellion against his father. As they say, the apple doesn't fall far from the tree. In spite of all that transpired, David was forgiven and restored to fellowship with God. As tragic as this story sounds, David actually did make a comeback. He got right with God and ended the race well. Isn't that what all of us strive for—to finish well with God?

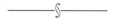

*God, we reap what we sow. And still, You are a God of second chances. The agony of our repentant hearts will be restored to ones of joy, through Your grace and mercy. We praise You, Lord.*

*Then David rested with his fathers and was buried in the City of David. He had reign* *forty years over Israel—seven years in Hebron and thirty-three in Jerusalem. So Solom* *sat on the throne of his father David, and his rule was firmly established.*

1 Kings 12:10-12 (NIV

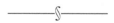

Yes, David had many good qualities. But because of David's sin ( shunning the Lord and taking Uriah the Hittite's wife, the Lord promise continuous dissention and upset in David's house. David's family wa certainly falling apart. With so many wives, brothers and sisters, hal brothers and half-sisters, things got pretty chaotic. Hatred; lies; deceit; ince: rape; and even murder were activities in which the king's family engage( Sadly, David had led by example many of these behaviors.

It is often hard for us to accept that it seems the innocent are made t suffer because of the sins of the guilty. The death of their son wa devastating to David and Bathsheba. Yet, God, our forgiving Father, late extended His mercy to them. In time, He blessed them with another sor Solomon. Considering the amazing events of his life, some might wonde why God thought so highly of David. Part of the answer is that, in spite c his lapses, David usually wholeheartedly sought God's will. He didn withdraw from the responsibilities of life. The biblical record shows tha the more conditions around David deteriorated, the more he grew i character. David remained faithful to God throughout his life. His loyalt to His Creator was beyond question—he truly was a man after God's ow heart.

*God, may we have a heart like David. Despite some mis-steps, his loyalty and devotio* *to You was beyond question. May we fall deeply into that pattern to cling to You with a* *our heart, soul, mind, and strength.*

# October 11                    Honor Government

*"Show respect for everyone. Love Christians everywhere. Fear God and honor the government."*                    1 Peter 2:17 (TLB)

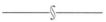

Ooh, this is a tough one! Today in America, many people have forgotten how to display the virtue of honor or respect to people and/or customs, i.e. our parents; marriage; children/family; the elderly; friends; teachers; church leadership; employers; law enforcement; military; and local/national government. What is even sadder is that our nation is failing in our willingness to honor God, upon Whom our founding fathers formed our nation's Constitution. First and foremost, God is the only One truly worthy of our honor and worship. We honor and love Him most when we are obedient to His authority.

Our obedience is also required as a way to honor others who are in positions of authority. This can sometimes be a challenge for us, especially when our personal views of the competency, decision-making, and opinions of the one(s) in authority differ from our own. Yet, we must be reminded that we are commanded to submit to governing authorities because it is God Who placed them in those positions (Romans 13:1). To do otherwise is to dishonor God. We should show respect to the office or position one holds, even though we are on opposite sides of the laws, policies, and decrees that they pass. We have means on which to change who holds those positions. We still have freedoms in this country—freedom to pray; and the freedom respectfully express our opinions; and the freedom to vote. Let's not let these freedoms go to waste.

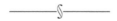

*God, help us to be faithful by living in this world as You want us to live; speaking as You want us to speak; and with humility conducting ourselves in all ways so that Christ can be seen in us. And help us show respect to those in authority over us, while being uncompromising in our commitment to obedience to Your rules.*

*"When justice is done, it brings joy to the righteous but terror to evildoers."*
Proverbs 21:15 (NIV)

———§———

It seems like we are living in a time where accountability and justice are on vacation. Yet, hypocrisy certainly has not taken a vacation. We see one side of the population arrested; indicted; or convicted for wrong-doing—or alleged wrong-doing—while the opposite side of the population is allowed to get away with doing the same wrongs. Law-makers and those who serve in the judicial system take an oath to uphold the laws and the Constitution of the United States. Those who honor their oath and see that true justice is done, bring pleasure and satisfaction to us and to God. When justice is not carried out, it is destructive and divisive to our communities, and nation as a whole.

When laws are adopted and/or enforced as written, the wicked cringe. They come kicking and screaming into the public square—often times with actions of violence and destruction. It as if the enemy himself is throwing a tantrum. On the flip-side, those of us who want to see fair and just laws enacted and upheld, rejoice when that is accomplished. It is just a reminder to elect people to positions of leadership who, when called upon, can enact laws and/or enforce such, to uphold what is said in our Preamble of the Constitution: *"We the People of the United States, in Order to form a more perfect Union, establish Justice, insure domestic Tranquility, provide for the common defense, promote the general Welfare, and secure the Blessings of Liberty to ourselves and our Posterity, do ordain and establish this Constitution for the United States of America."*

———§———

*Almighty God, we are blessed that You love justice and want to see it carried out for the good of all. We pray that more righteous people will be placed into positions of leadership to ensure that happens.*

# October 13                              Evil Doesn't Change

*"Evil people will not learn to do good even if you show them kindness. They will continue doing evil, even if they live in a good world; they never see the Lord's greatness."*
                                                                    Isaiah 26:10 (NCV)

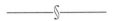

We are blessed to live in the greatest nation in the world—at least for now. Why do you think that lately millions of migrants are risking their lives to *illegally* cross our borders?  First of all, they know that they will not suffer any consequences for breaking our laws, and that they will receive unwarranted benefits—the likes of which our own citizens do not receive. Secondly, they come to our country because of the God-given freedoms and opportunities that are available—ones originally reserved for natural-born citizens and those who come to our country legally. This kindness originates from God.  Unfortunately, some leaders that are driven by power and greed, ignore the Source of kindness, even when it is bestowed on them.  Their hunger and thirst for more power and greed, seems to be a blatant desire to destroy all the goodness of our nation.  They live in basically a good world, but their evil is blinding them.  As a result, those of us who honor our Source of goodness and kindness, end up suffering the ill-effects of their evil.

We have an election coming up next month.  Please be in prayer as to how we can lean on the Lord for strength and guidance to rid our nation of the evil that has been dominating our government.  The blatant disregard for the laws we already have negatively impacts all citizens, as well as the immigrants who came to our country legally.

*Heavenly Father, we trust that You will look upon those who are enemies to Your people, and deal with them accordingly.  Give us the strength, courage, and will to honor our government through electing people who put You first in their lives and will steer our country back on a godly track.*

*"Don't be fooled by those who try to excuse these sins, for the anger of God will fall on a. who disobey him. Don't participate in the things these people do."*

Ephesians 5:6-7 (NLT)

———§———

The Bible tells us that positions of authority are placed by God. (Roman 13:1) The role of the government is to protect, seek, serve, and promote the common good of the people—not the good of the rulers. The role of government is to exercise justice based on truth; punish evil; and reward good. The role of government is to encourage law and order, and to hold accountable violations of such. But, keep in mind, government is to be limited. God's design was to prevent government over-reach. The institutions of church and family should be absent the over-rule of government.

God tells us to honor or respect government, (1 Pet. 2:17) but that becomes challenging when our government isn't behaving in the manner God intended. In recent years, we are experiencing an influx of lies from our leaders—amplified by a biased media. We are experiencing hypocrisy at levels we haven't seen before. We are seeing lawlessness run rampant with no accountability or consequences. We are seeing an unfettered illegal invasion of migrants, drugs, and gangs cross our borders, which are placing great harm to our citizens who end up paying dearly with their bank accounts and even their lives. What can we do? A few things come to mind—speak up; write letters to elected representatives; get involved with government and elections at a local level; of course, pray; and vote! Don't be fooled!

———§———

*Heavenly Father, we are frustrated. We are scared. We feel helpless. Every day we are exposed to the corruption, lies, and cover-up our government seems to be executing. We are not being fooled by them, or falling for their excuses. God, we are asking for solutions to restore our government to the way You intended.*

# October 15                          Wise Leadership

*"A nation falls where there is no wise leading, but it is safe where there are many wise men who know what to do."*            Proverbs 11:14 (NLV)

———§———

The Bible is pretty general in how it speaks about governments and their role. In other words, God hasn't given precise instruction on how we deal specific issues, such as: Reckless government spending; having so much pork in spending bills that put our nation in monumental debt; voting practices that are wrought with fraud; hypocrisy regarding judicial handling of wrong-doing based on political party affiliation; receiving large sums of money from foreign enemies in exchange for classified information— putting our national security at risk; government funding for Planned Parenthood so that millions of innocent babies can be ripped from the womb; indoctrinating our children with lies about our history and gender identity; taking away our energy independence; forcing green energy practices that are more harmful to the environment than what we have been using; career politicians who are lining their pockets with kickbacks from lobbyists and special interest groups; media withholding truth about events that impact elections—the list is endless.

It doesn't have to be this way. God was not specific regarding these issues, but He did tell us to seek wisdom above all else—His wisdom. In doing so, we can figure out how to address these concerns that are so disastrous to our nation. We need to do our homework; thoroughly vet candidates for all levels of government and leadership; and select those who have a proven record of operating with wisdom from God. We can't complain if we fail to do all we can to solve the problems and the path of godlessness our nation has been riding. Stand up; speak up; vet your candidates; pray; and vote for wise leaders.

———§———

*Heavenly Father, we pray that when we do our best to elect wise godly men and women to positions of leadership, that they remain true to You. We know that You place people in positions; we just ask that we could have some leaders who operate with integrity, transparency, fairness, and godliness. Our nation needs healing.*

*These events happened in the days of King Xerxes, who reigned over 127 provinc stretching from India to Ethiopia. At that time Xerxes ruled his empire from his roy. throne at the fortress of Susa.*               Esther 1:1-2 (NLT

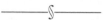

The Book of Esther is an account of the Jewish people living in exile i Persia, which was around 486 B.C. It recounts how the hatred of one ma for the Jews nearly resulted in the eradication of the Jewish people in th entire Persian Empire. It is the only book in the Bible that omits the wor "God"—yet, He is profoundly present throughout this story. The historic genesis for the drama played out between Mordecai, a Benjamite descendar of Saul, and Haman, an Agagite, goes back almost a thousand years whe the Jews exited from Egypt in 1445 B.C., and were attacked by th Amalekites, whose lineage began with Amalek, son of Esau. Go pronounced His curse on the Amalekites, which resulted in their tot elimination as a people. Although in 1030 B.C., Saul received orders to ki all the Amalekites, including their king Agag, Saul disobeyed the comman and failed to kill the Agagi—thus he incurred God's displeasure. Th prophet Samuel finally hacked Agag into pieces.

Because of his lineage from Agag, Haman carried deep hostility toward th Jews. The time of Esther arrived 550 years after the death of Agag. Bu despite such passage of time, neither Haman the Agagite, nor Mordecai th Benjamite had forgotten the tribal feud that still festered in their souls Ultimately, God's prophecy to extinguish the Amalekites, and His promis to preserve the Jews came to fruition.

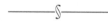

*Heavenly Father, since the beginning of Your chosen people, the Israelites, they hav experienced persecution, which remains today. We pray for Israel, and part of our praye is that they would come to realize that the Messiah has already come, and He will com. again.*

# October 17                                    Refusal

*On the seventh day, when King Xerxes was in high spirits from wine, he commanded the seven eunuchs who served him—Mehuman, Biztha, Harbona, Bigtha, Abagtha, Zethar and Karkas—to bring before him Queen Vashti, wearing her royal crown, in order to display her beauty to the people and nobles, for she was lovely to look at. But when the attendants delivered the king's command, Queen Vashti refused to come. Then the king became furious and burned with anger.*                    Esther 1:10-12 (NIV)

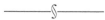

Eastern rulers enjoyed hosting lavish banquets because each occasion gave them opportunity to impress their guests with their royal power and wealth. Three banquets are mentioned in this chapter: one for the key military and political officers of the empire; one for the men of Susa; and one for the women of Susa, presided over by Queen Vashti. The name Vashti means "beautiful woman." Feeling no pain from the wine, King Xerxes ordered his queen to display her beauty to the assembled guests; but she refused to obey. Her response, of course, was a triple offense on her part. Here was a woman challenging the authority of a man; a wife disobeying the orders of her husband; and a subject defying the command of the king. Needless to say, king Xerxes was furious. Perhaps if had not been drunk, he may never have asked his wife to parade before his guests.

The fear or concern among Xerxes and the other men present at the banquet was that Vashti's actions were an offense, not only to her own husband, but to all the royal men of the empire. Therefore, the council recommended that an edict be issued that would (1) banish Vashti forever from the presence of the king; and (2) give her royal position to another. Her banishment would cause all women throughout the empire to respect their husbands. But would it? Are hearts changed because kings issue decrees or congress or parliaments pass laws? Not necessarily.

*God, like Vashti, may we not be used by the enemy to tempt others to do wrong. Please guard our hearts against such acts.*

*So his personal attendants suggested, "Let us search the empire to find beautiful young virgins for the king. Let the king appoint agents in each province to bring these beautiful young women into the royal harem at the fortress of Susa. Hegai, the king's eunuch in charge of the harem, will see that they are all given beauty treatments. After that, the young woman who most pleases the king will be made queen instead of Vashti."*

Esther 2:2-4 (NLT)

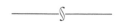

It had been four years since the king banished Vashti, and he was getting lonely. The advisors suggested that he assemble a new harem composed of the most beautiful young virgins in the empire. This was not a "beauty contest" where the winners were rewarded by having a chance for the throne. These young women were conscripted against their will and made a part of the royal harem. Every night, the king had a new partner; and the next morning, she joined the rest of the concubines. The one that pleased the king the most would become his new queen. Once they had been with the king, they belonged to him and could not marry. If the king ignored them, they were destined for a life of loneliness, confined in a royal harem.

This doesn't mean that God forced Xerxes to accept the plan, or that God approved of the king's harems or of his sensual abuse of women. It simply means that, without being the author of their sin, God so directed the people in this situation that would result in decisions being made that accomplished God's purposes. This is not necessarily a story of males versus female power, or sexual abuse and/or exploitation. Rather, it is a story about Persian power versus Jewish vulnerability in the world.

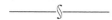

*God, we know that You don't command us to sin. Instead, You have given us the ability to choose our steps and directions. When we make bad choices, You use them for Your ultimate plan for us—with or without the consequences that come from those choices.*

# October 19                                    A Eunuch's Help

*At that time there was a Jewish man in the fortress of Susa whose name was Mordecai son of Jair. He was from the tribe of Benjamin and was a descendant of Kish and Shimei... This man had a very beautiful and lovely young cousin, Hadassah, who was also called Esther. When her father and mother died, Mordecai adopted her into his family and raised her as his own daughter.*                    Esther 2:5, 7 (NLT)

———§———

The name Mordecai means "little man; or bitterness of my oppression." Esther was Mordecai's cousin and adopted daughter. Her Persian name was Esther, which means "star," and her Hebrew name was Hadassah, which me means "myrtle." It's interesting that the myrtle tree bears a flower that looks like a star. Esther found favor in the eyes of Hegai, the king's eunuch and overseer of the harem. His favor was demonstrated by immediately providing her with cosmetics and yummy food. Up to this point, both Mordecai and Esther had not disclosed that they were Jews. Based on the fact that Esther did not refuse to eat the food that was not kosher, leads us to believe that both Esther and cousin Mordecai were passing themselves off as Persians, instead of following laws of Moses.

Hegai assigned her seven choice maids from the king's palace, and transferred her to the best place in the harem. Just as Joseph found favor in Egypt, so Esther found favor in Susa. God is so great that He can work even in the heart and mind of the manager of a harem! Hegai was a Gentile. He didn't know the true God of Israel. His job was to serve his king, by making sure the harem was to the king's satisfaction. Nevertheless, he played an important role in the plan that God was working out for His people. Even today, God is working in places where you and I might think He is absent.

———§———

*God, thank You when You use anyone and anytime for Your purposes. We may not be aware of it at the time, but when we think about all You do in our lives, we are grateful.*

# October 20                          Beauty Pageant

*Esther was taken to King Xerxes at the royal palace in early winter of the seventh year of his reign. And the king loved Esther more than any of the other young women. He was so delighted with her that he set the royal crown on her head and declared her queen instead of Vashti.*
                                                            Esther 2:16-17 (NLT)

———§———

Hegai had a year-long "beauty treatment" to prepare Esther and the other women for the king. It included a prescribed diet; the application of special perfumes and cosmetics; and probably a course in court etiquette. They were being trained to do one thing—satisfy the desires of the king. The one who pleased him the most would become his wife. Because of the providence of God, Hegai gave Esther "special treatment" and the best place in the house for her and her maids. *"Every day Mordecai would take a walk near the courtyard of the harem to find out about Esther and what was happening to her."* (verse 11) It's worth noting that Esther put herself into the hands of Hegai and did what she was told to do. Hegai knew what the king liked, and being partial to Esther, he attired her accordingly.

Esther had won the favor of everybody who saw her—and when the king saw her, he responded to her with greater enthusiasm than he had to any of the other women. At last, he had found someone to replace Vashti! The king personally crowned Esther and named her the new queen of the empire. Then he summoned his officials and hosted a great banquet. This is the fourth banquet in the book. The Persian kings certainly used every opportunity to celebrate! But the king's generosity even touched the common people, for he proclaimed a national holiday throughout his realm and distributed gifts to the people.

———§———

*God, Your watchful eye of protection that You provided for Esther, You provide for us, as well. Help us to be more in tune with You so we can actually see and enjoy Your work as it unfolds.*

# October 21                                    A Good Deed

*One day as Mordecai was on duty at the king's gate, two of the king's eunuchs, Bigthana and Teresh—who were guards at the door of the king's private quarters—became angry at King Xerxes and plotted to assassinate him. But Mordecai heard about the plot and gave the information to Queen Esther. She then told the king about it and gave Mordecai credit for the report.*            Esther 2:21-22 (NLT)

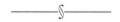

The phrase "sitting at the King's Gate" appears five times in the Book of Esther. Mordecai had received an appointment as a royal officer, perhaps a judgeship. It is not known if this appointment had been made prior to Esther becoming queen, or as a result of her influence on the king. In the East during those times, the gate was the ancient equivalent to our modern-day law courts, the place where important official business took place.

At that time two disgruntled royal guards were plotting the assassination of King Xerxes. Possibly they were seeking revenge for the ousting of the former queen Vashti. God in His providence enabled Mordecai to hear about the plot and notify Queen Esther. By making known to Esther what was about to happen, Mordecai saved the life of the king. The culprits were duly hanged, and the incident was recorded in the Court Chronicles of Persia—but Mordecai was not even thanked for his trouble.

A similar situation happened with Joseph when he interpreted the dream of a butler, a fellow prisoner in Egypt. (Genesis 40:23) The butler promptly forgot about Joseph, just as King Xerxes forgot about Mordecai. Yet, God made sure these facts were permanently recorded, so He would make good use of them at the right time.

$\S$

*God, sometimes we do good and righteous acts that seem unappreciated. That's okay because You are the really the only One we want to please.*

*Some time later King Xerxes promoted Haman son of Hammedatha the Agagite over all the other nobles, making him the most powerful official in the empire. All the king's officials would bow down before Haman to show him respect whenever he passed by, for the king had commanded. But Mordecai refused to bow down or show him respect.*

Esther 3:1-2 (NLT)

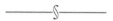

    The theme of chapter three of Esther is "anti-Semitism." This theme has been duplicated many times before—since—the events of Esther. When we read this chapter, we can almost substitute the name of Pharaoh, or even Hitler, in place of the name Haman. There has never been a time since Israel's captivity in Egypt; or since becoming a nation; and even to the present moment; that there has not been a movement somewhere to exterminate them.

    So, back to Haman. His name means "alone, solitary, or a rioter." He is one in the long line of those who have led in a campaign of anti–Semitism. King Xerxes sent out word that Haman had been appointed to the position of Prime Minister, to which people must bow to him. God permitted Haman to be appointed to this high office because He had purposes to fulfill through him. What people do with authority is a test of character. Do they use their authority to promote themselves or to help others? Do they glorify themselves or glorify God? The Prophet Daniel was given a high position similar to Haman's, but he used his authority to honor God and help others. Of course, the difference between Daniel and Haman is that Daniel was a humble man of God, while Haman was a proud man of the world. So, when we question people who God has placed in positions of power today, we can refer to the story of Esther to find hope for our future. God knows what He is doing—we just have to trust Him.

    *God, we're seeing this today in our nation. Some politicians, who You have allowed to hold positions, are proud, power-hungry, and corrupt. All we can do is trust You.*

*When Haman saw that Mordecai would not bow down or show him respect, he was filled with rage. He had learned of Mordecai's nationality, so he decided it was not enough to lay hands on Mordecai alone. Instead, he looked for a way to destroy all the Jews throughout the entire empire of Xerxes.*        Esther 3:5-6 (NLT)

———§———

Why did Mordecai refuse to bow down to Haman? What was there about being a Jew that prohibited him from doing what everybody else was doing? Even if Mordecai couldn't respect the man, he could at least respect the office and therefore the king who gave Haman the office. Most likely it was because Haman was an Amalekite, and the Amalekites were the avowed enemies of the Jews for centuries. The Lord swore and put in writing that He had declared war on the Amalekites and would fight them from generation to generation. (Ex. 17:16) How could Mordecai show homage to the enemy of the Jews and the enemy of the Lord? Mordecai's controversy with Haman was not a personal quarrel with a proud and difficult man. It was Mordecai's declaration that he was on God's side in the *national* struggle between the Jews and the Amalekites.

Keep in mind that the extermination of the Jews would mean the end of the messianic promise for the world. The reason God promised to protect His people was that they might become the channel through whom He might give the Word of God and the Son of God to the world. Mordecai is not the only person in the Bible who for the sake of conscience practiced "civil disobedience." The Hebrew midwives disobeyed Pharaoh's orders and refused to kill the Jewish babies. (Ex. 1:15–22) Daniel and his three friends refused to eat the king's food, (Dan. 1) and the three friends also refused to bow down to King Nebuchadnezzar's image. (Dan. 3) Mordecai was showing his loyalty to God.

———§———

*God, give us the courage and strength to stand up to those who are enemies of Yours. God, we will defend our faith at all cost.*

# October 24                                    Roll the Dice

*So in the month of April, during the twelfth year of King Xerxes' reign, lots were cast in Haman's presence (the lots were called Purim) to determine the best day and month to take action. And the day selected was March 7, nearly a year later.*   Esther 3:7 (NLT)

Haman was made aware of the insolence of Mordecai, and was pretty ticked off, to say the least. When Haman discovered that Mordecai's refusal to bow to him was based upon his religious convictions, he decided that a nationwide massacre of the Jews would solve his problem. Casting lots had been used in the ancient world, by various societies, as a way to make important decisions. Lots were usually small stones or pieces of wood, often with a carving of a letter or number. When thrown like dice, they would provide the decision concerning the impending matter.

So Haman went to the king and told him about a certain race that is *separate from everyone else*, and refused to obey the laws of the king. The king agreed with Haman's wish to have them destroyed. Like Satan, the great enemy of the Jews, Haman was both a murderer and a liar. To begin with, he didn't even give the king the name of the people who were supposed to be subverting the kingdom. His vague description of the situation made the danger seem even worse. The fact that these 'dangerous' people were scattered throughout the whole empire made it even more necessary that the king do something about them. Haman was correct when he described the Jews as a people whose "laws are different from those of all other people." Their laws were different because they were God's chosen people, who alone received God's holy law from His own hand. Moses asked, *"And what great nation is there that has such statutes and righteous judgments as are in all this law which I set before you this day?"* (Deut. 4:8)  The answer is: "None!"

§

*God, thank You that because of Jesus, Your chosen people now includes us. And, yes, we are separate from the "worldly" folks.*

# October 25            Great Mourning

*When Mordecai learned of all that had been done, he tore his clothes, put on sackcloth and ashes, and went out into the city, wailing loudly and bitterly. But he went only as far as the king's gate, because no one clothed in sackcloth was allowed to enter it. In every province to which the edict and order of the king came, there was great mourning among the Jews, with fasting, weeping and wailing. Many lay in sackcloth and ashes.*

Esther 4:1-3 (NIV)

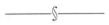

When Mordecai heard of the decree, he donned the garb of a mourner and went out into the city weeping loudly. He probably felt personally responsible for what had happened. By revealing his national identity, he thought he had brought this fate on his people. Mordecai was neither afraid nor ashamed to let people know where he stood. He had already told the officers at the gate that he was a Jew.

Mordecai stopped short of entering the king's gate because no one could enter the royal structures wearing sackcloth. When Jews throughout the empire heard about King Xerxes' edict, they duplicated Mordecai's mourning. Communication between the queen and Mordecai had to be through mediators, even when the forthcoming destruction of God's people was the topic. The utter trustworthiness of Hathach, the royal eunuch, is impressive. Those who waited on Esther knew of the bond between her and Mordecai, but were not to know that they were related. Also not yet known to the workers in the palace, was the king's edict, spurred on by the evil Haman, which had become the talk of the town outside the palace gates. Antisemitism is an awful thing—and it is still with us today. Satan hates the fact that the Jews transmitted the OT Scriptures. Satan hates God's special people, and as a result, the nations of the world at times are fanned into Satan's fury against these people.

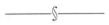

*God, our hearts break, as Yours does, that evil took the lives of so many of Your chosen people. Help us to get rid of anti-Semitism.*

*So Hathach went out to Mordecai in the square in front of the palace gate. Mordecai told him the whole story, including the exact amount of money Haman had promised to pay into the royal treasury for the destruction of the Jews. Mordecai gave Hathach a copy of the decree issued in Susa that called for the death of all Jews. He asked Hathach to show it to Esther and explain the situation to her. He also asked Hathach to direct her to go to the king to beg for mercy and plead for her people.*     Esther 4:6-8 (NLT)

———§———

When Esther received Mordecai's message, she told Hathach to relay her reply that nobody appears in the inner court of the king without being invited via the king's *gold scepter.*    Esther's reply was not an evasion but an explanation. She reminded Mordecai of what he already knew that nobody, not even the queen, could rush into the throne room and ask for an immediate audience with the king. If she were to do so, she would take her life in her hands. In order to protect the king's life from would-be assassins, this practice prevailed. The king would extend the scepter—a sign of kingly authority—only to those whom he knew and from whom he welcomed a visit.   Not only was the king of Persia sheltered from seeing sorrow and hearing bad news, but he was also protected from interruptions that might interfere with his schedule.

Mordecai sent the attendant back with an ominous message. He reminded Esther that she would not escape the general order to exterminate Jews just because she lived in the palace. He assured his adopted daughter that if she remained silent at this time, deliverance would arise for the Jews from another source. Here the faith of the old Jew in the covenantal position of the Jewish people shines through. Esther, however, should realize that *Providence* had placed her in her royal position for just such an emergency as this.

———§———

*God, there may have been restricted access to Xerxes, but we are blessed that our access to You is available to us anytime, anywhere, and for eternity.*

# If I Perish, I Perish

*Then Esther sent this reply to Mordecai: "Go, gather together all the Jews who are in Susa, and fast for me. Do not eat or drink for three days, night or day. I and my attendants will fast as you do. When this is done, I will go to the king, even though it is against the law. And if I perish, I perish."*                    Esther 4:15-16 (NIV)

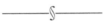

When we first met Esther and Mordecai, they were hiding their identity as Jews. Now Mordecai is enlisting other Jews in the struggle against Haman, and Esther is commanding her Gentile ladies-in-waiting to participate in the fast. Even though the name of God is not mentioned in the book, this act of humiliation was directed to the Lord and was certainly accompanied by prayer. Though prayer is not mentioned, it was always the accompaniment of fasting in the Old Testament. Fasting is a preparation for concentrated and humble prayer.

How should we interpret Esther's words, *"And if I perish, I perish."*? Do these words suggest unbelieving resignation, or trustful submission to the will of God? I vote for the latter. From the human point of view, everything was against Esther and the success of her mission. The law was against her, because nobody was allowed to interrupt the king. The government was against her, for the decree said that she, being a Jew, was to be slain. Her gender was against her, because the king's attitude toward women was a bit chauvinistic. The officers were against her, because they did only those things that ingratiated themselves with Haman. Yet, Esther put all her faith in God, to get through this challenge. Here's a news flash—He does the same for us.

*God, may we have the courage and fortitude of Esther and finish the work that You assign. May we fully submit to Your leadership and guidance to complete the mission and fulfill Your will.*

*On the third day Esther put on her royal robes and stood in the inner court of the palace in front of the king's hall. The king was sitting on his royal throne in the hall, facing the entrance. When he saw Queen Esther standing in the court, he was pleased with her and held out to her the gold scepter that was in his hand. So Esther approached and touched the tip of the scepter.*

Esther 5:1-2 (NIV)

————§————

Mordecai had both challenged and encouraged Esther to go to her husband King Xerxes, and somehow put an end to this perilous situation—a scheme that was conceived from the anti-Semitic beliefs of the evil Haman. Without hesitation, Esther took up the challenge. She requested that the Jewish people throughout the Persian Empire, identify themselves with her through fasting. Hope for the hopeless has emerged in the form of a courageous and sensible young woman, who up to this point, may have considered herself out of favor with the people that matter. However, the Jews are not out of the woods yet.

In a perplexing way, God is most present and most absent in this situation. What Esther did ranks among the great deeds of faith in Scripture and could have been recorded with the other faithful cited in chapter eleven of Hebrews. It wasn't enough for the Jews to fast, pray, and had to have faith that God would work. Somebody had to act. But Esther wasn't operating on blind faith. She knew the covenant promises God had made with His people to deal with their enemies. Unlike Esther, when we come to the throne of grace, we don't have to wonder what the Father thinks about us because He always loves us and welcomes us into His presence. Just as King Xerxes held out the scepter to accept Esther into his presence, God always extends His scepter of grace for salvation and the privilege of living in His eternal presence.

————§————

*God, we are so blessed that we can approach Your throne of grace anytime, anywhere. Your omnipresence is comforting. We praise You and love You.*

# October 29                              Let's Party!

*Then the king asked, "What is it, Queen Esther? What is your request? Even up to half the kingdom, it will be given you." "If it pleases the king," replied Esther, "let the king, together with Haman, come today to a banquet I have prepared for him.*

Esther 5:3-4 (NIV)

In light the impending doom that possibly awaited Esther, and all Jews, we would expect that Esther would immediately present her ultimate request to the king. But she worked it a bit—the king's ego—and set the stage for yet, another banquet. She wished for the king and Haman, the prime minister, to come to a banquet she had prepared. What an honor for Haman to attend a special banquet with the king and queen *alone* and in the queen's private apartment at that! It's unlikely that any official in the empire had ever been so honored. As Haman ate and drank with Xerxes and Esther, his confidence grew. He was indeed an important man in the kingdom, and his future secure.

The Lord restrained Esther from telling Xerxes the truth about her true identity and the evilness of Haman. God was delaying the great exposure until after the king had honored Mordecai, which we'll get to shortly. Esther, sensing that the time was not right to make her true appeal, simply invited the king and Haman back the next day to another banquet. At that time, she would reveal her true wishes. Haman left the banquet elated that the queen had included him in her invitation. But, on the way home at the king's gate, he encountered Mordecai. Haman was enraged when the old Jew did not pay homage to him by bowing. However, because he was riding high on the pseudo honor he had just received, he maintained his composure and went home.

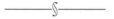

*God, when we grow anxious and impatient, please remind us that Your ways are not our ways, and Your timing is not our timing. When that sinks in, we can be comforted and find peace in knowing that You are always in control.*

# October 30                              Pride Before the Fall

*Then Haman called together his friends and his wife, Zeresh. He told them how wealthy he was and how many sons he had. He also told them all the ways the king had honored him and how the king had placed him higher than his important men and his royal officers. But all this does not really make me happy when I see that Jew Mordecai sitting at the king's gate." Then Haman's wife, Zeresh, and all his friends said, "Have a seventy-five foot platform built, and in the morning ask the king to have Mordecai hanged on it. Then go to the banquet with the king and be happy."*          Esther 5:10-11,13-14 (NCV)

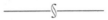

It has been said that pride is the only known disease that makes everybody sick except the person who has it.  Pride was not lacking in Haman.  His mind is full of thoughts about the recent honors, which give him prestige over every other subject in the kingdom.  Haman was so sure that his advancement made good sense that he did not suspect that Esther may have any ulterior motive in issuing a second invitation to dine with the monarch and herself.  Yet there is one little—or big—problem.  Haman is fixated on the only thing that doesn't feed into his pride—Mordecai.  Mordecai was making his life miserable!

Malice is that deep-seated hatred that brings delight if our enemy suffers, and pain if our enemy succeeds.  Malice can never forgive; it must always take revenge.  The insidious thing about malice is that it has to act— eventually it must express itself.  But when we shoot at our enemy, beware!  For the ammunition usually ricochets off the target and comes back to wound the shooter!  If a person wants to self-destruct, the fastest way to do it is to be like Haman and cultivate a malicious spirit.  Haman had infected his family and friends with his sinful hatred of the Jews.  So they suggested that he ask the king for permission to hang Mordecai.

*God, cleanse us of our pride, especially before it manifests itself into malicious thoughts or actions.  For all the heinous mistreatment Jesus endured, He was never prideful, nor malicious.*

# October 31            Insomniac Reward

*That night the king could not sleep; so he ordered the book of the chronicles, the record of his reign, to be brought in and read to him. It was found recorded there that Mordecai had exposed Bigthana and Teresh, two of the king's officers who guarded the doorway, who had conspired to assassinate King Xerxes. "What honor and recognition has Mordecai received for this?" the king asked. "Nothing has been done for him," his attendants answered.*        Esther 6:1-3 (NIV)

—————§—————

That very night, the sovereign hand of God was over the events at the palace. King Xerxes could not sleep. God accomplishes some of his greatest works during sleepless nights. Xerxes wasn't at a loss for sources of entertainment! He could have called a concubine from the harem, or he might have brought in the court musicians to play for him. He and his guards could have played a game of cards together, or he might have asked for a troubadour to entertain him with a ballad. His decision to have a book read to him was certainly of God. Xerxes ordered a scribe to read to him from the royal records. It was the book that chronicled the detailed events and decisions that took place during Xerxes reign as king. Now, that would put anyone to sleep!

In the course of this reading the king was made aware of how Mordecai had reported the assassination plot of the two doorkeepers. Now it had been several months, and possible years since this event happened. The records indicated that no honor had yet been bestowed on Mordecai for his loyalty to the crown. The king was bothered to learn that Mordecai had not been rewarded for his loyalty, and desired to remedy this oversight immediately. In the Persian culture rewarding deserving individuals was an opportunity to display a king's generosity. Xerxes wanted to honor the deserving individual—Mordecai, not Haman.

—————§—————

*God, the long time between Mordecai's good deed, and the king acknowledging it, often times is puzzling. But we are to remember that Your delays are not necessarily Your denials. Help us to trust Your timing in our lives.*

# November 1　　　　　　　　　　　　Role Reversal

*So Haman came in, and the king said, "What should I do to honor a man who truly pleases me?" Haman thought to himself, "Whom would the king wish to honor more than me?" ... "Excellent!" the king said to Haman. "Quick! Take the robes and my horse and do just as you have said for Mordecai the Jew, who sits at the gate of the palace. Leave out nothing you have suggested!"*　　　　　　　　　Esther 6:6, 10 (NLT)

When Haman first spoke with the king he was imagining himself as the beneficiary, Haman proposed a four-fold honor: The man whom the king wished to honor should wear a robe once worn by the king; ride on one of the king's own horses on whose head was a crown; be led by one of the king's most noble princes through the city square; and the prince should proclaim before the honoree that he was being honored by the king. After the way Mordecai had insulted him, Haman's imagination grew thinking he would now get double revenge: First Mordecai would see Haman honored by the king, and then Mordecai would be hanged on the gallows. Haman would then finish the day by feasting merrily with the king and queen.

What Haman intended for his personal honor became the greatest humiliation of his life. Haman left the court in utter shock. One can only imagine how he must have felt when he bestowed these honors on the man he had hoped to execute that very day. Haman was humiliated. But he had to suck it up  because he had one more of Esther's banquets to attend. Haman was still distressed because of the events of the day, but he composed himself and hoped to enjoy the banquet. One more thing, when they arrived at Esther's palace apartment, neither the king nor Haman knew that Esther was a Jewess. Another surprise awaited Haman.

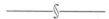

*God, You do not let evil go unpunished. It might not be immediate, but we must trust that in Your timing, Your promises will be fulfilled, and Your justice will reign.*

*Tell me what you want, Queen Esther. What is your request? I will give it to you, even if it is half the kingdom!" Queen Esther replied, "If I have found favor with the king, and if it pleases the king to grant my request, I ask that my life and the lives of my people will be spared. For my people and I have been sold to those who would kill, slaughter, and annihilate us…" Who would do such a thing?" King Xerxes demanded. "Who would be so presumptuous as to touch you?" Esther replied, "This wicked Haman is our adversary and our enemy."*      Esther 7:2-4, 5-6 (NLT)

———§———

Can't you see the jaw-dropping fear that came over the face of Haman? It was then that Esther reminded the king of the decree he had approved regarding Haman's proposal to wipe out the Jewish nation. Xerxes was smart enough to put two and two together and understand that Queen Esther was a Jewess, and he had unwittingly consented to her murder! God's delay in having the king learn of the foiled assassination attempt gave Xerxes opportunity to put all the pieces of the puzzle together—Mordecai was a Jew and that he deserved to be honored. If a Jew had saved the king's life, why should the king exterminate the Jews? He also learned that Mordecai and Esther were cousins.

As it turned out, the gallows Haman erected for Mordecai would be used for himself. The king put a stop to the edict to annihilate the Jews. And, an annual festival regarding these events is celebrated today—the Feast of Purim. Throughout the Old Testament, we see that God sometimes has used armies and/or flashy miracles in order to rescue His People. But He is not limited to just those strategies. He can just as easily use one obscure person—male, such as Joseph, or female, such as Esther—and manipulate the circumstances around them to allow them to be the agent of His salvation.

———§———

*God, the Jews have suffered persecution from the beginning. Yet we see in the Bible that every enemy that had attempted to destroy Israel, had been destroyed. We pray for Israel and know that her present-day enemies will one day pay the price for their persecution.*

# November 3        For Such a Time As This

*"Perhaps you have been made queen for such a time as this."*    Esther 4:14 (Voice)

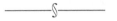

Before the truth was revealed, Mordecai gave this advice to Esther with the confidence that God would not allow the destruction of His people. The dictionary defines providence as: *"the protective care of God."* In other words, Providence is the means by which God directs all things—animate and inanimate; seen and unseen; good and evil—toward a worthy purpose. In other words, *His will must ultimately prevail.* Serving God and fulfilling the role to which He calls us is quite possible, even if we find ourselves in an environment where almost everyone around us is a heathen. And it can be done without attempting to change everyone around us. Joseph, Esther and Daniel all served totally pagan kings and won favor with them by their exemplary conduct and example. And they were thereby able to accomplish great deeds. God can use young women, like Esther, just as easily as young warriors, like David, to accomplish His plans for His people.

The Book of Esther shows the choice we all make between seeing the hand of God in our circumstances in life, and seeing things as merely coincidence. God is the sovereign Ruler of the universe and we can be assured that His plans will not be moved by the actions of mere evil men. Although His name is not mentioned in the book, God's providential care for His people, both individuals and the nation, is evident throughout. And He placed Esther in the palace *for such a time as this.*

*God, You have given each one of us a calling of some sort to contribute to Your Kingdom. We may not be aware of it, but whenever we live it out, it will be for such a time as this.*

# November 4          Discernment Required

*"Then you will again discern between the righteous and the wicked, between one who serves God and one who does not serve Him."*        Malachi 3:18 (MEV)

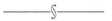

In this world it is often hard to discern between the righteous and the wicked. They are mingled together—so disguised, that we are often deceived in our opinions concerning one from the other. There are many who we think have their hearts right with God, only later to discover that their actions may prove otherwise. And, the opposite can be true—on the surface the ones who may appear to be as crooked as a dog's hind leg, turn out to have integrity beyond reproach. However, we must remember that God is the only One Who truly knows if one's heart is wicked or righteous. That doesn't mean we should bypass our use of discernment.

We have an election tomorrow (11/5/24). Elections are critical times where we must use the tool and/or guide of discernment. Elections are not simply popularity contests. Free and fair elections are our opportunity to truly voice our opinions through electing people who can genuinely represent us in a way that is in line with our Constitution, and in line with the virtues of God. When our nation was founded, undoubtedly there were some differences of opinion in laying our foundation. But, there was a majority of consensus that that foundation would be firmly rooted in God. Today, our nation is deeply divided. Please pray that our discernment will result in having elected representatives who will restore us back to God.

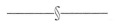

*Heavenly Father, we ask that You would place leaders in our communities, states, and federal government who have their hearts devoted to You and devoted to honestly serving those they represent. We have suffered dearly as a nation for the unrighteous actions that ungodly leaders have taken. We pray You will be restored to Your rightful place in our nation—that place is number one!*

# November 5                    God Bless America

*"Pray for rulers and for all who have authority so that we can have quiet and peaceful lives full of worship and respect for God."*                    1 Timothy 2:2 (NCV)

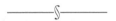

It is for the public good that there should be civil government, and proper persons entrusted with the administration of it. We pray that God will turn the hearts of those He has placed in authority, and direct them to lead our cities, states, and nation in honorable ways. We pray for our leaders so we can live in a secure society that allows us the freedom to focus on worshiping God. Since the beginning of having rulers over nations, God has seen His share those who operate with integrity and righteousness, and those who thrive in evil and corruption. He wants us to pray for all kinds of rulers.

There's power in prayer, whether we see the result of such immediately, or not. So, we need not only pray on this Election Day, but every day for those whom God has placed in positions of leadership. If a heart-change or attitude adjustment is in order—pray for such. If wisdom and discernment is needed for making good, fair, and beneficial decisions—pray for such. If there needs to be decisions and leadership that have a positive impact on our families, our churches, our schools, our laws, and our nation as a whole—pray for such.

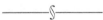

*Almighty God, at this moment, we don't yet know which candidates will be elected, but You do. We trust that those You place will be leaders who will keep our nation secure and embedded in Your guidance. We pray that our rulers will allow us peaceful lives and total freedom to worship You. We pray that new leadership will come in and dismantle the destruction that has been happening in the past several years. God, please bless America!*

# November 6                    Evil Education

*"But as for the wicked and the imposters, they will keep leading and following each other further and further away from the truth."*                    2 Timothy 3:13 (VOICE)

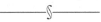

In his letter to Timothy, the Apostle Paul was mainly referring to those who taught false doctrine to the early Christians. The way of sin is downhill, which takes the wicked so far from the truth that they cannot get out of the cesspool of lies. Before we start thinking that "this doesn't apply to us today"—think again. There are countless imposters and wicked people in our society today—especially in our public education system. The enormously powerful Teachers' Union is hell-bent on re-writing our history—warts and all; indoctrinating our children into believing they should hate their country and hate themselves if they are Caucasian; strongly influencing young children to change their gender; and all the while purposefully hiding these heinous actions and ideology from parents.

They will not stop unless they are removed from the education arena, or unless parents remove their children from those toxic environments and place them in schools that teach truth. The light has been shown on this crisis, but the evil in the system is causing them to manipulate and cover-up their actions so it remains in darkness. This crisis seems malignant and requires the healing power of God to eradicate it. *"He took the children in His arms. He put His hands on them and prayed that good would come to them."* (Mark 10:16) As a former Speaker of the House once flippantly stated, "It's all about the children..." Well, *we the people* really mean it. What kind of a nation are we handing over to our children? One that is righteous, or one that is wicked?

*Almighty God, we pray that You would remove the wickedness under which some in our education systems are operating. Please protect our children from evil influences and imposters who intend harm.*

# November 7           Commissioned By God

*After the death of Moses the servant of the Lord, the Lord said to Joshua son of Nun, Moses' aide: "Moses My servant is dead. Now then, you and all these people, get ready to cross the Jordan River into the land I am about to give to them—to the Israelites."*

Joshua 1:1-2 (NIV)

———§———

Joshua, who had been the faithful servant and young assistant to Moses for the forty years the Israelites were wandering in the desert, was now commissioned by God to become the Israelite leader. But foremost, Joshua was an obedient servant to God. Joshua was called to boldness in God, to finally lead the people into entering the Promised Land. Joshua knew his own weakness. Joshua knew the limits of his ability, and here we find God offering encouragement. Three times He said to him, *"Be strong and courageous."* Why did He say that? God had commissioned Joshua to achieve three things: lead the people into the land; defeat the enemy; and to apportion the land to each tribe as its inheritance.

To accomplish these tasks, Joshua would definitely need courage and strength. God could have sent an angel to do this, but He chose to use a man and gave him the power he needed to get the job done. When he looked across that Jordan River, he could see the well–fortified city of Jericho and the enemies throughout the land, and he knew he would have to totally rely on God. When we are faced with a difficult task or challenge, we too need encouragement from the Lord. All we have to do is ask. God is always available to hear from us—He loves it when we rely on Him.

———§———

*Heavenly Father, You are our Shield, and our Source of strength. We often fail to tap into those valuable resources that You provide. May we be reminded to lean on You daily for strength and courage.*

# November 8 — The Heart of a Harlot

*Then Joshua secretly sent out two spies from the Israelite camp at Acacia Grove. He instructed them, "Scout out the land on the other side of the Jordan River, especially around Jericho." So the two men set out and came to the house of a prostitute named Rahab and stayed there that night.* Joshua 2:1 (NLT)

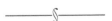

Only two women are personally named in Hebrews 11, "The Hall of Fame of Faith": *Sarah*, the wife of Abraham and *Rahab*, the harlot of Jericho. Sarah was a godly woman; the wife of the founder of the Hebrew nation; and God used her dedicated body to bring Isaac into the world. But Rahab was an ungodly Gentile who at times worshiped pagan gods and sold her body for money. Humanly speaking, Sarah and Rahab had nothing in common. But from the *divine* viewpoint, Sarah and Rahab shared the most important thing in life: They both had exercised saving faith in the true and living God.

Rahab took her life in her hands when she welcomed the spies and hid them, but that in itself was evidence of her faith in the God of Israel. True saving faith can't be hidden for long. Since these two men represented God's people, she was not afraid to assist them in their cause. Had the king discovered her deception, he would have slain her as a traitor. Rahab shared with these two men how everybody was afraid of the Israelites. For they had heard how their God was with them, and that God had parted the Red Sea so that they could safely come through. They heard how that they had previously destroyed the strong kings Sihon and Og. Thus, the fear of the God's people Israel had come upon all the inhabitants of the land.

*God, You are available to all who seek You and want an eternal relationship with You. We may not be harlots, but we came into Your family with plenty of sins of our own, and You graciously opened Your loving arms to each of us. Lord, we are so grateful.*

*But someone told the king of Jericho, "Some Israelites have come here tonight to spy o,*
*the land." So the king of Jericho sent orders to Rahab: "Bring out the men who have con*
*into your house, for they have come here to spy out the whole land." Rahab had hidd,*
*the two men, but she replied, "Yes, the men were here earlier, but I didn't know whe*
*they were from. They left the town at dusk, as the gates were about to close. I don't kno*
*where they went. If you hurry, you can probably catch up with them." (Actually, she ha*
*taken them up to the roof and hidden them beneath bundles of flax she had laid out*
*And as soon as the king's men had left, the gate of Jericho was shut.* Joshua 2:2-7 (NL)

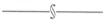

We are not to lie, but God is more interested in our *faith*, than He is *corre*
*behavior.* Again, we should not condone lying, but there are a few example
in the Bible where saying something mis-leading, or untruthful were done a
acts of faith. Take for example when the Israelites were in captivity in Egyp
and their population was exploding. Pharoah felt threatened and ordered th
Hebrew mid-wives to kill every new-born Hebrew boy they helped to delive
But the mid-wives chose to follow God's orders, rather than Pharoah's.

The supervisory mid-wives instructed the other mid-wives to purposefull
be *late* to the actual delivery, and explained to the Pharoah that these women
are "have their babies so quickly that we cannot get there in time." Did thi
mis-truth and manipulative act save a nation—God's chosen people? Yes
The same can be said about Rahab, a Gentile woman, who chose an immora
profession, but believed in the God of Israel. Her actions of hiding the spie
and lying about their whereabouts enabled the Israelites to eventually ente
the land God had promised. God honors faith, even when it doesn't com
packaged with a bow.

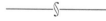

*God, we know that You don't like when we lie, or omit the truth. We also know tha*
*You love us regardless of our confessed sins, and it pleases You immensely when w*
*demonstratively express our faith in You.*

*"Now swear to me by the Lord that you will be kind to me and my family since I have helped you. Give me some guarantee that when Jericho is conquered, you will let me live, along with my father and mother, my brothers and sisters, and all their families." "We offer our own lives as a guarantee for your safety," the men agreed. "If you don't betray us, we will keep our promise and be kind to you when the Lord gives us the land."*

Joshua 2:12-14 (NLT)

    Being a Gentile, Rahab's understanding of God was limited. Yet with the little that she did know about Him at that point, she placed her total faith in the God of Israel. That evening Rahab went up to the roof confessed her faith in the Lord to the two spies and asked for a favor in return for her kindness she had bestowed on her guests. Rahab wasn't concerned only about her own welfare, for once she had personally experienced the grace and mercy of God, she was burdened to rescue her family. Rahab wanted assurance from the two spies that when the city was taken, they would guarantee her family's safety. The men gave her that guarantee in two ways: They pledged their word, and they pledged their lives that they would not break their word.

    Before the two spies left Rahab's house, they reaffirmed their covenant with her. Since the men didn't know God's plan for taking the city, they couldn't give Rahab any detailed instructions. Perhaps they assumed that the city would be besieged; the gates smashed down; and the people massacred. The men were certain that the city would fall and that ultimately the land would be taken. Details aren't important when we put our total trust in the Lord.

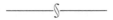

*God, we have the privilege of Your Word to understand more fully Who You are. So, it is inspiring to see the faith of someone like Rahab, who only heard a little about You.*

# November 11          Scarlet Cord of Faith

*They said to Joshua, "Surely the Lord has delivered the entire land into our hands, for all of the people in the land are overcome with fear of us."*      Joshua 2:24 (NCB)

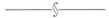

In the case of Rahab, the spies instructed her to hang a scarlet rope out of the window of her home, which was built into the wall. This scarlet rope would identify the "house of safety" to the army of Israel when they came to take the city. The color of the rope is significant for it reminds us of blood. Just as the blood on the doorposts in Egypt marked a house that the angel of death was to pass over, so the scarlet rope marked a house on the Jericho wall whose occupants the Jewish soldiers were to protect.

Rahab let the men down from the window with that rope and kept it in the window from that hour. This was the "sure sign" of the covenant that she had been made. The two spies escape unharmed, and return to report their findings to Joshua. Jericho was one of the strongest and most heavily fortified cities of Canaan. If Israel could conquer it, the whole land would be before them—but how did this spy trip help them with the eventual battle It didn't help them at all! The reconnaissance mission didn't help with military strategy, but it did help in encouraging the faith of these spies and the whole nation. This was far more important than a good battle plan. As it turned out, Rahab and her family were saved and her destiny was to marry an Israelite named Salmon, who would become the great, great grandfather of King David, who is in the lineage of Jesus Himself. God's providence is amazing. He is in complete control of all things—the universe as a whole; our physical world; the affairs of nations; and protection of His people.

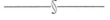

*Almighty God, thank You for another example of Your grace and mercy in the story of Rahab. Your grace is sufficient to transform a bad reputation and past into one that is pleasing to You. All that is required is faith. Rahab had amazing faith that resulted in her being in the lineage of Jesus Christ. That is amazing grace!*

# November 12 — Acquire Wisdom

*"Acquire wisdom. Acquire understanding. Do not forget. Do not turn away from the words that I have spoken."* Proverbs 4:5 (GW)

————§————

This Proverb from Solomon is one that speaks to a father instructing his child about wisdom. This is the primary way God has ordained for His truth to be preserved and invested from generation to generation. Children who have godly parents, grandparents, aunts, and uncles ought to give thanks to the Lord for their rich heritage, instead of scoffing at that heritage and abandoning it for the way of the world. The wisdom that is most valuable and lasting is God's wisdom.

Solomon was passing wisdom he had acquired from his father, David. When Solomon was grown up he not only remembered, but took a pleasure in repeating, the good lessons his parents taught him when he was a child. He was not ashamed of those teachings, nor did he look upon them as the childish things, Yes, both David and Solomon had committed their fair-share of sins. Guess what—so have we. At the same time, if we have acquired God's wisdom from our family, friends, or mentors, we are obligated to pass that wisdom on to another.

Parents and grandparents can teach us, but only *we* can receive the Word into our hearts; cherish it; or pay the price to not do so. It is our responsibility to digest and apply that wisdom in our day-to-day lives. When we receive God's truth into our heart, God renews our mind and enables us to think wisely

————§————

*Heavenly Father, we thank You for placing people in our lives that can share Your wisdom, Your truth, Your instruction, and Your love with us. We will not forget this wisdom and will commit to passing it on to others, so they can experience all that You are in their lives. We love and praise Your providential leading in our lives.*

# November 13        Cry Out for Wisdom

*"Cry out for wisdom, and beg for understanding. Search for it like silver, and hunt for it like hidden treasure. Then you will understand respect for the Lord, and you will find that you know God. Only the Lord gives wisdom; He gives knowledge and understanding.*

Proverbs 2:3-6 (NCV)

———§———

Obtaining spiritual wisdom isn't something we reserve for Sunday at church. It is a quest we make on a daily basis. With the internet and social media, it's easy to get distracted by all the worldly events pouring into our minds. This is risky because we are more vulnerable to fall prey to the enemy who lurks in our midst. In our times of so many lies; mis-truths; and evil propaganda bombarding us, we need to avoid mob-mentality and discern truth from lies.

God's Word is the best source through which to obtain the truth. Wisdom is a necessary quality if we are to persevere in our trials. Insight into the will of God, and the way it is to be applied in our life, are both given by wisdom. We need wisdom during our trials and temptations so we will not squander the occasions God is giving us to mature in our faith. Seeking wisdom and understanding isn't limited to times of trial, it is a daily discipline of a lifetime. These are gifts from God, through His truths in Scripture, and through His Holy Spirit. Yet, these gifts are only given when they are faithfully asked for with confident, unwavering trust in the Giver. If you don't ask in faith— don't ask at all. If we do ask, God has kept His promise to protect us from the enemy.

———§———

*Heavenly Father, help us to understand that the trials we endure are precisely for that purpose—to obtain wisdom. God, You are the only Source of the wisdom and understanding we need in all our circumstances. You have promised to give us these gifts, if we ask in faith. You never make a mistake, or a bad decision. God, we trust You, and cry out for Your wisdom, in all we do.*

*Jesus said, "There was a rich man who always dressed in the finest clothes and lived in luxury every day."*                                    Luke 16:19 (NCV)

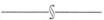

Jesus shared one of His parables about an un-named wealthy man who *dressed to the nines*, and lived a lavish life each day. How he acquired his wealth or if he was grateful or not for living in luxury is never mentioned. The Bible warns repeatedly about the tendency we have to live selfishly. Selfishness is that attitude of being concerned with one's own interests above the interests of others. However, the Bible commands us to *"do nothing from selfishness or empty conceit, but with humility of mind regard one another as more important than yourselves; do not merely look out for your own personal interests, but also for the interests of others."* (Philippians 2:3-4) In chapter nineteen of Matthew's Gospel, selfishness caused the rich young ruler to turn his back on Jesus because he could not separate himself from his wealth.

Selflessness, on the other hand, was exemplified in Jesus, Who came down from Heaven; put on human flesh; lived a sinless life; and took on every sin of mankind on the cross—all to selflessly offer us the eternal gift of salvation. None of us, young or old, can live a selfless life without a constant abiding in the Lord Jesus Christ, for it is only through Him that our attitudes can be changed and molded toward unselfish behaviors.

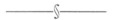

*Heavenly Father, we know it is not a sin to acquire wealth. We also know that it becomes a sin when we get lost in that wealth to the point of our failure to see the needs of others to whom we might be able to provide much-need help, instead of only providing for ourselves. May we be reminded of Your selflessness each day.*

*"And a very poor man named Lazarus, whose body was covered with sores, was laid at the rich man's gate. He wanted to eat only the small pieces of food that fell from the rich man's table. And the dogs would come and lick his sores."* Luke 16:20 (NCV)

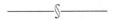

Here we have Lazarus, a godly man who was not only poor, but hungry, sick, and weak from his afflictions of sores on his body. He was forced to beg for the bread and scraps that he might possibly get at rich people's doors. His expectations from the rich man's table was simply a few crumbs that may have fallen on the floor, or scraps he was planning to give to his dogs. He silently laid at the rich man's gate without complaint or disruption. We are not told that the rich man mistreated or caused any harm to Lazarus—he simply ignored him.

Notice the rich man was nameless, yet in His parable, Jesus honored beggar with a name. Perhaps Jesus picked the name Lazarus because it is the Greek form of the Hebrew name which means *"God, the Helper.* Lazarus was clothed with painful sores that received no medical attention except from the dogs who licked his sores. These dogs were more kind to Lazarus than the anonymous rich man. Lazarus was righteous, not because he was poor, but because he depended on God.

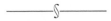

*Heavenly Father, thank You for all the blessings You bestow on us. Impress upon our heart and mind that it is not what we do with our wealth, it's what we don't do. Give us a heart for the poor and the suffering—a heart like Jesus.*

# November 16                    Eternal Chasm

*Finally the beggar died and was carried by the angels to be with Abraham in the place of the righteous dead. The rich man also died and was buried, and his soul went into hell. There, in torment, he saw Lazarus in the far distance with Abraham. "Father Abraham, he shouted, 'have some pity! Send Lazarus over here if only to dip the tip of his finger in water and cool my tongue, for I am in anguish in these flames." But Abraham said to him, "Son, remember that during your lifetime you had everything you wanted, and Lazarus had nothing. So now he is here being comforted and you are in anguish. And besides, there is a great chasm separating us, and anyone wanting to come to you from here is stopped at its edge; and no one over there can cross to us."* Luke 16:22-26 (TLB)

They died about the same time. Since Lazarus, the poor beggar, had trusted in Jesus Christ alone for his salvation, he immediately went to Heaven. The wealthy man died and found himself in the torment of Hell. This rich man had entirely devoted himself to the pleasures of the world, now found himself in misery and endless torment. He looked up and saw Abraham far away with Lazarus at his side. He begged and pleaded that Abraham would send Lazarus to him for just a moment so he could dip his finger in water and cool his tongue because he was in such agony. He was probably begging for help louder than Lazarus ever did outside his gate.

Abraham tells him that all hope is lost for the rich man. The great chasm between an eternal place for the righteous and a place for wicked is unpassable. That is a huge warning to all who have yet to put their faith in Jesus Christ. There is no hope for the rich man to escape the eternal torment—it is an irreversible situation. If this doesn't motivate us to make sure we—and all those we care about—end up on the correct side of that chasm, nothing will.

*Heavenly Father, this is a glaring picture of choosing eternity with You and failing to make that vital choice. We are grateful and blessed that we have made the correct choice and will one day meet Lazarus, who is now rich in You.*

*Then the rich man said, "O Father Abraham, then please send him to my father's home—for I have five brothers—to warn them about this place of torment lest they come here when they die." But Abraham said, "The Scriptures have warned them again and again. Your brothers can read them any time they want to." The rich man replied, "No, Father Abraham, they won't bother to read them. But if someone is sent to them from the dead, then they will turn from their sins." But Abraham said, 'If they won't listen to Moses and the prophets, they won't listen even though someone rises from the dead."*

Luke 16:27-31 (TLB)

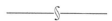

Can you feel the urgency and the passion of this proud, wealthy man to get this message out? Ah, but it was too late; there was now nothing he could do. Abraham explained to the man that not even someone who had died, returning to his family on earth would be of no benefit, because they wouldn't get it. If they didn't *get it* from the teachings of the prophets, the Torah, and especially Jesus' time on earth, they wouldn't get it now.

Not even a spectacular sign, like someone returning from the dead can change those whose hearts are set against God's word, as the response of many to the resurrection of Jesus was to show. In fact, Jesus told this parable knowing that He would appear to many people right after His resurrection, yet people today ignore those eye-witness accounts and haven't put their faith in Christ or the resurrection. They don't see with an eternal lens what lies ahead in their forever—a glorious life with God, or the torment of hell and separation from all that is good.

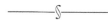

*Heavenly Father, what a wake-up call. For those in our life who have yet to make the most important decision for eternity, we must keep our foot on the pedal to share the goodness of You and all the goodness we have received, and will continue to receive long after we leave this world, with those who may not end up in Heaven. God, may Your Holy Spirit nudge their souls to learn eternal truth, so they don't end up on the wrong side of the chasm.*

*"Sometimes you can become rich by being generous or poor by being greedy. Generosity will be rewarded: Give a cup of water, and you will receive a cup of water in return."*
Proverbs 11:24-25 (CEV)

———§———

In God's economy, the greedy ultimately lose even the material things they try so hard to keep while the benevolent only prosper more and more. Those who hoard by their refusal to give, ultimately are hated by many—take Mr. Scrooge for example. Often times they have to face the poverty they dread—financial at times—but always spiritual poverty.

Let's face it, most, if not all of us, are rich when compared to the rest of the world. But God has not given us all of our material and spiritual blessings so that we could keep them just for ourselves. He wants us to be a blessing to others through joyful generosity. Giving to those in need is a matter of willingness; not wealth. It's an attitude; not an amount. If we live just for ourselves, we will never be content. Christ, Who is rich in grace, became poor; humbly served; and sacrificially gave of Himself. He had a global and eternal perspective, and wants us to have the same. The Apostle Paul described God's view of generosity by saying, *"For God is the one who provides seed for the farmer and then bread to eat. In the same way, he will provide and increase your resources and then produce a great harvest of generosity in you."* (2 Corinthians 9:10) God blesses the giving hand, thus turning it into a receiving hand.

———§———

*Father, we are blessed with the riches of Your mercy, grace and love. We ask for our hearts to be filled with the compassion, humility, and willingness to look beyond ourselves, so that we may be more like Christ. Help us to remove our blinders so we will truly see the level of poverty and injustice that exists in this world. Let us be reminded that You look at our hearts when it comes to what we give, and how we serve.*

# November 19        Resist Temptation

*"The temptations in your life are no different from what others experience. And God is faithful. He will not allow the temptation to be more than you can stand. When you are tempted, he will show you a way out so that you can endure."*

1 Corinthians 10:13 (NLT)

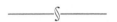

In Paul's letter to the church in Corinth, he was warning them not to succumb to the temptations that were all around them. Their city was plagued with corrupt and immoral behavior. The Corinthians were growing complacent in matters of self-discipline and falling more into the trap of self-indulgence. Anything that tests, tries, or encourages us toward sin is temptation. Temptations don't just happen. Satan, who is always an active participant, plans them.

Temptations are one of the most common experiences of our lives. If we succumb to temptation, the result is sin. The after-effects of our sin can be devastating. We risk our future; we hurt our loved ones; and we weaken our faith and intimate relationship with God. Having met temptation during His life on earth, Jesus left us with a sinless example for us to follow when we are tempted. He turned to God the Father, in Whom He trusted, Who showed Him a way out. We can do the same. Whenever we face temptation, pause and realize what's at stake. Then turn to the only One Who will show us a way out of the situation.

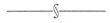

*Heavenly Father, thank You for Your love and protection. We ask that You would continue to guard our hearts from temptation, and our lives from sin. We want to serve You wholeheartedly. Through Your grace and Your Word, strengthen us in Your Holy Spirit that we may resist the temptations that Satan uses to separate us from You. Help us to pause and turn to you first, so that temptation does not turn into a sinful action. God, there is too much at stake when we fail to trust You to show us a way out.*

# November 20                     Jesus Can Relate

*"Because Jesus was tempted as we are and suffered as we do, He understands us and He is able to help us when we are tempted."*                     Hebrews 2:18 (NLV)

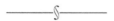

When Jesus put on human flesh and came to live among His people, He experienced every emotion we do; He faced many of the problems we do; and He faced Satan's temptations like we do. The difference is—He remained sinless.

Three of the most prevalent temptations we face are: meeting our own needs; gaining power by compromise; and putting God to the test. In chapter four of Matthew's Gospel, Jesus had to face these same temptations from the same tempter. And to all three He responded with Scriptural references. With unshakeable trust, He relied on God the Father. It is God Who supplies all our needs. It is God Whom we worship and serve. It is God Who will see use through the temptations we face—provided we ask Him. The responses by Jesus to temptation are relevant to us. He knows what it is like to be tempted, therefore He knows how to help us when we are being tempted. In His compassion, He is ready and willing to guide and comfort us when we are under temptation. In our lifetime, we will experience countless temptations. It is so comforting to know that we have Someone in our corner to fight back against the enemy, and turn our focus on God. We must not allow temptation to steal our trust in God.

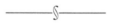

*Almighty God, we are so blessed that You are our Creator, Provider, Protector, and Deliverer. Thank You for the tremendous insight given us by Your Son in His temptation. May we trust the power and promises of You, and not seek to make life happen in our own ways. Help us to resist temptation by turning a deaf ear to the evil one; and instead placing our trust in You alone.*

*"They had not been faithful to God's promise. They refused to follow His teachings. They forgot what He had done—the miracles that He had shown them."* Psalm 78:10-11 (GW)

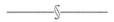

Israel had a habit of turning away from God—does that sound familiar in our time? Having been in the Promised Land for some time, the Israelites once again rebelled against God and failed to remember all the good and wondrous things He had done to get them out of Egyptian captivity in the first place. It was a shameful ingratitude they displayed to God for the amazing things He had done for them. God had performed miracle after miracle until Pharoah finally let the Israelites leave Egypt. He made a lane for them and gave them courage to pass through the Red Sea. He provided bread from Heaven—*manna*—and water in the desert to sustain them for their forty-year *spiritual* journey. He protected and guided them via the cloud by day, and the fire by night. In spite of all His mercies and blessings, the people still sinned; quarreled; and grumbled against God. Their hearts were hardened.

How often do we fail to remember all the good that God has done for us? How often do we take for granted His compassion, love, power, and guidance? How often do we grumble and complain when things don't go the *way* and *when* we would like them to? But, let's not forget that God is a compassionate and forgiving God, and it breaks His heart when we forget Him and what He has done. *"My heart is torn within Me, and My compassion overflows."* (Hosea 11:8)

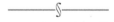

*Heavenly Father, we are just as guilty as the Israelites for the times we put in in the back of our minds, and fail to express our gratitude for all that You are and all You have done for us. Please forgive us. Help our nation as a whole to place You front and center in all that we do, say, think, and feel.*

# Don't Get Sidetracked

*"Don't get sidetracked; keep your feet from following evil."* Proverbs 4:27 (NLT)

————§————

Righteousness involves all parts of our being—mind; heart; speech; thought; attitude; and walk. It starts by learning, studying, and applying what God has told us in Scripture. We have to take care of the inside of us in order to apply His Word outwardly—our walk. Our spiritual journey can sometimes take us on some hazardous paths, full of temptations and distractions. So, we must plan ahead for those possibilities and keep our focus on God and His Word. We've seen the sad results of being sidetracked or distracted by texting while driving. This can have some deadly consequences. Yet, we have all been sidetracked by temptation to compromise what is righteous, for what is temporary, which can also have devastating consequences.

The Bible is full of examples of those who have done the same: Adam compromised God's law and fell right in with his wife's sin—he lost paradise. Esau compromised his birthright for a bowl of stew—he lost his rightful inheritance. David compromised his moral standard for a night of adultery—he lost his child. And Judas compromised his supposed love for Christ for thirty pieces of silver—he lost his eternal soul. On the other hand, the Bible has also provided us with examples of those who did not abandon the principles of God, i.e., Joseph, Daniel, and Jesus Christ. Life is too precious to be wasted on the temporary or transitory. On what path do we want to find ourselves on the day when Jesus returns?

————§————

*God, You have outlined the path we are to follow; yet we still get sidetracked from time to time. God, help us to understand and trust Your promise for a way out of every test or temptation we may face. We ask for strength and wisdom to make the right choice in every instance. Help us to live an uncompromising life results in courage, peace, and genuine faith.*

# November 23                    Torn Between Two Options

*"I'm torn between two desires: I long to go and be with Christ, which would be far better for me. But for your sakes, it is better that I continue to live."* Philippians 1:23-24 (NLT)

    The Apostle Paul is writing the Philippian from a Roman prison. While Paul rejoices in the good that his imprisonment has accomplished, he looks forward with eager expectation to being released soon. While Paul is optimistic about being released, he realizes that he has not been given a special revelation from God concerning this matter. It is possible that he will not be released—but instead executed.

    He was troubled with choosing what option would be best. If Paul had a choice between living or dying for Christ, he didn't know which to choose. Of course, the choice was really not up to him in the first place, and neither is ours. He wanted to know which would bring the most glory to God and therefore be to everyone's advantage in the long run. Paul did not tremble at the thought of death. He considered it to be a most welcome prospect. He expressed a desire to depart and be with Christ, which would be for Paul 'far better'. Such words seem very strange to many people these days. This life is generally regarded as being so very wonderful that we must cling to it at all costs. We would have no trouble agreeing with Paul if he had said, 'I would prefer to die than to continue in prison.' However, he didn't say it that way.

    We are all familiar with situations that are so dreadful that death is a relief. But Paul is not saying that death is better than the worst of life. He is saying death is better than the best of life. In other words, he was not longing for death as the way out of unbearable circumstances. He was longing for it as the way into unspeakably glorious circumstances.

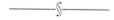

*God, we no longer are afraid of dying. While we enjoy our life on earth as we worship and serve You from a distance, we have no fear of leaving this to enjoy the splendor, gloriousness, and unthinkable joy that awaits us in Your presence.*

# November 24          A Laughing Matter

*"Is anything too hard for the Lord? I will return to you at this time next year, and Sarah will have a son."*         Genesis 18:14 (NLV)

Okay, let's get this out of the way. Sarah was 90 years old, and Abraham was 100 years old when their son Isaac was born. A year earlier, three visitors informed Abraham that Sarah, who had been barren up to this point, was going to give birth to a son. Overhearing this outlandish news, Sarah laughed to herself and questioned whether such a thing could happen to two elderly people. (Now, I'm guessing that we might all giggle at that news if we were their ages.) Abraham's laughter had been born out of joyful faith (Gen. 17:17); but Sarah's laughter was marked by unbelief, even though she tried to deny it. Sarah's reaction is what would be expected, given these circumstances. She looked at the promise from her perspective—and laughed. By the way, when their son was born, they named him Isaac, which means "he laughs, or laughter." We have to admit that God does have a good sense of humor!

Of course, whenever we doubt God, we are questioning both His truthfulness and His ability. Does He keep His promises? Does He have the power to do what He says He will do? The answer to both questions is yes! God can do the impossible! The promise to Sarah was the announcement of an impossible birth. The announcement to Mary of the birth of Jesus, likewise could not be understood how such a thing could be. In it all God expects His people to respond by faith and not doubt, for His Word is based on His nature.

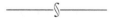

*Almighty God, forgive us for all the times we doubt You because are looking through our limited lens. Your ways are not our ways. But Your ways are the best ways. We praise You for doing what seems impossible, which sometimes result in a little laughter on our part. And, thank You for the gift of laughter which is music to our ears.*

# November 25                        Thankful Hearts

*"Don't worry about anything, but pray about everything. With thankful hearts offer up your prayers and requests to God."*                 Philippians 4:6 (CEV)

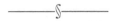

Christians are not to be filled with anxiety. We are rather to bring our problems and needs to the Lord with the confidence that He cares for us and His care is sufficient. We are to do so with thanksgiving, remembering how very gracious God has been to us. An ungrateful child always seeks more from his parents without giving thanks for what he has already received. We are not to be ungrateful children.

The caveat that the requests are to be offered with *thanksgiving*, the counterpart to rejoicing, rules out complaints or laments. Prayers like "God, please change them because they bother me" would not pass muster. Instead, the challenge is to thank God for the person or the situation— acknowledging that God is indeed sovereign and in control.

Of course, He already knows whatever we make known to God. So why are we to pray? Because as we bring our requests, which reflect every possible cause for anxiety, we are casting all our cares on God and are declaring our absolute dependence upon Him. When we carry our burdens and requests to God, He will bless us with a peace we cannot explain, nor can we experience any other way. For that, and so much more, we have thankful hearts.

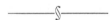

*Heavenly Father, whatever is going on in our lives, we want to always give You thanks for all things. Instead of worrying, we want to pray. Instead of worrying, we want to praise You and bask in the glory of Your wonderful, unexplainable peace. Help us to always have thankful hearts.*

# November 26                    Thank the Source

*"Enter his gates with thanksgiving; go into his courts with praise. Give thanks to Him and praise His name."*                    Psalm 100:4 (NLT)

Thankfulness is how we should always approach God. We're apt to firstly be thankful for all the blessings with which He has enriched our lives. Yet, that should be our second motivation, with the first being thankful for the Source of those blessings. Without God, there wouldn't be blessings; protection; guidance; salvation; and eternal life. Our hearts and minds focus a little more about thankfulness in this season of the year. What would happen if we carried this on throughout each year? It couldn't hurt.

We are living in unsettled and often evil times. It has undoubtedly been like that since the first sin in the Garden. But, we can be grateful to a God Who has never left our side, and has promised that one day we will be in His world—absent of evil and corruption. In the meantime, we should be thankful that we still have some freedoms remaining and pray that through His grace, God will restore our nation to one that puts Him first, and that He will put leaders in positions to make that a reality. Let's not take God's gifts and blessings for granted. When we receive them—the little ones and the big ones—do not hesitate to thank the Source from where they came with a gracious and devoted heart.

*Heavenly Father, thank You for Your sacrifice so that we could have an eternal life with You. Thank You for the freedoms that we have to openly worship You. Thank You for Your goodness, Your grace, Your protection, and Your love. Thank You for the wealth of blessings You pour on us each day. We praise You, our Source of all blessings.*

*"Give thanks to the Lord, for he is good! His faithful love endures forever."*
1 Chronicles 16:34 (NLT)

King David was elated and composed a thanksgiving psalm because the ark of God was finally going to come home to Jerusalem. There was singing and dancing to praise God for His wondrous works; for seeing the Israelites through their forty-year journey; for guiding them as they conquered the land God had promised; for His creation; for His ever-lasting covenant; and thanksgiving for His love that endures forever.

This celebration, this demonstration of adoring praise, should not be limited to a single day of the year. God is with us; protecting us; disciplining us; developing us; guiding us; and loving us every moment of every day. Should we then only give Him thanks one day in November? Yes, the original thanksgiving celebration was held by the Pilgrim settlers in 1621. But, that wasn't *actually* the first time for a Thanksgiving celebration. God had established various feasts and festivals in the time of Moses, some of which to celebrate and be thankful for their harvests. Of all the gifts for which to be thankful is the gift of His Son, Jesus Christ. He was tortured; died on a wooden cross; buried; and resurrected—all to pay our debt of sins. Now that's something about which we should be thankful—always!

*Lord Jesus, we can only imagine the suffering, the shame, the grief You took upon Yourself—all for us. Your mercy and grace is without measure. May we acknowledge that and express our gratitude each day. We love You and praise You, for You are good and Your love endures forever.*

# November 28          Joyful, Prayerful, Thankful

*"Always be joyful. Never stop praying. Be thankful in all circumstances, for this is God's will for you who belong to Christ Jesus."*          1 Thessalonians 5:16-18 (NLT)

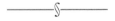

This side of Heaven, not all of our circumstances are going to be the kind that would naturally lead us to react joyfully. But, feeling joy really comes down to *choosing* to be joyful. It seems impossible, yet it's worth a shot to *choose* joy. What's the worst that can happen? Now prayer, on the other hand, is definitely a choice—one where we have no excuse for not making that choice. Praying is simply talking with God. We can do that anytime, anywhere, silently or aloud—in other words we can pray without ceasing. If we never stop praying, it makes it much easier to be thankful in all circumstances. Notice, it doesn't say thankful *for* all circumstances; it says be thankful *in* all circumstances. God is with is in all circumstances. Our joy is not determined by our circumstances or dampened by difficulties. We don't rejoice only when we have happy experiences. Even in sorrow and suffering, we have joy because all is well with our souls.

Take Jesus, for example. In the night of His arrest, He broke bread with His disciples. Then, *He took some bread and gave thanks to God for it. Then He broke it in pieces and gave it to the disciples, saying, "This is My body, which is given for you. Do this in remembrance of Me."* (Luke 22:19) Jesus didn't thank His Father based on His present circumstance of facing brutal torture and crucifixion. He was thankful to His father for the grace and glory that was to come because of the cross—and that gave Him joy.

*Heavenly Father, there is no finer example to follow than Jesus to show us how to be joyful, prayerful, and thankful in all our circumstances. Help us to be mindful of that each and every day. We look to the joy You have set before us, and we are eternally grateful.*

# November 29        A Change of Heart and Mind

*Peter said to them, "Repent, and each one of you be baptized in the name of Jesus Christ for the forgiveness of your sins, and you will receive the gift of the Holy Spirit."*

Acts 2:38 (NET)

Too often, we overlook the importance of repentance. It is the action of our faith. What, then, does repentance mean? It is a very interesting word. Our word *repent* comes from a Latin word that means "to think again." But the corresponding Greek word for repentance means "a change of mind." It's what the Gospel calls us to do. Repentance means thinking in a new way. Peter was preaching to the people to reflect on the miracle of healing the lame man and to see the revelation of the power of our risen Savior and of God our Father. Think again, start afresh.

Jesus Christ said the same thing. That is why He told the parable of the prodigal son. Our Lord was telling the Pharisees in effect, "Your ideas about God are all wrong. You are the teachers about God, but you are wrong. It is a vile travesty. It is an insult to Him. This is God—He is like the father of the prodigal son." But thinking again is not enough. We must *admit* we are wrong. Confess it; tell God about it. That is repentance. When we repent, we turn our backs upon the world; the flesh; and the devil. We do not become perfect, but we turn our backs on it all; we no longer want it in the way we once did. We may, in our folly, be enticed to look back over our shoulders; we may fall into sin; but we know we do not belong there. Like the prodigal, we have gotten up and have gone home.

*Heavenly Father, we are grateful that You are merciful to allow us to think again, or have a change of mind. Thank You that when we surrender our life to You, that our confessed sins are forgiven. It doesn't get any better than that.*

# November 30           Gimme, Gimme, Gimme!

*There was a man who had two sons. The younger one said to his father, "Father, give me my share of the estate." So he divided his property between them. Not long after that, the younger son got together all he had, set off for a distant country and there squandered his wealth in wild living.*       Luke 15:11-13 (NIV)

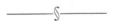

The parable of the prodigal (or lost) son is thought to be one of the most beautiful stories to exemplify the forgiveness and love of God. Here we have two sons, both of whom are loved by their father. The older son seems perhaps more reserved and possibly introverted. The younger son, is much different from his brother. He is impetuous, demanding, daring, and seems to possess and an entitlement mentality—does this remind you of a generation of folks today?

At any rate, the younger son demands that his father give him his share of the father's estate. This was not totally uncommon in those times that a father would allocate property or wealth to their children before he died. His father kindly grants his wish and the young son is out the door in a heartbeat—off to a distant land to live life hard and fast on drugs, sex and rock 'n roll. All the while, the elder son remained at home and continued working. Before we judge, just remember we are all sinners, and have sinned in all sorts of ways. The young man ran away some distance to be sinful. He not only was running far from his earthly father, he was running far from his Heavenly Father.

*Heavenly Father, we were all lost at one time in our life, until You called us into Your family. We, too, have squandered the gifts and blessings You have bestowed a time or two. We are blessed and grateful to have a loving Father Who forgives our mistakes and wrong choices.*

# December 1                                          Wallowing with Pigs

*"After he had spent everything, there was a severe famine in that whole country, and h*
*began to be in need. So he went and hired himself out to a citizen of that country, wh*
*sent him to his fields to feed pigs. He longed to fill his stomach with the pods that the pig*
*were eating, but no one gave him anything."*                    Luke 15:14-16 (NIV)

————§————

While living the wildlife, he suddenly found himself completely broke
There's no mention of any feelings of guilt, but he realized he was truly or
his own and had to actually work. Here he was in a foreign land with nc
financial support, yet worse he had no spiritual support. So, the only job
the lost son was able to find was feeding pigs in a pigpen. What a job for a
Jew! Pigs were considered unclean animals according to Levitical Law. He
becomes so desperate and hungry that he pines for the husks and pods the
pigs were eating—so desperate, he took to begging but was offered nothing.

When we depart from God and are at the end of our rope, we cry out. But
if we cry out to the world, they will not have anything that will feed and
nourish us physically or spiritually. He is lost—lost to his family; lost to his
friends; lost to his faith; and worst of all lost to God—to Whom he should
really be crying out.

Too bad many Americans who have been living large on the government's
free money chose to put work on someone else's shoulders. They didn't run
away to another land to squander their so-called government inheritance.
They stayed right at home watching TV and eating bon bons. But they are
aliens to God in living this way. What will they do when that spigot of free
money is finally closed?

————§————

*Heavenly Father, we may know of people in our life who are in a desperate state, far from*
*You. We pray that they will come to their senses and see that You are the only way out*
*of their darkness. There are plenty of lost souls in our world who need our prayers.*

# December 2                                    Returning Home

*When he came to his senses, he said, "How many of my father's hired servants have food to spare, and here I am starving to death! I will set out and go back to my father and say to him: Father, I have sinned against heaven and against you. I am no longer worthy to be called your son; make me like one of your hired servants." So he got up and went to his father.*                                    Luke 15:17-20 (NIV)

————§————

When we are alienated from God, we are always alienated from ourselves. Running from God is always a running *from* ourselves. On the flip side, repentance is running *to* God. When this young man finally "came to his senses" he realized he had left the greatest thing ever—God and his family. Humility settled in and he realized that returning home was the best choice to make. His desperate state brought him to repentance. He realized not only that he had made a mess of his life but also that he was unworthy to be called his father's son. He was fit only to be a servant, and he was prepared to humble himself and seek re-entry to the home at that level. He was willing to return home, not as a son, but as a servant or day laborer.

This humbleness is vital to all true faith and remains in it to the very end, even after the sinner has been pardoned. The young man had the hope that his father would receive him, and perhaps forgive him. As humans, we have the ability to change. We do not have to remain in the pigpen. We do not have to continue to live as sinners. We can become responsible for our lives. We can quit our wild living. We can confess our sinfulness. We can repent and change our ways. We can return to our Heavenly Father because we will definitely need His help. We can come home.

————§————

*Heavenly Father, thank You for the gift of Your Holy Spirit Who points out our sin; helps us to confess; and guides us in the journey of repentance. Like this young man, sometimes we don't feel worthy to be Your child. But, You are a good, good Father.*

# December 3        Open Arms

*But while he was still a long way off, his father saw him and was filled with compassion for him; he ran to his son, threw his arms around him and kissed him. The son said to him, "Father, I have sinned against heaven and against you. I am no longer worthy to be called your son." But the father said to his servants, "Quick! Bring the best robe and put it on him. Put a ring on his finger and sandals on his feet. Bring the fattened calf and kill it. Let's have a feast and celebrate. For this son of mine was dead and is alive again; he was lost and is found." So they began to celebrate. Meanwhile, the older son was in the field. When he came near the house, he heard music and dancing. So he called one of the servants and asked him what was going on. "Your brother has come," he replied, "and your father has killed the fattened calf because he has him back safe and sound."*

Luke 15:20-27 (NIV)

————§————

The father saw his son from a long way off because he had been waiting and watching for his son's return. The father did not wait for his son to reach him, he raced to his son with a compassionate kiss and embrace. In that day and age, it was unusual for older men to run. But the compassion the father had for his lost son propelled him into a full-on sprint to greet his son.

This is a great cause for a celebration—the son who was lost has now been found. There was no hesitation of the father to fully forgive his once-wayward son. The prodigal came home between hope and fear—fear of being rejected and hope of being received. But his father was not only better to him than his fears, he was better to him than his hopes. He not only *received* him, but received him with forgiveness and respect. This is a picture of our Heavenly Father, and how He celebrates when we sinners repent. Heaven is full of repentant sinners. The celebration never ceases. The arms of Jesus are always open.

————§————

*Heavenly Father, we can just imagine the joy You felt when we surrendered our life to Christ. It make us joyous to think about the fact that You have accepted us with open arms.*

*The older brother became angry and refused to go in. So his father went out and pleaded with him. But he answered his father, "Look! All these years I've been slaving for you and never disobeyed your orders. Yet you never gave me even a young goat so I could celebrate with my friends. But when this son of yours who has squandered your property with prostitutes comes home, you kill the fattened calf for him!" "My son," the father said, "you are always with me, and everything I have is yours. But we had to celebrate and be glad, because this brother of yours was dead and is alive again; he was lost and is found."*
                                              Luke 15:28-32 (NIV)

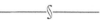

The older brother was angry, jealous and a bit self-righteous. Was he also *lost?* All this time the older brother had enjoyed shelter and provision from his loving father. Perhaps the older brother had been serving his father begrudgingly. The father reminded him that the younger brother had received all he was ever to receive regarding his inheritance, and that the older brother would be receiving twice as much, as was with Jewish tradition. So, what did the older brother do next? We are left to our imaginations to determine his final response.

Are we the younger brother, needing to repent and seek reconciliation and forgiveness? Are we the father, who was sinned against and who must have been tempted to respond in hatred and alienation? Are we the older brother—who resembled the self-righteous Pharisees—refusing to have anything to do with the sinful younger brother? Are we lost? Do we share God's mercy and compassion for the lost? Are we part of Jesus' mission, coming to seek and to save that which is lost? This parable reminds us that no one escapes the gracious love of God. We once were lost, but now we have been found.

*Abba Father, You may have stood for a long time until You saw us coming down the road to You. Thank You for Your patience; Your forgiveness; Your love; and Your celebration for our return.*

# December 5          Bad Company Corrupts

*Do not be misled: "Bad company corrupts good character."* 1 Corinthians 15:33 (NIV)

The Apostle Paul was warning those in the Corinthian church not to get too close with non-believers—specifically those who denied the resurrection of Jesus. Paul was concerned that associating with such unchristian thinkers would corrupt not only the Corinthians' doctrine but their behavior as well. In America today, we too, need be aware of those people and/or organizations that can corrupt good character, such as our education system. Public schools, as well as a handful of private and Christian schools, have become a spiritual battleground for children. Additionally, they can have damaging affects on how children view their own race, gender, history, their view of our country, and their own self-image.

There have been numerous incidents of corrupt, evil, and immoral teachers who have indoctrinated young children with lies, propaganda, and evil curricula that is completely inappropriate for young children, let alone any student. What's worse is that they are directing the students to withhold these activities and information from their parents. Now that some of it has finally been exposed, some teachers and their school administrators are going to great lengths to covertly continue these heinous actions.

The teacher's union has become way too powerful and is used to putting a muzzle on parents and patriotic citizens. We shall not remain silent any longer. We can peacefully, yet directly speak up; speak out; and expose the truth. If at all possible, place your children in learning environments where bad company can no longer corrupt one's good character.

———§———

*Almighty God, we need Your help to fight back against this evil and corruption in our educational system. It has infected all levels of education, but mainly we want to protect the very young.*

# December 6            Crucial Crossroads

*This is what the Lord says: "Stand by the roadways and look. Ask about the ancient paths, 'Which is the way to what is good?' Then take it and find rest for yourselves." But they protested, "We won't!"*       Jeremiah 6:16 (CSB)

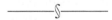

We've all heard the phrase, "My way or the highway!" Well God was telling the Jews, through the prophet Jeremiah, that it was "His way, period!" But like many of us, we don't always heed His warnings, or we blatantly tell Him, "We won't!"

The ancient paths is the biblical path, which has clearly been marked out in the Scriptures. It was the divine path laid out to the Patriarchs—the never changing, always the perfect path. Jeremiah's advice for people at the crossroads was to walk in the ancient path of biblical faith. We can learn from the past without living in the past. God's truth is as applicable today, as it was in ancient days. When a nation, a church, or an individual comes to a crucial crossroad, or a fork in the road, it helps to have good road signs, good directions, or a good map. These can only be found in God's Word.

But like the people in Jeremiah's day, the people refused. Our society now stands at the crossroads. We have started down the road to destruction with the ethical dilemmas. Will we cherish the lives of the un-born, or will we permit abortion on demand? Will we protect the lives of the defenseless, or will we allow involuntary euthanasia? Will we preserve the sanctity of marriage, or will we tolerate LGBTQ+ nonsense? These are the questions a culture faces at the crossroads.

-------§-------

*Heavenly Father, so often we are standing at a crossroad in life that absolutely requires to go in the correct direction. Help us to remember that when we are in those situations and know that we can rely on Your Word to guide us on the same path—the ancient path—that has stood the test of time, and is always the perfect path to take.*

# December 7                             A Time for War

*"There is a time to love, and a time to hate; a time for war, and a time for peace."*

Ecclesiastes 3:8 (NLV)

Solomon reminds us that in God's sovereignty, He controls time, which imposes itself on us. To everything there is a season, and we do not possess the power to change that. There is an appointed time when we are born and when we are to die. There's a time to laugh, cry, dance, heal, reap, speak, kill, search, weep, embrace etc. There is also a time for love, hate, war and peace.

As we celebrate the anniversary of the attack on Pearl Harbor, we must acknowledge that as surprising as it was to America, it was no surprise to God. While war can never be considered good, the Bible reveals that God has a purpose for it, as well as an appointed time for it to occur. In fact some wars in which our nation has chosen to engage in are proxy wars. In fact, in some of the conflicts we have participated in have cost Americans billions of dollars and depleted the armament that our military should actually have—political theater at its best. A time for war is also made in reference with end times. Jesus told His disciples, *"You will hear of wars and rumors of wars, but see to it that you are not alarmed. Such things must happen, but the end is still to come. Nation will rise against nation, and kingdom against kingdom.* (Matthew 24:6) As for peace, God has promised that as well. Our peace on earth may be sporadic and momentary, yet Jesus' promised peace that awaits us is eternal. Even in the most hostile situations, over which we have little or no control, we can know peace by trusting and resting in God, knowing that He orders our times according to His good pleasure.

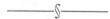

*Heavenly Father, everything is in Your hands and in Your control. We honor those who died in the Pearl Harbor invasion, as well as those who survived (such as my Dad.) Whether we are in a physical war, or not, we are always in a spiritual one. We are comforted to know that You are with us through it all.*

*"Whatever you do, work at it wholeheartedly as though you were doing it for the Lord and not merely for people."*                    Colossians 3:23 (ISV)

————§————

Each of us is uniquely gifted and shaped by God to serve other people in unique ways. Ministry is not something done just by pastors. Every Christian is a minister, called to serve in the name of Jesus. Any time we use our talents, abilities, background, or experience to serve somebody else, that is ministering. This is a major purpose that God has for each one of us. *Every* ministry is important. This high calling makes no distinction between pleasant or unpleasant tasks; dull or challenging; menial or interesting. The humblest service can be glorified and dignified when it comes from the heart, in serving in God's Kingdom. Often times, the work done behind the scenes is actually the most important, because in God's book, there is no menial service.

God did not call and gift us to sit on the bench, but He called us to find a position; accept our role; and say, "I'm all in!" Let us all be faithful servants for Christ, through our service to others. The same amount of effort we put into serving others, we can also pour into our careers, and our societal responsibilities. The more involved we are in our community, the better chance we have of keeping God front and center in our community and nation. Wouldn't this be a better world if we put as much energy into things that matter, as we do with our electronic devices? Give it a try. Can't hurt!

————§————

*Lord, all the blessings we have in this life come from You. You have uniquely molded us and given us special talents that we may utilize to serve others and glorify You. Help us to remove all the excuses we may have for not coming forth in serving Your Kingdom. God, open our eyes, ears, and hearts to the numerous opportunities that exist where we can become faithful servants.*

# December 9                 Standing Before the Judge

*"He will judge everyone according to what they have done."*   Romans 2:6 (NLV)

We might think that God will judge only those who are really evil. But Paul reminds us that the same judgment we call down on others falls on us as well. That's the part that makes us squirm. We all want justice for the world, but we each carry within us a standard of righteousness based on our own perceived goodness. Furthermore, we will tolerate only as much evil in the world as we can accept within ourselves. When we feel resentment toward God for not eradicating sin and/or evil in the world, we forget that eliminating *all* of it would mean the end of us too! So, from now on we'll have to say what we really mean. "Lord, get rid of all evil *that's worse than what's inside of me.*"

Each person will be judged by his or her deeds, not *saved* by them. Paul's point is simple: "There is no partiality with God" (2:11). All have equal opportunity to stand before the Judge to present evidence of their own righteousness. And the standard will be the same for all. At the end of days there will be a terrifying courtroom scene involving every human being who ever took a breath on earth. The deeds of each man and woman will be laid on a scale and weighed against the holy character of God—the very definition of righteousness. Wealth, power, position, race, nationality, heritage, and philosophy will count for nothing. Religion will count for nothing, but faith will. The standard will be the same for all.

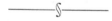

*Lord, only You are the real Judge of our sins and accomplishments. We are thankful that because of our relationship with You, that You won't be throwing us out of Heaven. Help us to be mindful to behave in ways that please You, and not to judge others for their sin.*

# December 10                                    Jesus Weeps

*"Jesus wept."*   John 11:35 (KJV)

———§———

In the shortest verse in the Bible, we are given a glimpse into the utter humanity of Jesus. We celebrate His deity—and justly so. He is the Wonderful Counselor, Mighty God, the Everlasting Father, and the Prince of Peace. But He is also a man, and here is a true indication of that in this verse. What prompted this sorrow from the Lord? Since He was about to restore Lazarus to life, He probably wasn't weeping over his death. Instead, He saw Mary and others weeping, and He was touched. Jesus wept because He noticed their weeping. He was moved by their sorrow. In the same way, when He sees our tears, He is touched.

But what if Jesus were to take on flesh again and pay an in-person visit to America today? Would our spiritual and moral condition move Him to tears? It certainly would—as it does us. The moral decay and radical policies and points of view are shifting our democratic republic to one of socialism— which has not worked out well for several countries. We will completely destroy America if we don't address our failing education system; opioid and fentanyl crisis; open-border illegal migrant crisis; voter fraud; failing military due to woke policies; lies about COVID and the untested harmful vaccines; violent crime and failure of radical DA's to prosecute; energy crisis from shutting down our energy independence; hypocrisy and corruption in the Dept. of Justice; a White House administration that withholds truth or out-and-out lies to Americans; promoting the murder of babies in the womb; funding corrupt wars in other countries, while ignoring our war at the border; gender nonsense forced on young children; our failing economy, mainly due to endless spending on useless things and ending our energy production; and most of all, removing God from everything. It's highly likely that Jesus weeps today for us.

———§———

*Jesus, we are weeping with You. Help us to turn our country back to its founding principles. Please cast out the demons in our nation.*

# December 11                    Mystery of God's Love

*"Thanks be to God for His gift that is too wonderful for words."*
2 Corinthians 9:15 (NCV)

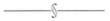

Gifts are given with the hope that they will be well received and found useful. In Christ, we have been given the most exceptional gift—a gift beyond our ability to ever fully comprehend. The gift of God's love, through Jesus, is ours. His gift of salvation, through Jesus, is ours. His gift of eternal life with Him, is ours. It is ours whether we are aware of or not. It is ours whether we believe it or not. It is our gift, but until we *receive* it; *accept* it; and make it part of our living, it is not fully ours. The gift of a new life, that God offers, is not meant to be returned; exchanged for something better; used only for a season; or wrapped up and stored away because it is "too nice." God wants us to let our lives show the wondrous mystery of His love, and that He is the center of our life.

The mystery of the Holy Trinity is the mystery of God's Love. We live in this Love—the Love of the Father Who creates and sustains us; the Love of the Son, the merciful One Who became one of us and Who overflows with compassion for each of us; and the love the Spirit, the One Whose presence within us gives us the ability to love as God loves. So now what? Will we receive and the greatest gift ever, and give your life fully to the Giver?

*Our gracious Father, You have given Your very Self—in creation; in sending Your Son to live among us; and in Your Holy Spirit that is with us today. We are eternally grateful for Your precious gift and what it means to each of us now, and eternally. Help us to truly receive the gift of You and Your love, and share it with others.*

# December 12                                    Word Became Flesh

*"And the Word became flesh and dwelt among us. And we saw His glory, the glory as of the Father's only Son, full of grace and truth."*                    John 1:14 (NCB)

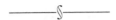

This is a statement about eternity; before there was life; before there was a nation called Israel; before there was a garden called Eden. *"In the beginning was the Word, and the Word was with God, and the Word was God."* (John 1:1) This verse bears a striking parallel with the opening words of Genesis. For centuries, God had His patriarchs, judges, prophets and kings to represent His authority and His voice on earth. Then after 400 years of silent nights, at a moment that God had long prepared by His own methods, God became flesh in the person of Jesus—with a mysterious mixture of grace, truth, and love.

It was more than a ribbon-cutting ceremony when the Word became flesh. It was not just a symbolic act when He identified with human beings and extended His offer of salvation to us, only to be resurrected to His exalted station of glory in heaven. He didn't come into being—He just came to be flesh never ceasing to be fully God. He became vulnerable to those natural human weaknesses that accompany our flesh—hunger, thirst, physical weakness and pain. He experienced the emotional traumas we experience—disappointment, sorrow, hurt, loneliness, and rejection. He did this without a taint of sin. Just as the silence of the 400 years was broken by His first coming, so the present silence will be broken by His second coming. That should fill us with hope and peace. But let's face the truth. If we feel that He is currently being silent, who's fault is that? Look in the mirror, America! We have put a gag order on God in our country—not all of us, but enough to cause this silence. We need to stand up, and cry out for God to break the silence!

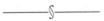

*Jesus, thank You for stepping out of Heaven to show us how to live and for showing us how much You love us. Thank for Your saving grace and allowing us to spend eternity in the presence of Your glory. We need Your presence more than ever. Please break the silence.*

# December 13                                    Promised Savior

*"And it is one of King David's descendants, Jesus, who is God's promised Savior of Israel! ...This message of salvation has been sent to us! "*                    Acts 13:23, 26 (NLT)

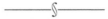

The Gospel is not a new message; it was promised in the Old Testament, beginning in Genesis and periodically through other books of the Bible. God also made His promise to David that the Savior of the world would come from David's lineage. The prophet Jeremiah foretold of this as well. *"The days are coming," declares the Lord, "when I will raise up for David a righteous Branch, a King who will reign wisely and do what is just and right in the land."* (Jeremiah 23:5) Jesus Christ, Who is the center of the Gospel message, is identified as a man; a Jew; and the Son of God—fully human and fully God.

How amazing it is that Christ's family tree comprises every kind of sinner—adulterers; prostitutes; liars; and murderers to name a few. That's just the point—we, as sinners, are the reason we all need a Savior. God keeps His promises, and He kept His promise to David. The Gospel is for *everyone*. No one is excluded from the great grace and mercy of God in Christ. We are all created in His image; all fallen; all in need of a radical redemption and rescue. Every single person on the face of this planet is lost, destined to hell, apart from saving faith in the Person and work of Jesus Christ. The Savior has been given as a gift to all of us. Let us joyfully receive this awesome gift with humble gratitude as this month we worship the birth of our Savior.

*Almighty Savior, we celebrate You with joyous and thankful hearts. You are everything that has been promised—the suffering Savior and the glorious King. Your birth; Your sinless life; Your death; Your resurrection; Your ascension; Your intercession; and soon Your return, are all promises that have been and will be fulfilled. We thank You that Your grace, mercy, and forgiveness is available to every sinner. Jesus, we ask that every heart would be open to You and would know You as Savior and Lord.*

# December 14           Purchased Freedom

*"But when the right time came, God sent his Son, born of a woman, subject to the law. God sent him to buy freedom for us who were slaves to the law, so that he could adopt us as his very own children. And because we are His children, God has sent the Spirit of His Son into our hearts, prompting us to call out, 'Abba, Father.'"*

Galatians 4:4-6 (NLT)

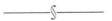

Christmas is a time for us to cherish the fact that God sent His Son to be born of a virgin woman to redeem us. This mission, which He had planned from the beginning, was to also to adopt us—all who believe—into His family. The word "redeem" was often used to speak of buying a slave's or debtor's freedom. Christ's death—because it was a death of substitution for sin—satisfied God's justice and exhausted His wrath toward His people, so that Christ actually purchased believers from slavery to sin, and from the sentence of eternal death.

The Holy Spirit's work is to confirm to believers—by His presence in our hearts—that we are truly God's sons and daughters. What a gift! Our Abba Father has chosen us to have a deep, personal, and intimate relationship with Him forever. We have the privilege of communicating with our Heavenly Father—our Abba, Father. The word "Abba" is Aramaic for "Father." Yet, it is more intimate; it is similar to the English word, "Daddy." Through our adoption, God has made available to us the riches of His grace; the riches of His glory; the riches of His wisdom; the riches of His truth; the riches of His goodness; and the riches of His unconditional love. The best part of our inheritance is yet to come!

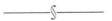

*Abba Father, You are powerful, awesome and mighty. You alone deserve all glory, honor and praise in this universe. As Your adopted children through Christ Jesus, we praise You for Your love and faithfulness to us. We find our only true comfort in You as our Spiritual Father in Heaven. We are so blessed that You chose each of us.*

*"Don't be afraid, Mary," the angel told her, "for you have found favor with God! Yo*
*will conceive and give birth to a son, and you will name him Jesus. He will be very grea*
*and will be called the Son of the Most High. The Lord God will give him the throne*
*His ancestor David. And He will reign over Israel[1] forever; His Kingdom will neve*
*end!"*
                                                                  Luke 1:30-33 (NL)

It's highly likely that if an angel were to suddenly appear to us, that w
would be fearful. So, imagine what this young teen-age virgin, who wa
doing her daily chores in her family's home in Nazareth, experienced tha
day. Then, the angel simply announces God's plan for Mary's life—that sh
will conceive and give birth to the Messiah! It goes without saying that thi
was not how Mary thought her life's plan would unfold. One of the thing
we learn from the Christmas story is that God does not always conform to
human expectations. When God interrupts our life's plans and asks us to
do great things for Him, how do we respond? Do we treat it as an
inconvenience and reject His invitation, or do we faithfully and obedientl
embrace it? Well, we can learn a thing or two from the way Mary responded

Despite her initial fear and confusion, she didn't run from the situation
She didn't question God's call on her life—she only asked for clarification
"How could that be?" (v.34) Neither God, or Gabriel demanded of Mar
that she must understand everything. What is required of her is only this—
that she believes, and willingly submits in obedience. Nothing is impossibl
with God. If we find favor in God's sight (as did Mary); if He chooses to
use us for the fulfillment of His purposes; then the outcome will be Hi
responsibility. God doesn't choose us and then leave us on our own. Goo
chose Mary and then watched over her. We find favor with God when we
trust in Him.

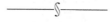

*Heavenly Father, we pray that, like Mary, we will take the angel's "fear not" at fac*
*value by obediently surrendering to Your will. We pray we will find favor with You always*

# December 16                                     Righteous Joseph

*So her husband, Joseph, being a righteous man, and not wanting to disgrace her publicly, decided to divorce her secretly. But after he had considered these things, an angel of the Lord appeared to him in a dream, saying, "Joseph, son of David, don't be afraid to take Mary as your wife, because what has been conceived in her is from the Holy Spirit."*

Matthew 1:19-20 (CSB)

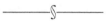

Just for a moment, try to put yourself in Joseph's place. You are betrothed to Mary, which is the same as a legal marriage, except there is no physical intimacy until the actual marriage ceremony. All of a sudden, you learn that she is pregnant—and you are NOT the father! Yet, instead of reacting in anger, Joseph responded with love and compassion toward Mary. He sought a way to sever their relationship without publicly humiliating her. But, God had a plan, and Joseph was part of that plan. Joseph's daytime resolution to quietly dismiss Mary had given way to a night of dreaming; pondering; and wrestling. Joseph's view of Mary, her pregnancy, and even himself had been enlarged and opened. From the mouth of an angel, Joseph was instructed to *fear not*, and go ahead with the wedding plans, because Mary had not been unfaithful after all, and that the Holy Spirit had conceived the baby.

For a righteous man like Joseph, this was a lot to ask. Was he prepared to lose his reputation in the community; his reputation in the synagogue; and his loyal customers of his carpentry business, on the say-so of an angel? Verse 25 tells us that Joseph was a man willing to place the will of God ahead of his own. Joseph did not hesitant in his obedience to God. He began to see this situation—this scandalous pregnancy—through the eyes of faith, rather than through the stares of the villagers. Joseph didn't take the easy path; he took the RIGHT one. He pleased God through his obedience.

*God, we pray for Joseph's level of faith, and that our desire to please You replaces our concern for what the world thinks.*

# December 17                                    Humble Birth

*"At that time the Emperor Augustus ordered a census of the Roman Empire. This was the first census taken while Quirinius was governor of Syria. All the people went to register in the cities where their ancestors had lived. So Joseph went from Nazareth, a city in Galilee, to a Judean city called Bethlehem. Joseph, a descendant of King David, went to Bethlehem because David had been born there. Joseph went there to register with Mary. She had been promised to him in marriage and was pregnant. While they were in Bethlehem, the time came for Mary to have her child. She gave birth to her firstborn son. She wrapped him in strips of cloth and laid him in a manger because there wasn't any room for them in the inn."*                                    Luke 2:1-6 (GW)

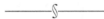

Joseph and Mary made the seventy-five-mile journey to follow the Emperor's order to register. Because of this census, Bethlehem was bustling with people, so there was no room for them to spend the night. The labor pains were beginning and the only place available to them was a cave or manger where animals were fed. It's highly likely that it wasn't the scene that is often depicted on Christmas cards—but more like a dark, smelly, musty cave. *"Bethlehem Ephrathah, you are too little to be among the family groups of Judah. But from you One will come who will rule for Me in Israel. His coming was planned long ago, from the beginning."* (Micah 5:2) This prophesy from Micah was announced more that 700 years prior to its fulfilment.

With all that time to plan a birth, perhaps God could have prepared a better place for His Son to come into this world. That's how our minds work, but God's providence and wisdom far exceed ours. How amazing that our King—the Lord of lords, and Savior of the world—was born in a feed trough. His humble birth brought glory to His Name.

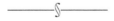

*Heavenly Father, what a birth! What a gift! What a Giver! We praise You, our Savior and King.*

# December 18                                    Joy Went Viral

*That night, some shepherds were in the fields nearby watching their sheep. Then an angel of the Lord stood before them. The glory of the Lord was shining around them, and they became very frightened. The angel said to them, "Do not be afraid. I am bringing you good news that will be a great joy to all the people. Today your Savior was born in the town of David. He is Christ, the Lord."*                    Luke 2:8-11 (NCV)

––––––§––––––

During the time of the Patriarchs, shepherding was a noble occupation. Yet, during the Jews' 430-year captivity, Egyptians prejudiced the Israelites' attitude toward shepherding. In Christ's day, shepherds were ranked at the bottom rung of the social ladder, along with lepers and tax collectors. The nature of their calling prohibited them from frequent participation in the religious rituals of their day. They were considered to be unscrupulous and untrustworthy. So, how amazing is it that their testimony, although worthless in law courts of the day, was valued by God? He entrusted to them the first human proclamation of the Gospel of Jesus Christ.

In the midst of an ordinary night, the lowly and ordinary shepherds encountered an extraordinary God. The shepherds became the metaphor for the kind of people Jesus came to save. We can only imagine their amazement and fear when the landscape magnificently displayed the glory of the Lord to these lowly shepherds. The glorious news of Jesus' birth drove away their fear, and replaced it with an unspeakable joy! Joy went viral that night! So what did the Shepherds learn at the manger? They learned that they were important to God. They learned that they could know the Savior personally. They learned that God has wonderful news for all who will believe. And they learned that the Good News is not something that they could keep to themselves.

––––––§––––––

*Heavenly Father, the birth of Jesus brought joy to the world. Help us to be more than a spectator of the Nativity and participate with You in Your Gospel. We need that same joy today in our nation.*

# December 19             Treasure These Things

*"But Mary treasured up all these words, pondering in her heart what they might mean."*
Luke 2:19 (NET)

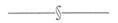

Christmas calls us to ponder in sacred silence that God's love was born in a barn to a poor teenage peasant girl. Jesus is God's Christmas gift of love—which none of us deserve. Despite the possibility of rejection by Joseph, and her own family and community, Mary surrendered herself—first to the Lord—and then to His plan. There's no "Why me?" or "This is not what I planned!" from Mary. Instead, she just rejoiced! So now what? Following nine months of pregnancy, and an arduous seventy-five-mile trip from Nazareth to Bethlehem, she found herself having given birth to the Son of God in a cold, dark, damp, and smelly manger.

Soon after, an unlikely group visited Mary, Joseph, and baby Jesus—the shepherds who responded to the Lord's invitation to find the Christ child. Imagine some of the things Mary was now pondering as she cradled her child not only what had led up to this moment, but what the future held. Of all the women of Israel she was the mother of the Messiah. All the while, Mary kept her focus on what God was doing and kept her heart open for the next step of obedience. As we celebrate the birth of our Savior, it would please God if we *pondered*—for just a moment—the story of His life in the flesh. The truths of Christ are worth keeping; and the way to keep them top of mind, and always in our heart, is to ponder them; to meditate on them; and to treasure them.

*Almighty God, we rejoice as we honor and celebrate the great historic moment when You sent Your Son into this world as a baby. We thank You that we have come to know You personally; and that You live in us; You bless us; You forgive us; and You fill us with peace, hope, and joy. God, we are in awe of Your greatness and grace, and that You have given us the promise of eternal bliss in heaven with You. May we ponder all of these truths this Christmas season, and throughout our lifetime.*

# December 20                                    Wise Faith

*When Jesus was born in the village of Bethlehem in Judea, Herod was king. During this time some wise men from the east came to Jerusalem and said, "Where is the child born to be King of the Jews? We saw His star in the east and have come to worship Him."*

Matthew 2:1-2 (CEV)

———§———

Little notice was taken of the obscure birth of Jesus, with a few exceptions: the shepherds, Simeon, and Anna. Yet from a distant land, a few wise men, or astrologers, were divinely prompted to follow a special star that would lead them to the Christ child. Perhaps these Gentile Magi had read prophetic Scripture from the time the Jews were in exile in Babylon and Medo-Persia, and were not going to ignore the signs presented to them. They traveled miles and miles for one distinct purpose; to pay homage; to worship this child; and to offer gifts to the King of the Jews—the Savior of the world. God had directed their journey. By the first appearance of the star God gave them the understanding where they would find this King.

How is it that these strangers would be the ones to announce His birth, instead of the Jews, who had anticipated the coming of the King of Kings? How is it that the Magi would receive and believe in the Messiah, while the chief priests and teachers lacked faith? The Magi came to where Jesus was bearing gifts. The gifts they gave were entirely appropriate. They gave gold—gift for a king. By giving it they acknowledged that Jesus was and is the King. They gave frankincense—a gift for a priest. This was incense the priests used in Temple. By giving it they acknowledged that Jesus was a Priest, the One who would bring us to God. They gave myrrh—a gift for the dead. This was a fragrant ointment used to anoint a body before burial. By giving it they acknowledged that Jesus had come to die for the sins of the world.

———§———

*Lord Jesus, may we have the same purpose and determination to go the distance to seek, receive, believe, and worship You, as did those wise men from the east. May Your Word make us wise, as well.*

# December 21                    Despised and Rejecte·

*"He was despised and rejected—a man of sorrows, acquainted with deepest grief. W·*
*turned our backs on him and looked the other way. He was despised, and we did not ca·*
*But He was pierced for our rebellion, crushed for our sins. He was beaten so we could·*
*whole. He was whipped so we could be healed."*                    Isaiah 53:3, 5 (NLT·

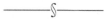

Chapter 53 of the Book of Isaiah foretells the life; death; burial; ar·
resurrection of Jesus. The child is born—God taking on human flesh on·
to be rejected by those He came to save. Israel was no Garden *of Eden* whe·
Jesus was born. Both politically and spiritually, it was kind of messy. Soun·
a lot like our nation today.   He did not come as a great tree but as a *tena·*
*plant.* He was born into poverty in Bethlehem and grew up in a carpenter·
shop in Nazareth. Because of His words and works during His earth·
ministry, He attracted large crowds; but His physical appearance made Hi·
no different from any other Jewish man.

It is good to remember that Jesus succeeded without the glamour, glitz an·
good looks so many people rely on today. The people were ashamed of Hi·
because He was not the kind of king they were expecting; and did not favc·
the things that they placed as priorities in their lives, like wealth; entitlemen·
social prestige; greed; and power. Again, America has rejected Him for th·
same reasons today. Jesus was beaten, bruised, whipped, pierced, an·
crushed by the burden of humanities sin. Sin is rampant in our society toda·
and it won't get any better the longer we have our backs turned on our Savic·
Let's renew our hearts and minds to bring Jesus back to our nation and worl·

*Lord Jesus, we are no better as a society than when You stepped down from Heaven t·*
*first time. Our nation once had You firmly placed in our foundation, which has sin·*
*eroded. Jesus, we need You. Those of us who believe in You have our faces toward Yo·*
*and ask for Your guidance to turn others around in the same direction.*

# December 22                    Wonderful Counselor

*"For a Child is born to us, a Son is given to us. The government will rest on His shoulders. And He will be called: Wonderful Counselor..."*                    Isaiah 9:6 (NLT)

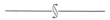

In this verse, the prophet Isaiah declares both the humanity and deity of Jesus Christ. As *Counselor*, He has the wisdom to rule justly—something that is desperately needed in our nation today. Jesus stands ready to lead our life, if we are ready to follow Him. He draws us to Himself through His compassion and wisdom. We serve a God Who doesn't object to getting His hands dirty with the muck of our lives. He doesn't change this fallen world—He steps into it and changes us.

In Christ, we have a Wonderful Counselor Who personally guides us through the potholes and pitfalls of life, which we all experience from time to time. He already knows our struggles and is waiting for us to honestly open up to Him for healing and guidance. We must listen to His voice through His Word; through prayer; and through others He uses to impart His advice, warnings, commands, and promises. If we are willing to seek His counsel, then we must be willing to follow the counsel, wisdom, and plans He has conveyed. God wants us to walk with Him and have our lives be guided by Him. That is why He has given us a *Wonderful Counselor.*

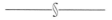

*Lord Jesus, You are the One and only perfect and Wonderful Counselor, Who fully accepts us; understands our situations; empathizes with us; speaks truth to us in love; and helps us to experience Your grace and mercy in every circumstance. Only You are the perfect Counselor, with Whom we can fully place our trust. Lord, open our hearts so we may honestly seek Your counsel to guide us through the ups and downs of life.*

# December 23                    Mighty God

*"For a Child is born to us, a Son is given to us. The government will rest on His shoulder. And He will be called: Mighty God..."*                    Isaiah 9:6 (NLT)

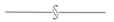

When we think of might and power, the last thing that comes to our mind is a baby. But Jesus was not an ordinary baby—He is Almighty God, Who took on flesh. He has the power to execute His wise plans. His omniscience knows no bounds. He knows every detail of our heart and mind. His omnipotence is always evident. He offers change in us; for us; and through us in His birth, life, death, and resurrection. He offers us renewed strength and new life from His inexhaustible strength and omnipresence as the Mighty God.

We see that He is Mighty over nature, which He created. We see He is Mighty over sickness and disease. And most importantly, we see that He is Mighty over sin. That is the reason this *'Child is born to us.'* God has graciously given us this Gift—that is the Christmas story. The Gift is available to all. God asks only that we open it; receive it; and invite Jesus into our life. Let us take time to celebrate His birth, and His gift of salvation from our Hero, our Mighty God.

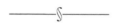

*Lord Jesus, You are all powerful and all consuming. You have demonstrated Your power and might by blessing us with Your most precious gift—Yourself. As our Mighty Savior You have conquered and defeated sin and death, allowing us eternal life in Your Holy presence. Lord, all our hope is in You to receive Your strength and power, as Your Holy Spirit works in us; for us; and through us. May Your power and might create changes in us that please You, so we may share Your gift of salvation with others. May our nation return to You. Thank You for being our Mighty God.*

*"For a Child is born to us, a Son is given to us. The government will rest on His shoulders. And He will be called: Everlasting Father..."*
                                                 Isaiah 9:6 (NLT)

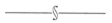

The Prophet Isaiah makes visible the paternal nature of God through the advent of Jesus, Who is marked by fatherly compassion and tender care. He loves us endlessly. He is before, above and beyond time. And, because He owns eternity, He can give us eternal life. Our heavenly Father was willing to pay any price in order to save us. He does not treat us as our sins deserve, or repay us according to our iniquities. He is always ready to meet our needs as our Provider, and offer refuge as our Protector.

Our Everlasting Father loves us so much that He is willing to discipline us to bring us to Christian maturity. And amazingly, He does not make His love for us conditional upon our love for Him. Whether or not we have been blessed with having an amazing earthly father (as I was) may we delight in the fact that our *Everlasting Father* loves us in ways we can hardly fathom, and He is always available. He is abounding in love, compassion, mercy, and grace.

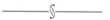

*Abba Father, thank You for loving us with a love that will last for eternity. How grateful we are that You, the One Who created the heavens and the earth with the power of Your Word, want us to be Your sons and daughters in Your kingdom. May we never forget this privilege came at an incredible cost. Your Son, who knew no sin, took upon Himself the full weight of our sin when He died upon a cross. That unimaginable sacrifice has allowed us to have an intimate relationship with You, our Everlasting Father.*

# December 25                                    Prince of Peace

*"For a Child is born to us, a Son is given to us. The government will rest on His shoulders. And He will be called: Prince of Peace."*                          Isaiah 9:6 (NLT)

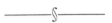

The Hebrew word for peace is "Shalom" which means: "completeness; wholeness; health; well-being; rest; harmony; and the absence of agitation or discord." We long for peace among nations; peace within our own nation; peace with our neighbors; peace within our families; peace within ourselves; and most importantly peace with God. Interestingly, the opposite of *shalom* is not war, but *chaos*. As the Prince of Peace, Jesus brings order and wholeness into the chaos of our world and the chaos of our lives.

Because of our sin, we were all separated from God. Yet, He sent us a *Prince of Peace* to restore us to having shalom with God. This magnificent gift has been given to us. As a Wonderful Counselor, He provides divine guidance for us. As a Mighty God, He provides everything we need for salvation in this life and the next. As the Everlasting Father, He watches over us and shapes us into His image. And as the Prince of Peace, He takes our broken lives and makes us complete with shalom that is uniquely His.

This verse also speaks to the second-coming of Jesus. This King of kings will irradicate all systemic evil forever. In His government peace will be eternal. In the meantime, we need to return to God as a nation and restore His Kingship in our current government.

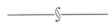

*Almighty Father, how absolutely blessed we are that You have given us the gift of Jesus, our Prince of Peace so that we are reconciled with You because of His work on the cross. Jesus, You are the Prince of Peace Who can calm every storm in life and give us a supernatural peace that transcends circumstances, as well as our understanding. You are in control of everything. We trust You.*

# December 26                    Return to the Lord

*"Though you are such wicked rebels, My people, come and return to the Lord."*
                                        Isaiah 31:6 (NLT)

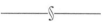

As the Lord spoke to Isaiah about the Israelites, He is also speaking to us today. As individuals, and as a nation, we have turned our backs on God. We have put everything else in the place of God—our careers; status; material possessions; power; greed; or whatever idol we worship instead of God. Our faith is in man, not in God. We turn to the world for all our answers and all our help.

Israel's enemy at the time was Assyria. Despite the condition of the hearts of the Israelites—wicked, corrupt, and rebellious—God promised that He would deliver them from anything their enemy would throw at them. We, too, have global enemies, such as China, Iran, or Russia. But our biggest enemy is ourselves. We must return to God—immediately!

Repentance starts in the mind and becomes a reality in how it shows up in our life. God warned Israel then, and He warns us now turn from our idolatrous and evil ways before He takes any action for our defense against our enemies—foreign or domestic. We started off as a nation where God was first in all aspects of our American lives. We need to bring Him back so we can be a nation that is protected by Him; influenced by Him; governed by Him; and restored by Him. It starts with each one of us individually—expanding into a group effort that reaches from sea to shining sea.

*God, we want so desperately to turn from our wicked ways as a nation. Equip us with the courage and the means to fight the evil and corruption we are experiencing, and give us wisdom and strength to bring You home.*

*"While I was with them, I protected them and kept them safe by that name You gave M*
*None has been lost except the one doomed to destruction so that Scripture would be fulfilla*
John 17:12 (NI'

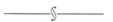

    This is part of Jesus' beautiful prayer for His disciples. Thankfully, Jest
loves us; preserves us; and intercedes for us. So clearly, we are preserve
protected, and kept by the power of God. Although God will keep us, w
must *want* to be kept. Which brings up an interesting aspect of Jesus' praye
He mentioned Judas Iscariot, who had already left to betray Him. It wasn
that Judas was a believer who fell away. From the start, Judas never was
believer. Jesus *keeps* all whom the Father has given to Him. Even so, tł
Bible tells us, *"Keep yourselves in God's love as you wait for the mercy of our Lo*
*Jesus Christ to bring you to eternal life."* (Jude 1:21) This shows us that clear
there is God's part, and there is also ours.

    We don't keep ourselves *saved*, but we do keep ourselves *safe*. Thoug
God's love is unsought, undeserved, and unconditional, it is possible for u
to be out of harmony with His love. Simply put, we are to keep ourselv
from all that is unlike God. We are to keep ourselves from any influenc
that would violate His love and bring sorrow to His heart. It means keepin
ourselves in a place where God can actively show and pour out His love i
our lives.

*Heavenly Father, we are blessed and grateful that You keep watch over us, and keep*
*safe every moment of every day. We thank You for Your Holy Spirit that guides us an*
*intercedes on our behalf. We also pray that our nation as a whole would return to Yo*
*so that we could be protected and kept safe from the evil influences of this world. We prai.*
*You.*

# December 28       Sanctification from Temptation

*"These are the ways of the world: wanting to please our sinful selves, wanting the sinful things we see, and being too proud of what we have. None of these come from the Father, but all of them come from the world."*       1 John 2:16 (NCV)

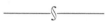

When we pray, as Jesus taught, *"Lead us not into temptation..."* (Matthew 6:13), we're asking the Heavenly Father to help us so we won't tempt ourselves by deliberately placing ourselves in volatile situations. We are living in an environment, which is alien and hostile toward our faith. It's called the world. We need to remember that, because sometimes we get a little too comfortable in this world. Our goal is to be in the world, but not of it—or of the evil one. Even as a ship is to be in the ocean, we should not allow the ocean to be in the ship.

No matter where we go, temptation will be there, waiting for us. Therefore, we must learn to take hold of God's divine resources to resist temptation. We should seek to influence others as we live our lives for the glory of God. If Jesus had wanted to, He could have immediately transported us to heaven on the day of our conversion. But instead, He has chosen to keep and preserve us in this world. The reason is so that we can reach it with the Gospel. Jesus prayed we would be sanctified—set apart—for God's purposes. The dynamic behind sanctification is truth, which is the Word of God read; heard; understood; and applied.

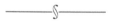

*Almighty God, Your process of sanctification is the same as Your "keeping" process. You don't leave that solely up to us. You are there working in us and through us. We are eternally grateful for Your Presence.*

*"Trust in the Lord with all your heart, and lean not on your own understanding."*
Proverbs 3:5 (NKJV)

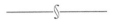

All the wisdom a person may acquire can never replace the need for full trust in God's superior ways. We must trust Him not only for the salvation of our souls, but for the direction in every aspect of our lives—our physical; emotional; professional; relational; financial; intellectual; and spiritual aspects of our lives. Next, there must be a healthy distrust of self; an acknowledgement that we do not know what is truly best for us; and that we are not capable of guiding ourselves to be in alignment with His will. That's the role of God's Holy Spirit in us. When we lean on Him in all we do, God will be with us every step of the way, and remove all obstacles that impede our direction and progress.

We can be tempted to trust the wisdom of the world rather than rely upon divine revelation. By nature we are inclined to foolishly rely upon our own inclinations and desires. We make crucial life decisions in areas such as marriage, finances, and vocation not based upon God's revealed Word or through prayer, but instead rely on our feelings. Feelings are unreliable, and often fickle. When we choose our own way instead of trusting exclusively in God, we are arrogantly claiming that we know better than God. That is pretty laughable! We must lean on God and trust Him to guide our path. He is our pillar of cloud that will lead us to the Promised Land.

*Heavenly Father, You are our Creator Who knows us far more than we will ever know ourselves. You have a perfect plan for each one of us. Forgive us when we fail to acknowledge that truth. Help us to see that when we seek Your will, and seek guidance from Your Holy Spirit, that our souls can experience a peace and comfort in knowing that You are in control. We love You and trust You, Lord.*

*"In all your ways acknowledge Him, and He shall direct your paths."*
Proverbs 3:6 (NKJV)

———§———

God's will and purpose should be our most important pursuit in life. We have problems with this process when we resist God and determine to go our own way. If we choose to do it our own way, then we must be prepared for the discontent, frustration and conflict that our soul will experience. When we neglect to acknowledge Him and seek His will, we act in faithlessness and pride—we put the flesh ahead of the Spirit. We send God the message that we know best. Yet, when we choose to take the path that God has planned, we will experience a satisfaction in our soul that doesn't come from something—but from Someone. The knowledge of His will is to live a life that pleases Him. God wants us to know His will more than we want to know it. Jesus is our example of being obedient to God's will. The cross was a horrific thing to go through, but Jesus went through it because it was the Father's will that we might be saved.

In addition to guidance from God, it means He removes the obstacles, making a smooth path or way of life, in order to reach our intended destination. We can all recall times when we didn't seek God's will and made decisions that caused us to get off His path and end up in a ditch. The path we choose on our own will be dimly lit, and full of potholes. The path that God lays out for us to take will be well-lit; freshly paved; and free of congestion. Choose wisely!

———§———

*God, we are so incredibly blessed that You desire each of us to seek Your counsel in every facet of our lives. You love us that much! You want our paths to be virtuous, peaceful, joyful, and prosperous. God, help us to see that we need to lean completely on You for that to happen. Father, we pray that our government would seek Your guidance and lean on You to give them direction on the correct path.*

# December 31                           Glorious Ending

*"Look, I am coming soon! My reward is with Me, and I will give to each person according to what they have done. I am the Alpha and the Omega, the First and the Last, the Beginning and the End."*                                    Revelation 22:12-13 (NIV)

———§———

This is truly a glorious ending. God alone knows the exact moment of Christ's return, but from our perspective, it could come at any moment. That has been true from the time Jesus uttered those words. Christ's second coming is certain and imminent; it could be this very day, or centuries from now. Yet again, we are not to guess—we are just to be alert.

When the Lord Jesus returns to earth, He will bring judgment to those who rejected His free offer of salvation by grace alone through faith alone. The time for repentance will have run its course and each person's eternal destiny will be sealed. The unsaved will receive what he or she deserves for their sins, regardless of fame, wealth, title, or status. In other words, Christ's reward will be just, never prejudiced. But for those of us who believe, it will be *Paradise*. The entire book of Revelation, in fact, can be regarded as a large invitation to separate oneself from the pollution of the world and its wickedness and to join God's eternal banquet. The Lord's ultimate reason for revealing future events is to draw people to Himself. The implied invitation woven throughout the book is made explicit in these last words.

Thank you all for going on this year-long journey with God. Pray that our nation will return Him to His rightful place. May we all find comfort in knowing that ultimately, it ends well.

———§———

*Heavenly Father, our hearts are bursting with our love for You. Thank You for Your grace, mercy, and love. We pray this—and all the prayers in this devotional—in the precious Name of our Savior, Jesus Christ. AMEN!*

Look for other titles from
Mist Carter:

*Our Crumbling Foundation: Will God Cancel Us?*

*God's Truth About America: A Sequel to "Our Crumbling Foundation…Will God Cancel Us?*

Available from LeRue Press, LLC
Bulk discounts available
www.thebookgallerynv.com
www.LrpNv.com

Or find them online at:
www.hisword.parable.com

Also available at Amazon, Barnes & Noble
and many independent bookstores.

Printed in the USA
CPSIA information can be obtained
at www.ICGtesting.com
CBHW070804201223
2784CB00007B/293